Learn Excel 2002, Brief

John Preston
Sally Preston
Robert L. Ferrett

Prentice Hall

Upper Saddle River, New Jersey 07458

Acquisitions Editor: David Alexander
VP Publisher: Natalie Anderson
Managing Editor (Editorial): Melissa Whitaker
Assistant Editor: Kerri Limpert
Editorial Assistant: Mary Ann Broadnax
Developmental Editor: Joyce Nielson
Media Project Manager: Cathleen Profitko
Marketing Manager: Sharon Turkovich
Marketing Assistant: Jason Smith
Manager, Production: Gail Steier de Acevedo
Project Managers: April Montana & Tim Tate
Associate Director, Manufacturing: Vincent Scelta
Manufacturing Buyer: Natacha St. Hill Moore
Design Manager: Pat Smythe
Interior & Cover Design: Judy Allen
Full-Service Project Management & Composition: PrePress Co. Inc.
Printer/Binder: RR Donnelley & Sons Company
Cover Printer: Phoenix Color Corp.

Microsoft and the Microsoft Office User Specialist logo are trademarks or registered trademarks of Microsoft Corporation in the United States and/or other countries. Prentice Hall is independent from Microsoft Corporation, and not affiliated with Microsoft in any manner. This publication may be used in assisting students to prepare for a Microsoft Office User Specialist Exam. Neither Microsoft Corporation, its designated review company, nor Prentice Hall warrants that use of this publication will ensure passing the relevant Exam.

Acceptable coverage of all content related to Core level Microsoft Office Exam entitled, "Word 2002," "Excel 2002," "Access 2002," or "PowerPoint 2002"; and sufficient performance-based exercises that relate closely to all required content, based on sampling of text.

Microsoft Excel, Solver, and Windows are registered trademarks of Microsoft Corporation in the U.S.A. and other countries. Screen shots and icons reprinted with permission from the Microsoft Corporation. This book is not sponsored or endorsed by or affiliated with Microsoft Corporation.

Copyright © 2002 by Pearson Education, Inc., Upper Saddle River, New Jersey 07458. All rights reserved. Printed in the United States of America. This publication is protected by Copyright and permission should be obtained from the publisher prior to any prohibited reproduction, storage in a retrieval system, or transmission in any form or by any means, electronic, mechanical, photocopying, recording, or likewise. For information regarding permission(s), write to: Rights and Permissions Department.

10 9 8 7 6 5 4 3 2
ISBN 0-13-061314-2

Learn Excel 2002, Brief

SERIES EDITORS **John Preston, Sally Preston, Robert L. Ferrett**

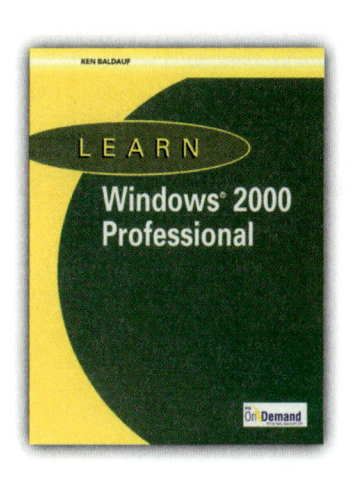

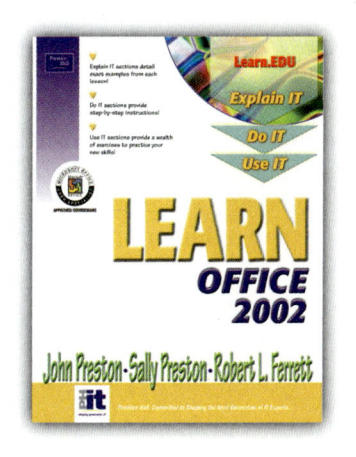

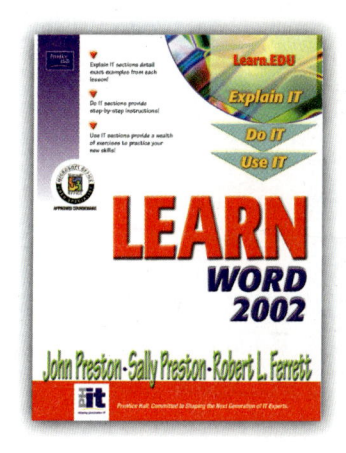

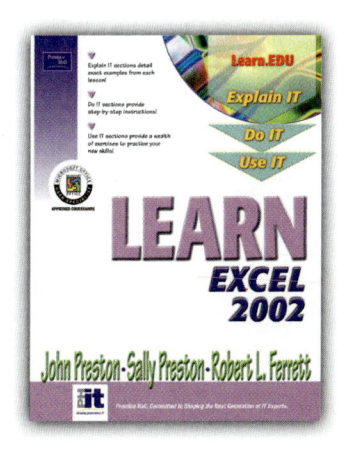

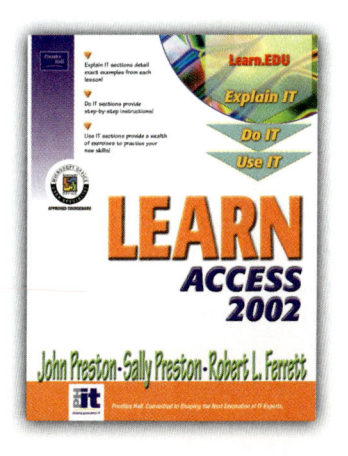

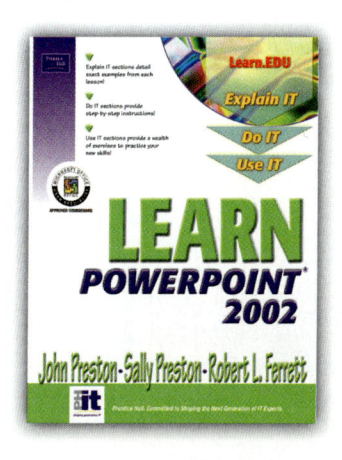

About the Authors

John Preston is an associate professor at Eastern Michigan University in the College of Technology, where he teaches microcomputer application courses at both the undergraduate and graduate levels. He has been teaching, writing, and designing computer training courses since the advent of PCs, and he has authored and co-authored over 40 books on Microsoft Word, Excel, Access, and PowerPoint. He is a series editor for the *Learn 97, Learn 2000*, and *Learn XP* books. Two books on Microsoft Access he co-authored with Robert Ferrett have been translated into Greek and Chinese. He has received grants from the Detroit Edison Institute and the Department of Energy to develop Web sites for energy education and alternative fuels, and has also developed one of the first Internet-based microcomputer applications courses at an accredited university. He has a B.S. in physics, mathematics, and education from the University of Michigan, and an M.S. in physics education from Eastern Michigan University. His doctoral studies are in instructional technology at Wayne State University.

Sally Preston is president of Preston & Associates, which provides software consulting and training. She teaches computing in a variety of settings, which provides her with ample opportunity to observe how people learn, what works best, and what challenges are present when learning a new software program. This diverse experience provides a complimentary set of information, which is blended into the *Learn* series books. Sally has been a co-author on the *Learn* series since its inception. In addition, she has authored books for the *Essentials* and *Microsoft Office User Specialist (MOUS) Essentials* series. Sally has an MBA from Eastern Michigan University and graduated magna cum laude. When Sally is away from her computer, she is often found planting flowers in her garden.

Robert L. Ferrett is the director of the Center for Instructional Computing at Eastern Michigan University, where he provides computer training and support to faculty. He has authored or co-authored more than 40 books on Access, PowerPoint, Excel, Publisher, WordPerfect, and Word, and he was the editor of the *1994 ACM SIGUCCS Conference Proceedings*. He has been designing, developing, and delivering computer workshops for nearly two decades, and is a series editor for the *Learn 97, Learn 2000*, and *Learn XP* books. He has a B.A. in psychology, an M.S. in geography, and an M.S. in interdisciplinary technology from Eastern Michigan University. His doctoral studies are in instructional technology at Wayne State University. As a sidelight, Bob teaches a four-week Computers and Genealogy class and has written books on genealogy and local history.

Contents

Using Common Elements in Office — CE1

Explain It — CE1
Introduction — CE1
Visual Summary — CE2

Do It — CE3
Task 1   Starting and Exiting an Office Application — CE3
Task 2   Opening and Saving an Existing Document with a New Name — CE6
Task 3   Using the Taskbar to Work in Multiple Windows — CE9
Task 4   Using Menus and Toolbars — CE11
Task 5   Printing a Document Using the Toolbar Button and the Menu — CE16
Task 6   Using the Office Assistant to Get Help — CE18

Use It — CE22
Comprehension — CE22

Lesson 1: Learning the Basics of Excel — 1

Explain It — 1
Introduction — 1
Visual Summary — 2

Do It — 3
Task 1   Navigating a Workbook — 3
Task 2   Selecting Individual Cells — 5
Task 3   Entering Text and Numbers into Cells — 7
Task 4   Fixing Simple Typing Errors — 9
Task 5   Summing a Column of Numbers — 12
Task 6   Saving a Workbook, Printing and Closing a Workbook — 13

Use It — 17
Comprehension — 17
Reinforcement — 19
Challenge — 21
On your Own — 23

Lesson 2: Formatting the Worksheet — 25

Explain It — 25
Introduction — 25

Do It — 27

Task 1	Selecting Groups of Cells	27
Task 2	Formatting Large Numbers, Currency, Decimal Plates, and Dates	29
Task 3	Adjusting Columns and Cells for Long Text or Numbers	32
Task 4	Aligning Text in a Cell	34
Task 5	Changing the Font, Size, and Emphasis of Text	36
Task 6	Adding Lines, Borders, Colors, and Shading	37

Use It — 40

Comprehension	40
Reinforcement	42
Challenge	44
On Your Own	47

Lesson 3: Using Formulas — 49

Explain It — 49

Introduction	49
Visual Summary	50

Do It — 51

Task 1	Adding, Subtracting, Multiplying, and Dividing Using Cell References and Numbers	51
Task 2	Using Formulas with More than One Cell Reference	53
Task 3	Combining Operations and Filling Cells with Formulas	55
Task 4	Filling Cells with Relative and Absolute Formulas	60
Task 5	Applying Basic Formulas to a Loan Payment	63
Task 6	Using Built-In Financial Formulas	64

Use It — 70

Comprehension	70
Reinforcement	72
Challenge	74
On Your Own	80

Lesson 4: Understanding the Numbers Using a Chart — 81

Explain It — 81

Introduction	81
Visual Summary	82

Do It — 83

Task 1	Creating a Chart to Show a Trend	83
Task 2	Creating a Chart to Show Contributions to a Whole	86
Task 3	Creating a Chart to Make Comparisons	89
Task 4	Editing the Elements of a Chart and Adding a Callout	91
Task 5	Printing a Chart	96

Use It	***99***
Comprehension	99
Reinforcement	101
Challenge	103
On Your Own	106

Lesson 5: Integrating Excel with Word and the Internet — 107

Explain It — ***107***
Introduction	107
Visual Summary	108

Do It — ***109***
Task 1	Deleting, Inserting, Renaming, and Moving Sheets	109
Task 2	Designing a Summary Sheet	110
Task 3	Linking the Results of Several Sheets to a Summary Report	112
Task 4	Pasting a Worksheet into a Word Document	115
Task 5	Saving a Worksheet as a Web Page	117
Task 6	Previewing the Web Page	119

Use It — ***121***
Comprehension	121
Reinforcement	123
Challenge	125
On Your Own	128

Glossary — 129

Index — 131

Preface

PHILOSOPHY OF THE *LEARN* SERIES

The Preston-Ferrett *Learn* series is designed for students who want to master the core competencies of particular software in an efficient and effective manner. We use the rubric EDU to organize the text into sections labeled "Explain It," "Do It," and "Use It." The books use extensive visual cues to provide immediate feedback to the students. Each step is accompanied by a figure displaying the result of doing that step. Highlights and callouts identify key screen elements. Steps are divided into paragraphs that give specific directions and paragraphs that explain the results of those actions. Special fonts and colors are used to identify the objects of actions and what the student should type. Deeper understanding is provided in asides called "In Depth." Places where students are likely to go astray are identified by asides labeled "Caution." The series uses visual elements, such as buttons and icons, to make it easier for beginners to learn the software. However, it recognizes that students who need to use the software at work are interested in speed. Asides called "Quick Tips" give directions on how to use keyboard shortcuts to accomplish tasks that are likely to be common in the workplace. The exercises at the end of each lesson promote increasing levels of abstraction similar to those described in Bloom's taxonomy. The "Comprehension" exercises test students' knowledge of the facts and their ability to recognize relationships and visual elements. The "Reinforcement" exercises provide the opportunity to apply these new skills to a different assignment with less-detailed instructions. "Challenge" exercises require students to learn a new skill that is related to the skills covered in the lesson. "On Your Own" provides students with guidelines for applying the newly acquired skills to a unique project of their own. The guidelines specify general requirements to give the student and the instructor a common ground for evaluation but otherwise allow for creativity and innovation. Books in this series give beginners very detailed step-by-step instruction while providing challenging options for more advanced learners.

STRUCTURE OF A *LEARN* SERIES BOOK

Each of the books in the *Learn* series is structured the same and contains elements that explain what is expected, how to do the tasks, and how to transfer this knowledge into daily use. The elements—"Explain It," "Do It," and "Use It"—are described in detail below.

Explain It

Students are provided with a cognitive map of the lesson where they see a list of the tasks, an introduction, and a visual summary.

Introduction

The EDU design relates to the lessons.

Each lesson has an introduction that describes the contents of the lesson to provide an overview of how the tasks are related to a larger concept that is identified by the title of the lesson.

Visual Summary

A visual summary displays the expected results of performing the tasks. Callouts are used to show the student and the instructor where to look in each file to identify the results of following the instructions correctly.

Do It

Once students are oriented to the objective of the lesson and are aware of the expected outcome, they proceed with the task. Tasks begin with an explanation of the relevance of the tasks and are followed by step-by-step, illustrated instructions on how to "Do It."

Why would I do this?

The authors draw upon their experience in education, business, government, and personal growth to explain how this task is relevant to the student's life. Students are motivated to learn when they can relate the task to practical applications in their lives.

Step-by-step instruction

Instructions are provided in a step-by-step format. Explanations follow each instruction and are set off in a new italicized paragraph.

Figures

Each step has an accompanying figure that is placed next to it. Each figure provides a visual reinforcement of the step that has just been completed. Buttons, menu choices, and other screen elements used in the task are highlighted or identified.

Special Notes

Three recurring note boxes are found in the Preston-Ferrett *Learn* series:

> **CAUTION** — An area where trouble may be encountered, along with instructions on how to avoid or recover from these mistakes.

> **IN DEPTH** — A detailed look at a topic or procedure, or another way of doing it.

> **QUICK TIP** — A faster or more efficient way of achieving a desired end.

Use It

The end-of-lesson material, "Use It," consists of four elements: "Comprehension"; "Reinforcement"; "Challenge"; and "On Your Own." Students are guided through increasing levels of abstraction until they can apply the skills of the lesson to a completely new situation in the "On Your Own" exercise.

> **"Comprehension":** These exercises are designed to check the student's memory and understanding of the basic concepts in the lesson. Next to each exercise is a notation that references the task number in the lesson where the topic is covered. The student is encouraged to review the task referenced if he or she is uncertain of the correct answer. The "Comprehension" section contains the following three elements:

"True/False": True/false questions test the understanding of the new material in the lesson.

"Matching": Matching questions are included to check the student's familiarity with concepts and procedures introduced in the lesson.

"Visual Identification": A captured screen or screens is used to gauge the student's familiarity with various screen elements introduced in the lesson.

"Reinforcement": These exercises which provide practice in the skills introduced in the tasks, generally follow the sequence of the tasks in the lesson. Since each exercise is usually built on the previous exercise, it is a good idea to do them in the order in which they are presented.

"Challenge": These exercises test students' abilities to apply skills to new situations with less-detailed instructions. Students are challenged to expand their skills set by using commands similar to those they've already learned.

"On Your Own": This exercise is designed to provide students with an opportunity to apply what they have learned to a situation of their choice. Guidelines are provided to give students and the instructor an idea of what is expected.

Glossary

New words or concepts are printed in italics and emphasized with color the first time they are encountered. Definitions of these words or phrases are provided in the text where they occur and are also included in the glossary at the back of the book.

MOUS Certification

Students may wish to become certified by Microsoft in the core competencies by taking the Microsoft Office User Specialist (MOUS) examination in Word, Excel, PowerPoint, or Access. There is a separate book for each of these applications that covers all of the skills required for core-level certification. The first four or five lessons of each of these books are included in the *Learn Office XP* book. Students may purchase one of the individual topic books on their own, or instructors may request that the additional chapters from one or more of those books be bundled with the *Learn Office XP* book to provide a complete set of lessons covering all of the MOUS core objectives in one or more of the applications.

Learn Themes

Personal note from the authors to the student: Microsoft Office is a tool that we have used in our professional and personal lives for many years. This experience helps us explain how each lesson in this book relates to practical use. Between the three of us, our interests range across a broad spectrum of activities. We have chosen four themes throughout the *Learn* series that are based on our personal use of Microsoft Office. We hope that one or more of these themes will be of interest to you as well.

Business: Sally's financial experience and Bob's personal experience in pool and spa sales provide the background for the exercises dealing with business. We use a fictional company named Armstrong Pool, Spa, and Sauna Company to illustrate the use of Microsoft Office XP in a business setting. Armstrong is a regional company that was founded in 1957 in Ypsilanti, Michigan. They have expanded to eight locations in Michigan, Indiana, and Ohio, and have sales of around $10 million a year. Armstrong has been trying to improve the communication between their locations and has recently installed Microsoft Office XP. You will see how a company can use Office XP to communicate with customers, manage finances, organize data, and make presentations.

Travel: All three of us love to travel, so we created the fictional Alumni Travel Club, which is an organization that provides travel packages to the alumni of a local college. This theme illustrates how an organization can benefit from the use of Microsoft Office XP. The pictures used for this theme were taken by either Bob or John.

Social Science: Bob's personal interest in genealogy and historical research provides the background for several lessons. Bob's family is from Alcona County, which is a small rural community in the thumb of Michigan. Immigrants from Canada, England, Germany, and other predominantly European countries settled there in the late 1800s. Bob Ferrett and his brother Don gathered data from U.S. government census records for that period of time and have published a book on the subject. This information provides interesting clues about the life of people in a rural community before the 20th century and gives us insight into how much the role of women has changed. You will see how Microsoft Office XP applications can be used to explain, tabulate, record, and illustrate research data for a social science project.

John teaches several classes on the Internet and has written papers on how this new form of communication affects the way we learn. These documents are used in the *Learn Word 2002* chapters where you practice formatting long documents.

Science/Environment: John's physics background and interest in energy and the environment are the source of material for several documents and presentations. Every summer he teaches a class on utility power generation to junior high school science teachers.

Bob collaborates on weather-related research and has published articles on the risks associated with tornadoes and lightning. We have included a database of all the tornadoes in the United States from 1950 to 1995 so that users of this book can learn how to use Access and Excel to answer real research questions using a real database with over 38,000 records. We enjoy the excitement of doing this type of research with the tools found in Office and hope to share this excitement with our readers.

SUPPLEMENTS PACKAGE

There are lots of supplements available for both students and teachers. Let's take a look at these now.

Student Supplements
Companion Web site (www.prenhall.com/phmoustest): Includes student data files as well as test questions that allow students to test their knowledge of the material and get instant assessment.

Instructor Supplements
Instructor's Resource CD-ROM: Includes Instructor's Manual, Test Manager, PowerPoint presentations, and the data and solution files for all four applications, which are available for downloading.

TRADEMARK ACKNOWLEDGEMENTS

All terms mentioned in this book that are known to be trademarks or service marks have been appropriately capitalized. Prentice Hall cannot attest to the accuracy of this information. Use of a term in this book should not be regarded as affecting the validity of any trademark or service mark.

ACKNOWLEDGEMENTS

We would like to acknowledge the efforts of the finest team of editing professionals, with whom we have had the pleasure of working. We have worked with editors from four other publishing firms, and none have done as thorough and professional a job as the people who have labored diligently on this series.

Our most frequent contact was with Melissa Whitaker. She did an outstanding job of coordinating the efforts of a diverse team, spread across the country, working around the clock in an all-electronic environment. Melissa has been ably supervised by David Alexander, who kept in touch with the project and was available when an executive decision needed to be made. The executive editor, Mickey Cox, deserves credit for assembling a team of this caliber and doing the work behind the scenes, of which we are gratefully ignorant.

Other team members include:

Kerri Limpert – Assistant Editor
Mary Ann Broadax – Editorial Assistant
Cathi Profitko – Media Project Manager
April Montana – Project Manager, Pearson
Gail Steier – Manager, Production
Pat Smythe – Design Manager
Jen Carley – Project Manager, Pre-Press

The authors wish to acknowledge the contributions of students at Eastern Michigan University. These students, most of whom are in the Technical Writing Degree Program, worked under the instruction and guidance of Professor Nancy Allen to ensure the accuracy of the final product. The students who participated in this project are:

Tom Barthel
Carrie Bartkowiak
Sandy Becker
Maureen Cousino
Lisa DeLibero
Julie Gibson
Bill Inman
Jyoti Lal
Jill Money
Ines Perrone
Matt Phillips
Brian Rahn
Darcey Schafer
Jeri Vickerman
Tracy Williams
Christine Zito

Learn.EDU Features

Books in the *Learn 2002* series follow the Learn.EDU philosophy: Explain It, Do It, and then Use It.

*E*xplain It
EXPLAIN IT sections begin each Lesson. Students learn up front what will be covered in a Lesson and what they can expect to learn from it.

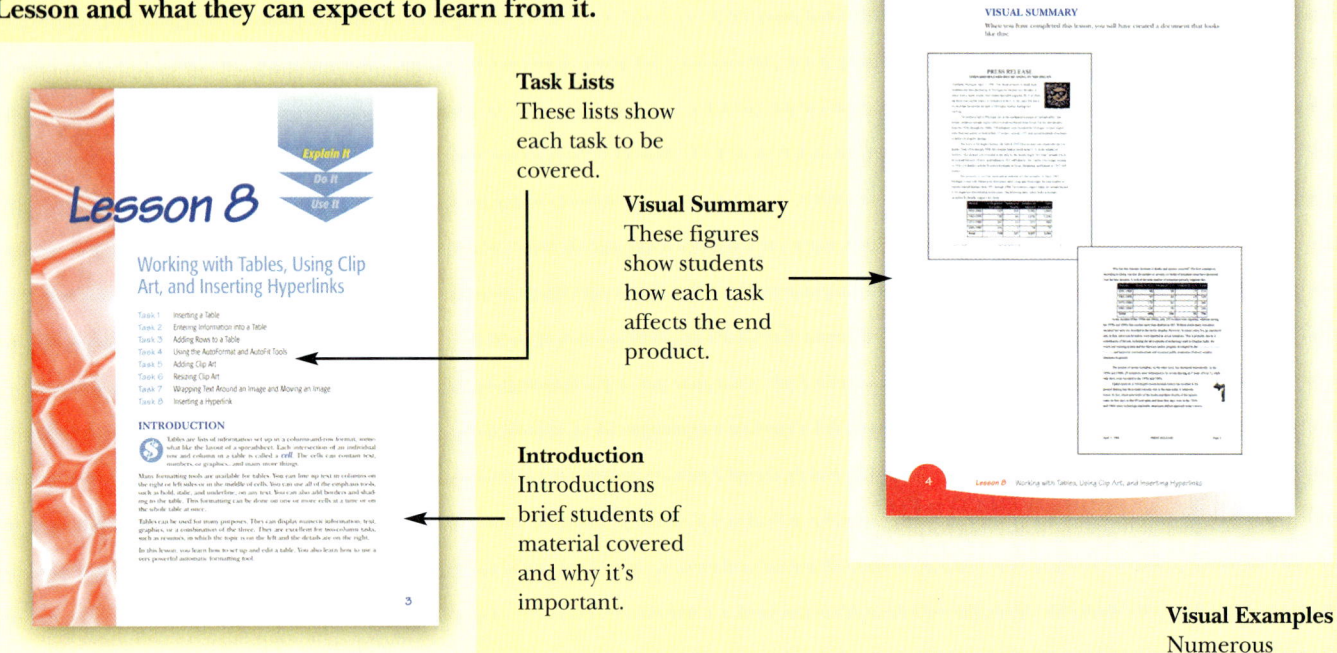

Task Lists
These lists show each task to be covered.

Visual Summary
These figures show students how each task affects the end product.

Introduction
Introductions brief students of material covered and why it's important.

*D*o It
DO IT sections contain numbered steps that walk students through each task, allowing them to do the work themselves along with the instruction.

Why would I do this?
These sections explain the relevance to the student of each concept covered.

Numbered Steps
Students are guided through each task in a step-by-step format with explanations in italics.

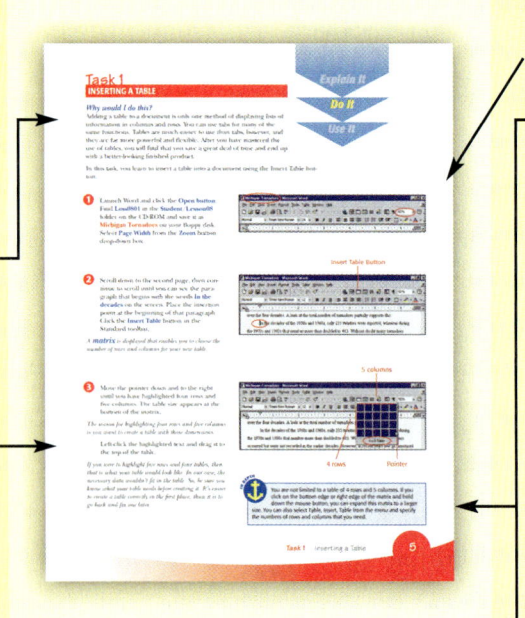

Visual Examples
Numerous screen captures show how the student's own screen should look.

Quick Tip
A faster or more efficient way of doing something.

In Depth
A detailed look at a topic or procedure, or another way of doing something.

Caution
Troubleshooting tips that point out common pitfalls.

Use It
USE IT sections give the student opportunities to evaluate and practice skills learned in the Lessons, furthering their knowledge, comprehension, and understanding of the topics.

Comprehension
Comprehension exercises, comprised of True-False, Matching, and Screen ID sections help the student transfer knowledge from short-term to long-term memory.

Reinforcement
These exercises provide practice in skills introduced in the tasks.

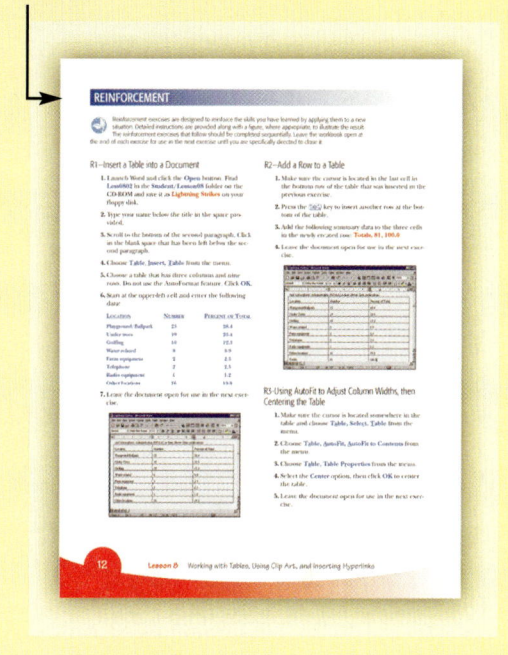

Challenge
The exercises test the student's ability to apply their skills to new situations with less-detailed instructions.

On Your Own
Students are provided with guidelines on how to apply the skills acquired to a project of their choice.

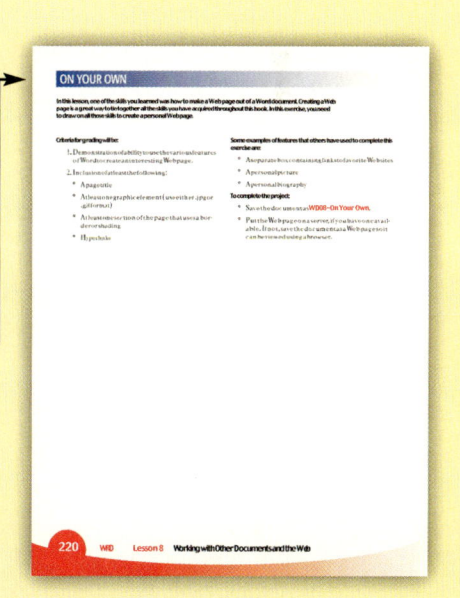

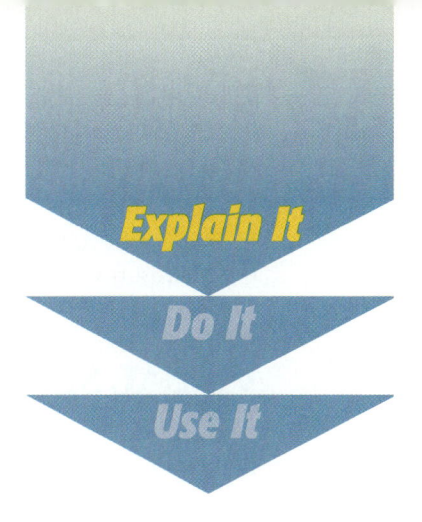

Using Common Elements in Office

Task 1 Starting and Exiting an Office Application
Task 2 Opening and Saving an Existing Document with a New Name
Task 3 Using the Taskbar to Work in Multiple Windows
Task 4 Using Menus and Toolbars
Task 5 Printing a Document Using the Toolbar Button and the Menu
Task 6 Using the Office Assistant to Get Help

INTRODUCTION

Many of the techniques and procedures you use in one Microsoft Office application will work in most or all of the other applications. (Note: The term *application* refers to one of the parts of the Office suite, such as Word or Excel. In this book, it is used synonymously with the word *program*). For example, you use the same procedures to activate a menu in Word as you do in Excel and PowerPoint. The toolbars are also used in the same way, and some of the more common buttons (Print, Copy, Paste, Undo, and several others) that you learn about in the following lessons are exactly the same in every application.

There are also differences between the applications. No two have exactly the same menu options, although all have many similarities. Some buttons are common to many of the programs, but are missing from one or two others. Some features are available in several programs, but absent from others. For example, Word, PowerPoint, and Excel have a feature that enables people who are collaborating on a document to write screen comments to each other. You cannot attach comments in Access, however.

One of the main strengths of the Microsoft Office suite is the consistency of the programs and the way they work together. A chart created in Excel can easily be inserted into a Word document or a PowerPoint presentation. An outline in Word can be used as the backbone of a PowerPoint presentation. A table of information in Access can be sent to Excel for numerical analysis.

Another strength of the Office suite is the capability to save files in a format that can be read on the World Wide Web. You can create a Web page using many of the programs. You can even create a Web slideshow using PowerPoint, and you can publish Access data files that can be read, searched, and sorted by people all over the world.

In this lesson, you will look at some of the features common to all (or nearly all) of the Microsoft Office applications.

VISUAL SUMMARY

By the time you have completed this lesson, you will have worked with a document that looks like this:

Task 2: Save a document with a different name

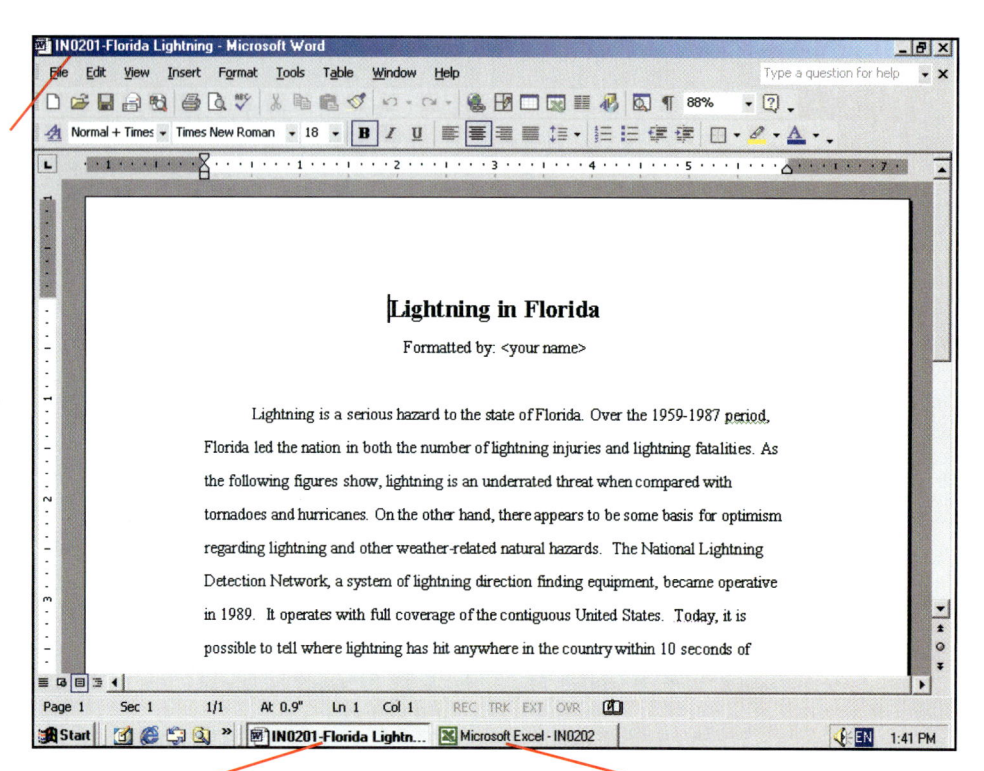

Task 3: Open an Excel spreadsheet and a Word document at the same time

Task 2: Open a Word document

2   CE   Lesson 2   Using Common Elements in Office

Task 1
STARTING AND EXITING AN OFFICE APPLICATION

Why would I do this?
To work in one of the Microsoft Office applications, it first needs to be opened. Starting an application is also referred to as launching the program. This is usually done using the **Start button** on the taskbar. The Start button provides an easy way to open programs and utilities, activate Windows Help, move quickly to recently used documents, and even shut down your computer. All Office applications can be started in the same way. The exit procedure is also consistent for all Office applications.

In this task, you start and exit Microsoft Word.

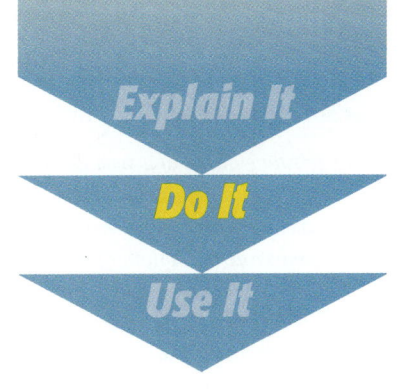

1 Click the **Start** button and move to the **Programs** option.

A submenu displays. It doesn't matter if Windows Explorer or any other program is open. You can launch any Office application with one or more programs open.

> ⚠ **CAUTION**
>
> The Microsoft Word option might not be available in the Programs submenu. If not, look for a Microsoft Office option that has another submenu.
>
> If the Start button does not activate the Start menu, it probably means that you are working in a lab in which security software has been installed. In this case, you will probably need to use a shortcut on the desktop to open programs. Check with the lab manager for further instructions.

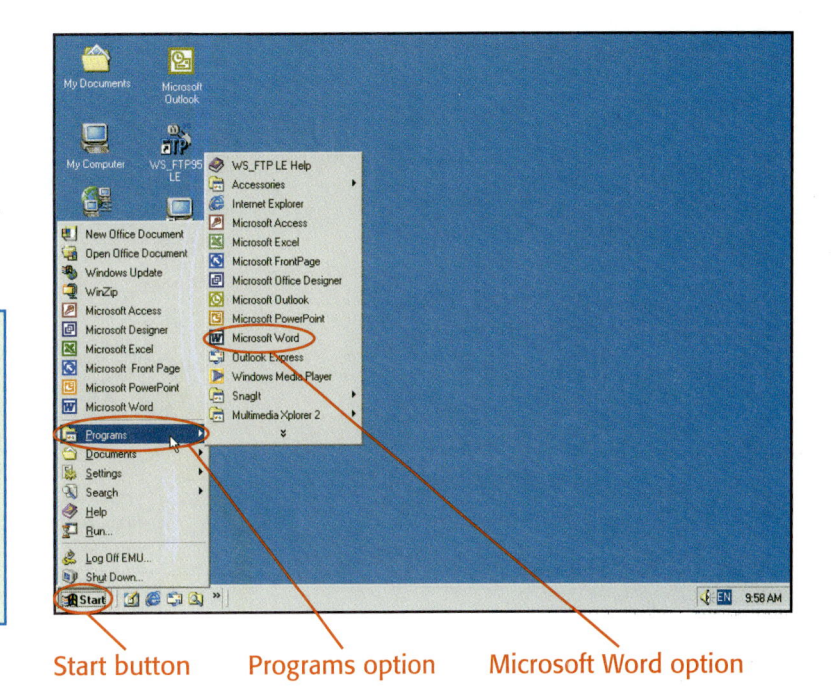

Start button   Programs option   Microsoft Word option

2 Select **Microsoft Word** from the submenu.

The Microsoft Word window opens to a new document. The document is given a default name, such as Document1. The document name is displayed in both the title bar and the taskbar at the bottom of the screen. A task pane also appears on the right side of the screen, displaying recently edited documents and program options. This feature can be turned on and off by selecting View, Task Pane from the menu.

Callouts (labels pointing to the Word window screenshot):
- Toolbar
- Menu bar
- Close Task Pane button
- Close Window button
- Close button
- Default name in the title bar
- Work area
- Recently edited documents
- Task pane
- Default name in the taskbar button
- Horizontal scroll bar
- Vertical scroll bar

> **IN DEPTH**
>
> You may have only one toolbar displayed instead of the two that are shown in the figure. This issue is addressed in Task 4. Your work area may also look different. There are several different views you can choose when working in Word, and the one that is displayed is the last one that was used on that machine. Finally, the rulers may also be turned off.
>
> In some of the applications, such as Access and PowerPoint, you will have to answer questions before you get to the window in which you will enter information. In Word and Excel, however, a blank document (or worksheet) is displayed as soon as the program is started.

> **CAUTION**
>
> You may not see the default document name in the taskbar if the taskbar is hidden. If the taskbar is hidden, move your pointer to the bottom of the screen. The taskbar will pop up. If you want to display or hide the taskbar, right-click in an open area of the taskbar and select Properties from the shortcut menu. Click the Auto hide check box to turn the Auto hide feature on or off. The taskbar will be displayed in the figures through the end of this lesson, and then hidden for the rest of the book. This gives you the maximum viewing area for the figures.

3 If the window is not maximized, click the **Maximize** button in the title bar.

The Maximize button is the middle button on the right end of the title bar. When the window is maximized, the Maximize button changes to a Restore button. Maximizing the work area will give you the largest area in which to work.

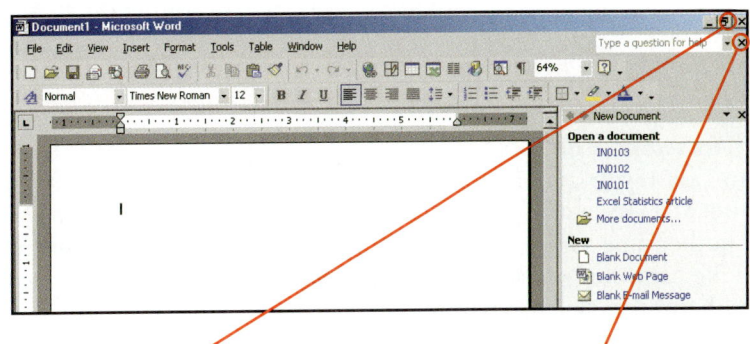

When the window is maximized, the Maximize button changes to a Restore button

Close Window button

4 Click the **Close Window** button on the right edge of the menu bar.

The Close Window button is just below the Close button in the title bar. The document closes, leaving the Microsoft Word window open.

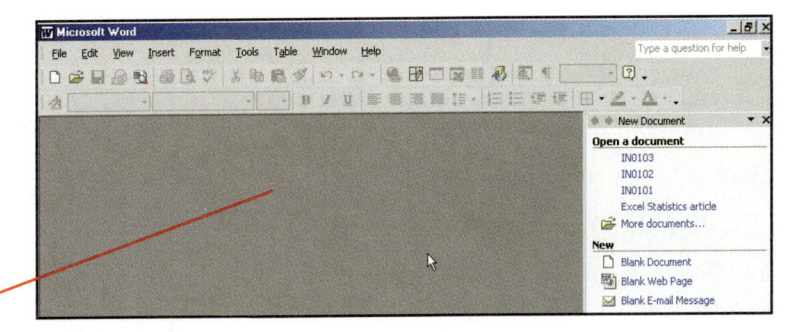

No document is active

5 Click the **Close** button in the upper-right corner of the Microsoft Word window.

This closes Microsoft Word and takes you back to the screen you saw just before you opened Word.

No programs are running

> **IN DEPTH**
>
> There are several ways to start an Office application. The most common is to use the Start menu, where you can get to the program using the Programs option. You can also add Office application shortcuts to the top of the Start menu or to the desktop. Use Windows Help if you would like to use one of these shortcut methods. In this book, you will be instructed to start the application. It is up to you which method you use.

Task 1 Starting and Exiting an Office Application

Task 2
OPENING AND SAVING AN EXISTING DOCUMENT WITH A NEW NAME

Why would I do this?
In Task 1, you launched Microsoft Word, which automatically opened a blank document. Once a document is created and saved to a disk, you may want to open it at another time so you can edit it or print it. After you have given an active document a file name and chosen a storage location, you will be able to save the file quickly with just the click of a button.

In this task, you use the Open dialog box to copy a file from its storage location (which may be a hard drive, a network drive, a Web site, or a CD-ROM disc) to your floppy disk. You then open the document, save it with a new name, make a change, and save the change. This is the document you will be using for the rest of this lesson.

1 Click the **Start** button, choose **Programs**, and then select **Microsoft Word**.

Word opens to a blank document.

Click the **Open** button on the toolbar.

The Open dialog box displays. The files contained in your Open dialog box are likely to be different than the ones shown in the figure.

Open button

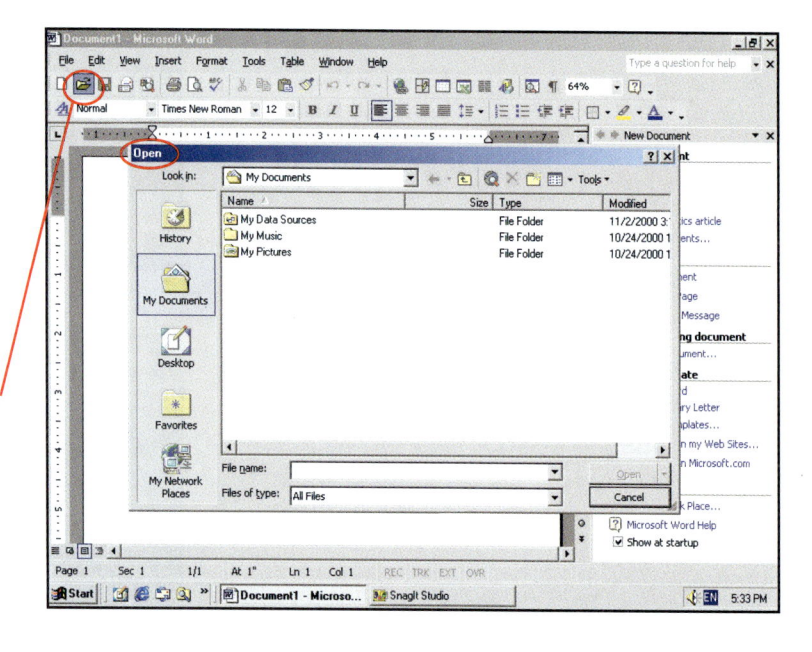

2 Click the down arrow at the end of the **Look in** box, and select the location of the student files from the list.

The folders (in this case on a CD-ROM disc) are displayed.

Double-click the **Student** folder to display the contents of the folder.

The files you see will not be exactly the same as those shown in the figure.

Student folder selected

Look in box

Down arrow

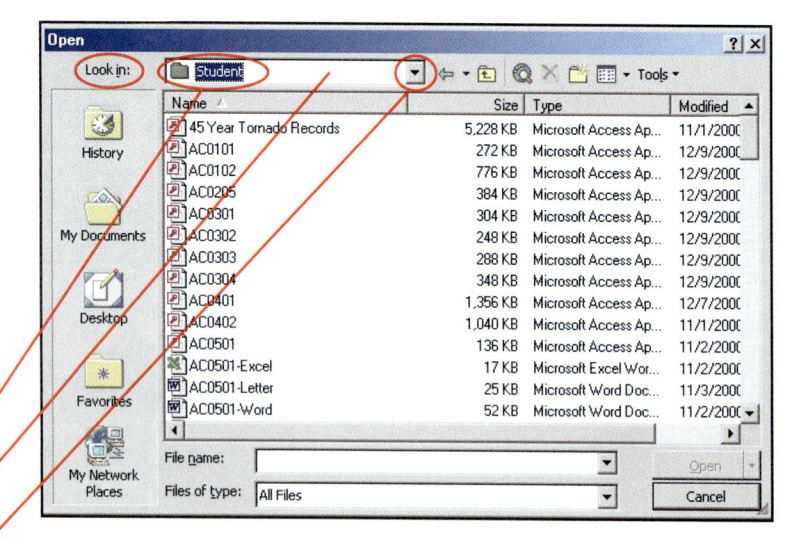

6　CE　Lesson 2　Using Common Elements in Office

3 Use the vertical scroll bar to scroll down. Select **IN0201** and click the **Open** button.

If you are using a file from a CD-ROM, it will be in a read-only format that does not allow you to modify it. This may also be true of files downloaded from a network server. Before you can begin to use this file, you need to save it with a new name. In the example that follows, a floppy disk is used.

Title bar indicates whether the file is read-only

4 Click the **File** option in the menu bar, move the mouse pointer down the options that are displayed, and click **Save As**.

The Save As dialog box opens showing a list of Word files in the Student folder. The Open dialog box and the Save As dialog box are very similar except one is used to open files, and the other is used to save files. To save this file, you need to choose a location for the file and a new file name. For this example, use a formatted floppy disk. If you don't have one available, use a folder on a hard drive or a network drive. (Note: You will learn more about using menus in Task 4.)

With your formatted floppy disk in the **A** drive, click the down arrow at the end of the **Save in** box and select **3½ Floppy (A:)**.

The contents of the disk in the A drive are displayed.

5 Click-and-drag across the name in the **File name** box, and then type **IN0201-Florida Lightning**.

The new file name replaces the old one.

> **IN DEPTH**
> If you want to create a new folder to store your new file, you can click the Create New Folder button on the toolbar. The New Folder dialog box will ask you to type a folder name, and then creates the new folder when you click OK.

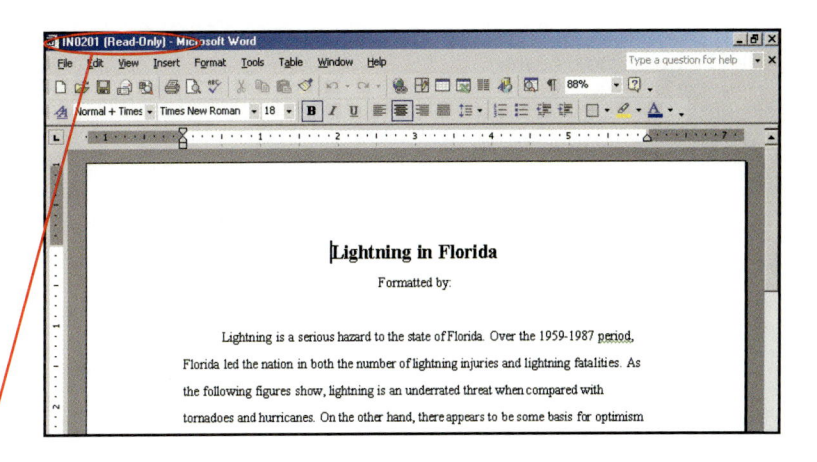

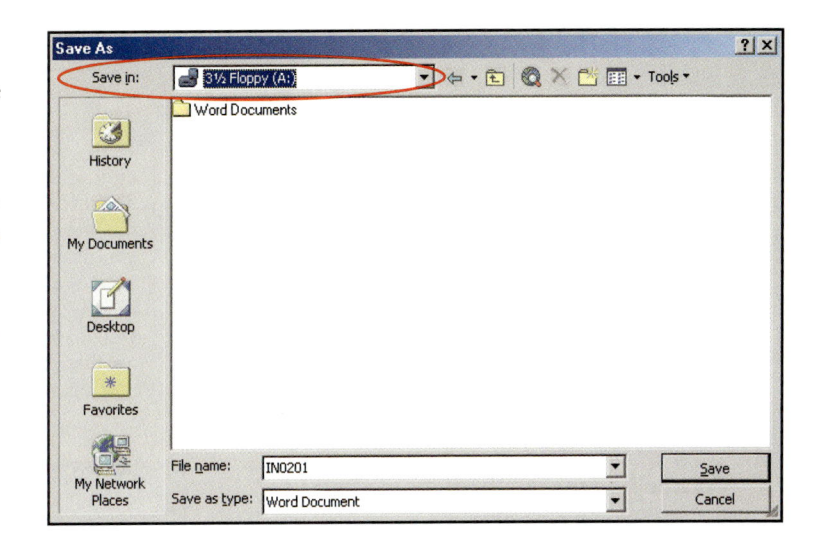

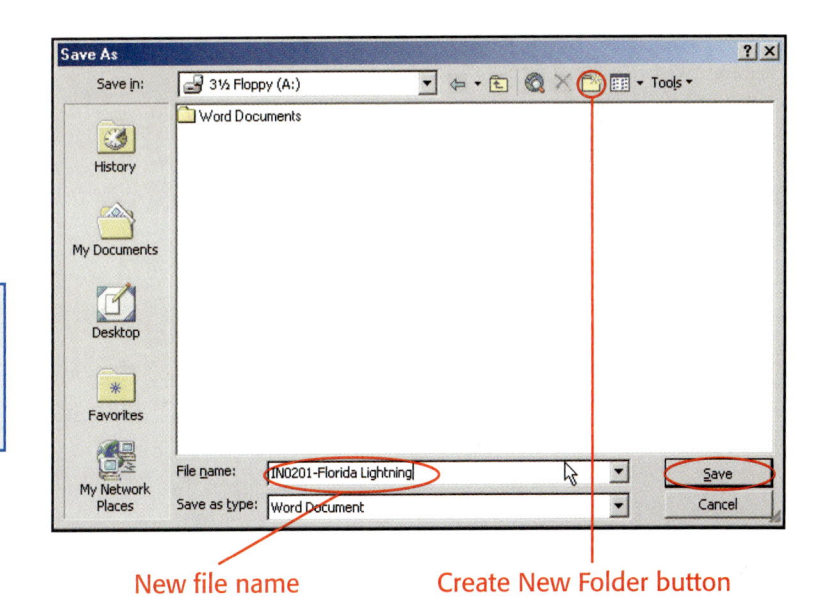

New file name   Create New Folder button

Task 2 Opening and Saving an Existing Document with a New Name   CE   7

6 Click the **Save** button.

The file is saved with the new name on your floppy disk, and the title bar no longer indicates it is a read-only file.

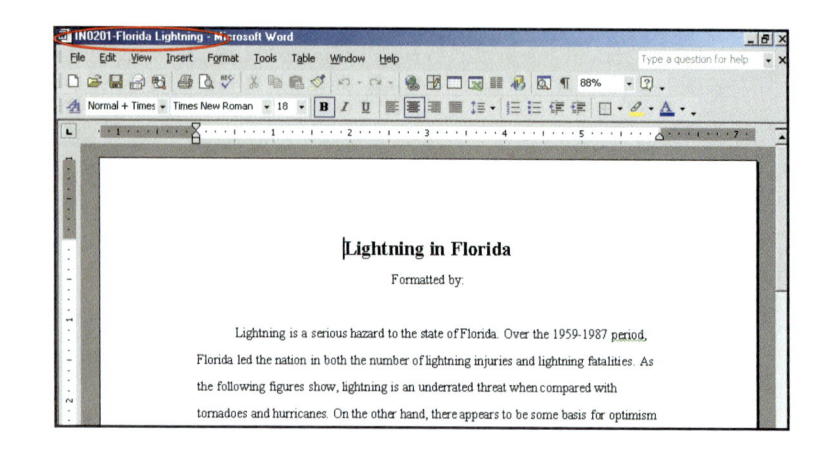

CAUTION

When using a floppy disk to save your work, make sure that the disk has enough room for your file before you save it. Always keep an extra disk handy. If you try to save your work and get an error message that the disk is full, click OK. Replace the floppy disk with one that has enough room and use the File, Save As procedure to select the new disk. If you do not have another disk available and are using a lab computer, you can right-click on one or more unneeded files in the Save As dialog box and select Delete from the shortcut menu. This will free up space to save your current document. If all else fails, save your work to the My Documents folder on the lab hard drive and go get another disk!

7 Click the pointer to the right of **Formatted by:** and type your name.

*The pointer is now in the form of an I-bar. When you position the I-bar pointer and click with the left mouse button, a flashing vertical line is inserted. This is known as the **insertion point**. When you start typing, the text will appear at the insertion point, not at the pointer location. This is true in all Office programs.*

Click the **Save** button on the toolbar.

The changes you just made to the document are saved. Leave the document open for the next task.

Save button
Type your name here
Insertion point
Pointer

QUICK TIP

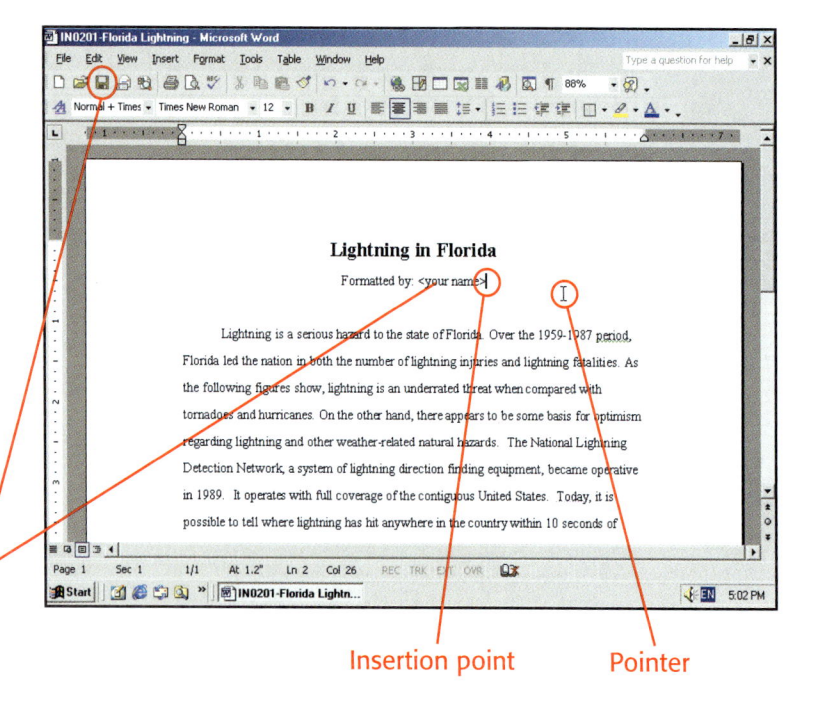

Once you have the document saved on your floppy disk, there is a quick method to open it in the future. Open Windows Explorer or my Computer, find the file, and double-click it. The application that created the file (in this case Word) is launched automatically and the document opens.

Task 3
USING THE TASKBAR TO WORK IN MULTIPLE WINDOWS

Why would I do this?
There will be times when you need to have two or more applications open at the same time. For example, you may be working on a Word document, but occasionally need to refer to data in a database or calculations in a spreadsheet. Also, you might want to copy a chart from Excel into a PowerPoint presentation. You can open one application, get the information you want, close it, and then open another application. It is much easier, however, to open multiple documents at the same time. To do this, you need to know how to effectively use the taskbar.

In this task, you learn how to keep several documents open at the same time and how to move from one to the other.

1 With the **IN0201-Florida Lightning** document open from Task 2, click the **Start** button, choose **Programs**, and then select **Microsoft Excel**.

Microsoft Excel opens and a blank worksheet displays. The toolbars might be displayed in either one or two lines.

Click the **Open** button on the toolbar.

The Open dialog box displays. The files and folders contained in your Open dialog box are likely to be different than the ones shown in the figure.

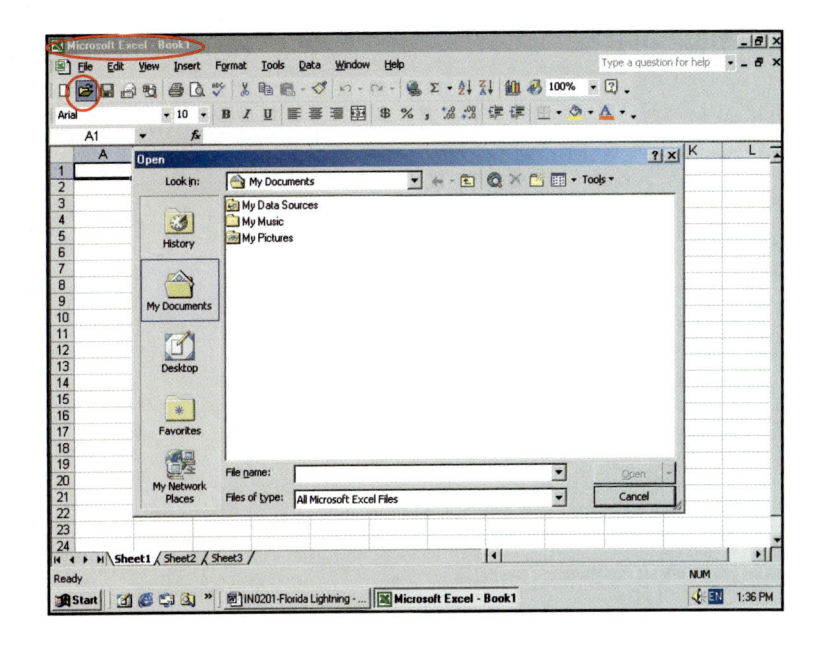

2 Select the location of your student files.

The Student folder displays.

Double-click the **Student** folder to display the contents of the folder.

The files you see will not be exactly the same as those shown in the figure.

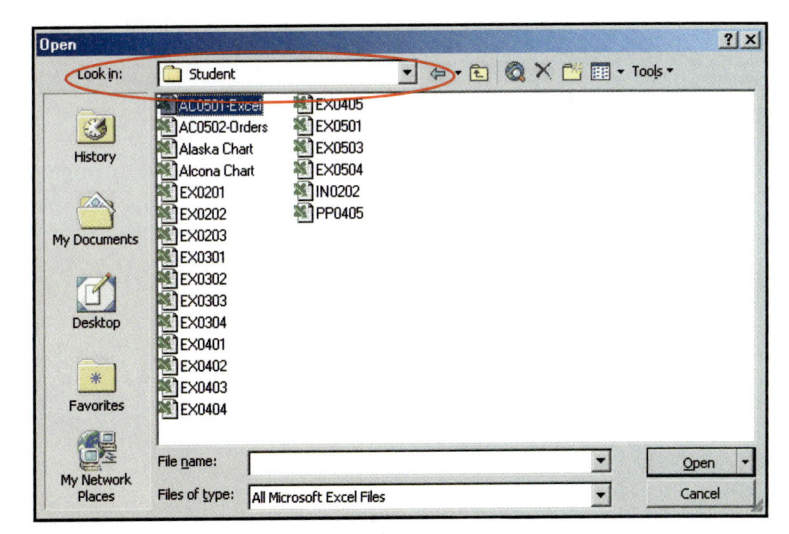

Task 3   Using the Taskbar to Work in Multiple Windows   CE   **9**

3 Select **IN0202** and click the **Open** button.

The file opens. Because you will not be making any changes to this file, you do not need to make any modifications if it opens as a read-only file.

Examine the taskbar.

Notice that you now have two open documents created by two different applications, even though only one is displayed.

Two programs are open at the same time

4 Click the **Microsoft Word** button on the taskbar.

You return to the Word document, leaving the Excel document open and conveniently available.

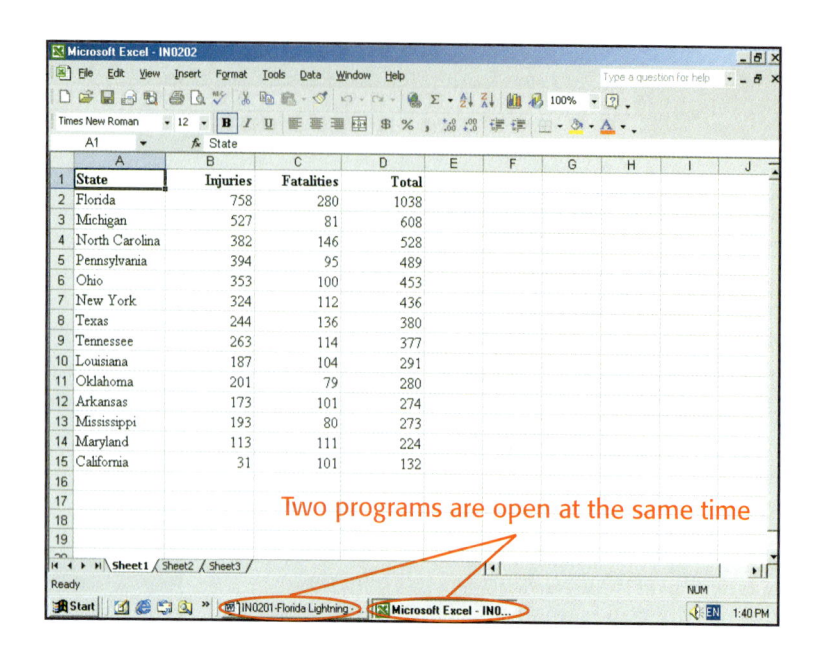

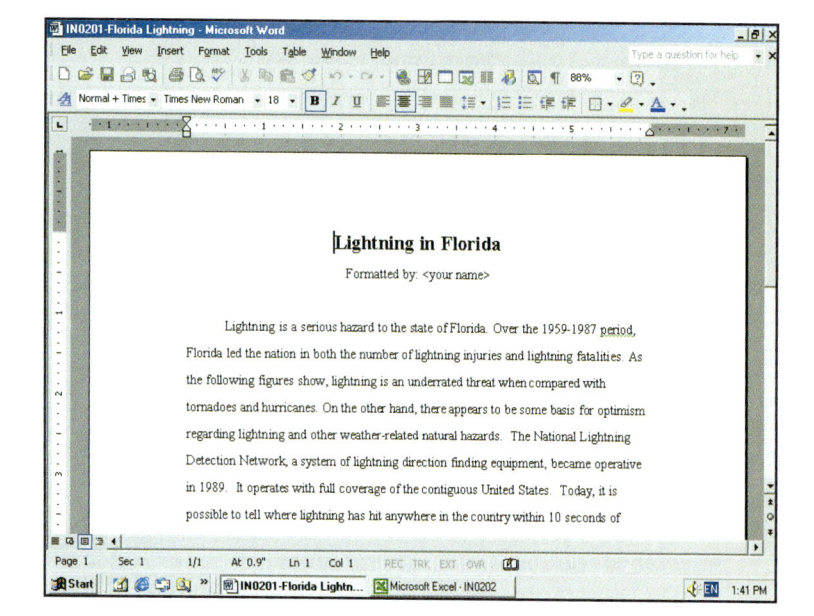

10   CE   Lesson 2   Using Common Elements in Office

5 Click the **Microsoft Excel** button on the taskbar, and then click the **Close** button in the upper-right corner of the Excel title bar.

Excel closes, and the screen reverts to the most recently open window, in this case the Word document. There is only one open document shown in the taskbar.

Leave the IN0201-Florida Lightning document open for the next task.

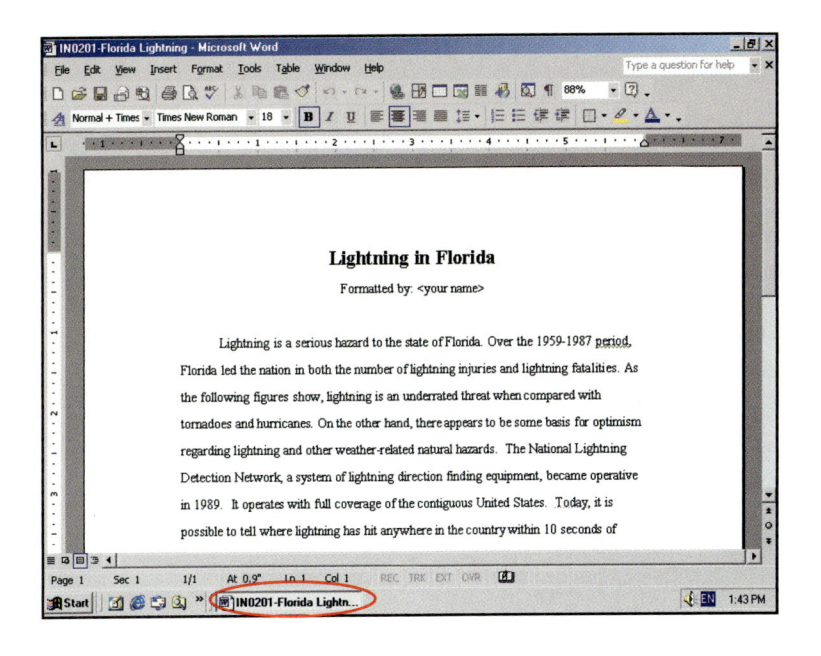

Task 4
USING MENUS AND TOOLBARS

Why would I do this?
You have already used both menus and toolbars in the introductory tasks of this book. For example, you used the File menu option in Task 2 to save a document using a different name. On occasion, you have also been asked to click buttons in a toolbar. The toolbars and menu bar have features that you will need to know to understand the way Microsoft Office works. (Note: The Standard and Formatting toolbars are shown on one line for this task.)

In this task, you learn how to use the menu bar and how to use and modify a toolbar.

1 With the **IN0201-Florida Lightning** document open, click the **Tools** option in the menu bar.

A fairly short drop-down menu displays. The options shown are the most commonly used Tools options and the ones most recently used on your computer. There are other Tools options that are not visible yet. The look of the menu displayed on your computer will depend on which options have been used recently.

The Tools drop-down menu

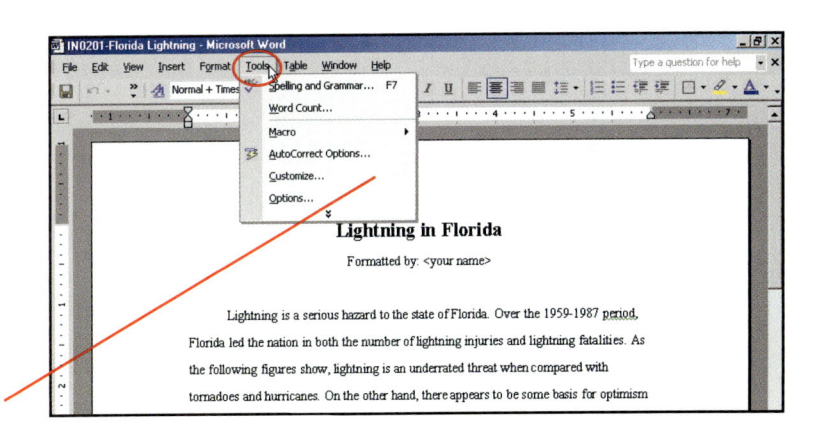

IN DEPTH
The letter that is underlined in the menu option refers to a keyboard shortcut for that option. An alternative way to activate the menu is to press and hold [Alt] and press the underlined letter, which activates the drop-down menu. You can press [Alt]+[T], for example, to activate the Tools menu. You can then use the up and down arrows to move to menu choices and press [↵Enter] to select a command.

2 Leave the pointer on the **Tools** menu option for a couple of seconds.

The Tools drop-down menu expands. The options with the light gray background on the left are the commands that were visible in the unexpanded drop-down menu. Those with a dark gray background on the left are less commonly-used commands. This feature enables you to choose from the most commonly-used commands in a short menu, but adds other options to be used when necessary. If you use one of these other options on a regular basis, it will appear in the short drop-down menu.

Notice that some of the commands in the Tools menu have arrows on the right side. This means that there is a submenu for that menu option.

Items on the short version of the menu
Arrow indicates a submenu

3 Move the pointer anywhere in the document and click.

When you have a menu open and want to close it, clicking outside the menu will turn it off. You can also press Esc *to turn off a menu.*

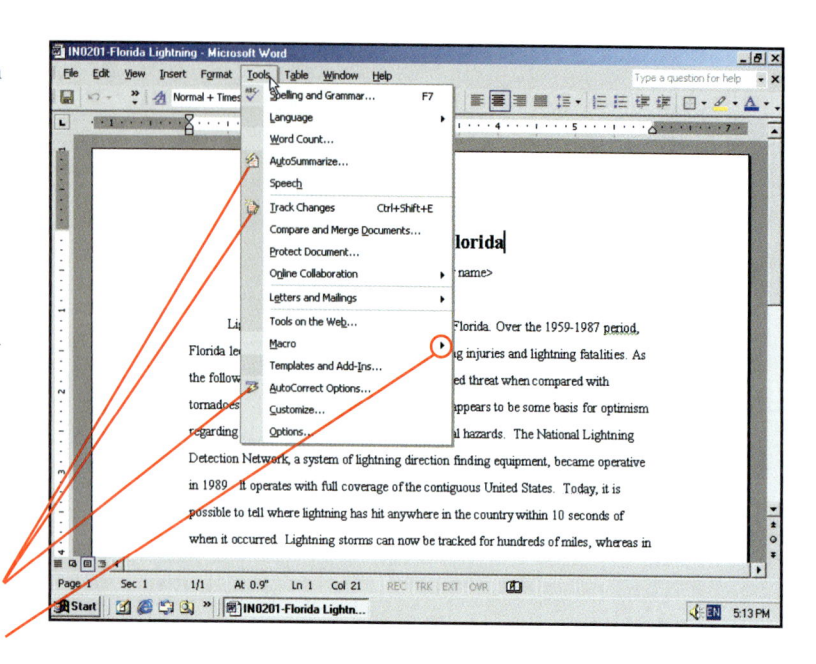

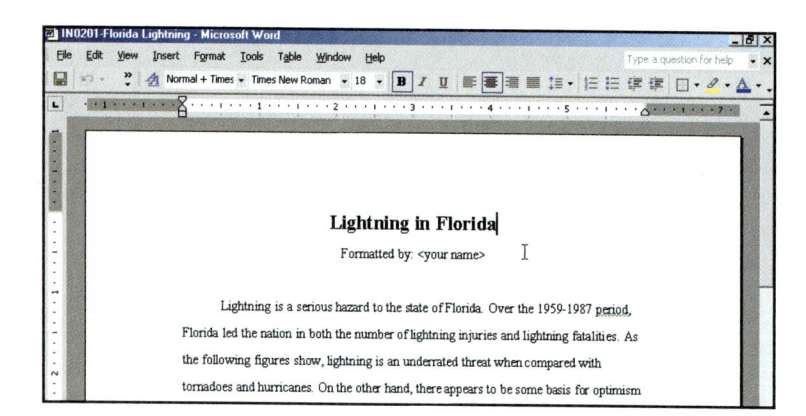

12 CE Lesson 2 Using Common Elements in Office

4 Click **View** from the menu and move the pointer down to the **Toolbars** option.

A submenu displays showing the toolbars that are available. The ones that are displayed on the screen have check marks to the left. There is also a Customize option at the bottom of the submenu.

View drop-down menu

Toolbars option

Pointer

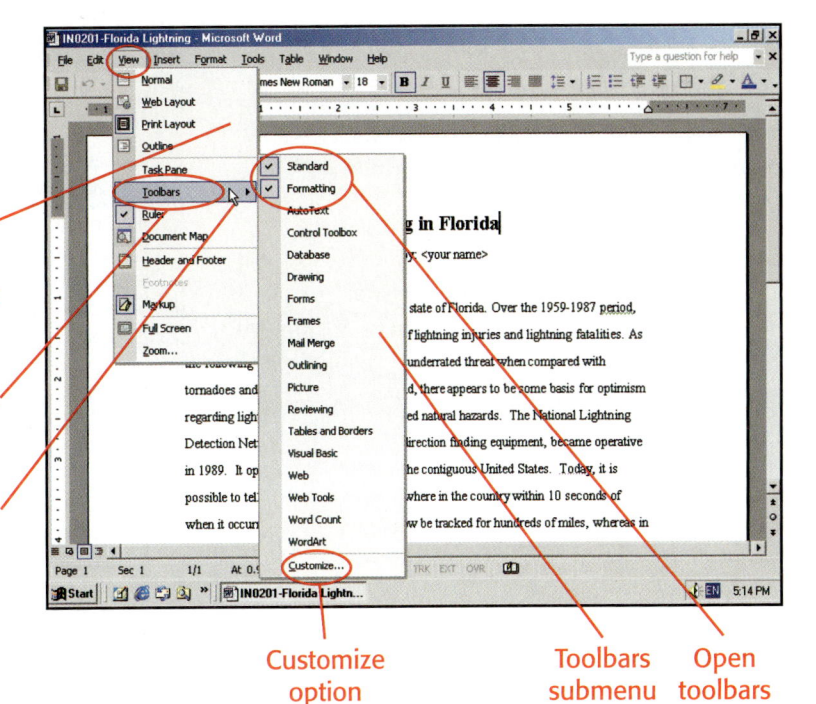

Customize option

Toolbars submenu

Open toolbars

IN DEPTH

Both the Standard and Formatting toolbars are on the same line in the figure. This is the default toolbar setting for several Office programs, including Word, Excel, and PowerPoint. You can stretch or shrink each toolbar by clicking the double vertical bars at the left end of the toolbar and holding down the mouse button, and dragging to the left or right. The problem with using a single line for the two most commonly-used toolbars is that you probably don't recognize each of the buttons or remember where they are located. It is much easier to use these two toolbars on separate lines so you can see all of the buttons.

If your screen shows the toolbars on separate lines, follow the rest of these steps to familiarize yourself with the procedure for turning this option on and off.

Task 4 Using Menus and Toolbars

5 Move the pointer to the **Toolbars** submenu and select **Customize**.

The Customize dialog box displays. This dialog box consists of three tabs—Toolbars, Commands, and Options.

Tabs used to access different pages of the dialog box

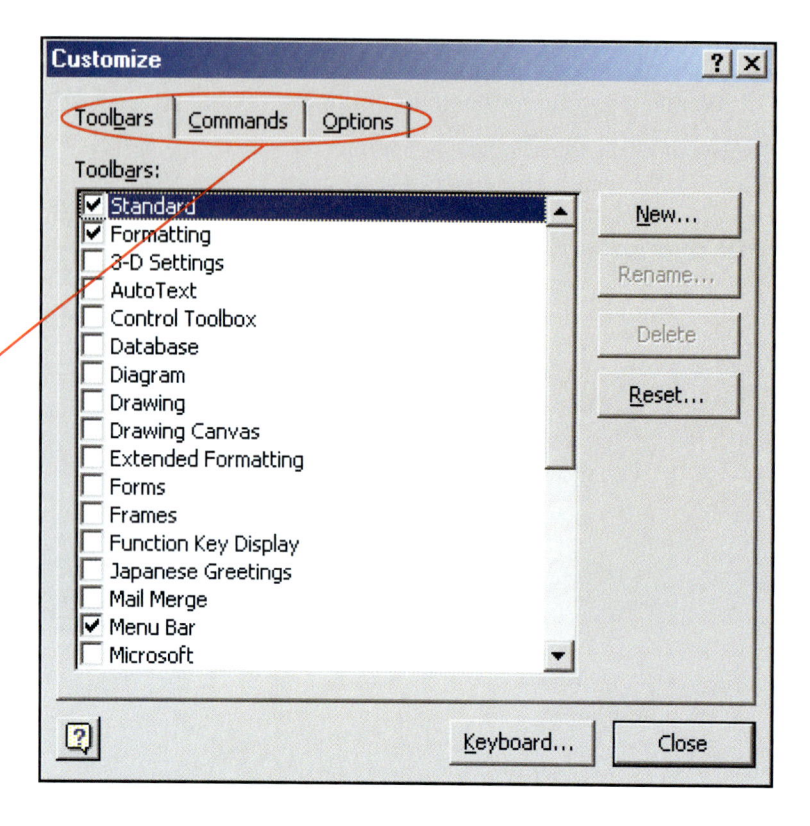

6 Click the **Options** tab to bring it to the forefront, if necessary.

The various toolbar options are shown.

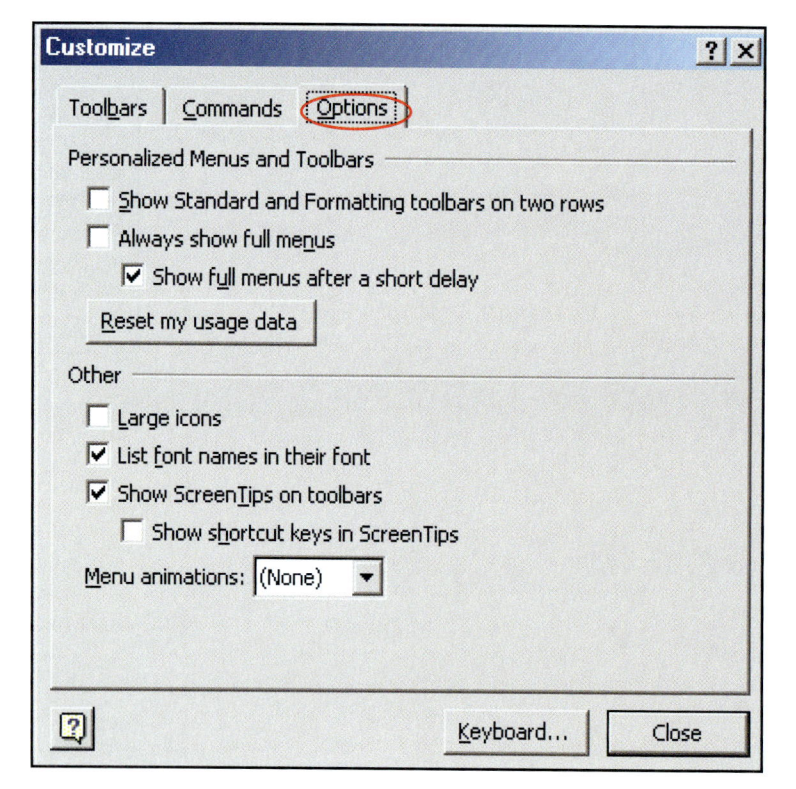

14 CE Lesson 2 Using Common Elements in Office

7 Click the check box to turn on the **Show Standard and Formatting toolbars on two rows** option, if necessary.

This causes the Standard and Formatting toolbars to display on separate rows. The second toolbar decreases your work area slightly, but the convenience of seeing all of the buttons more than makes up for a smaller work area. All of the figures in this book show the double toolbars when appropriate.

The toolbars will be displayed on two rows

Close button

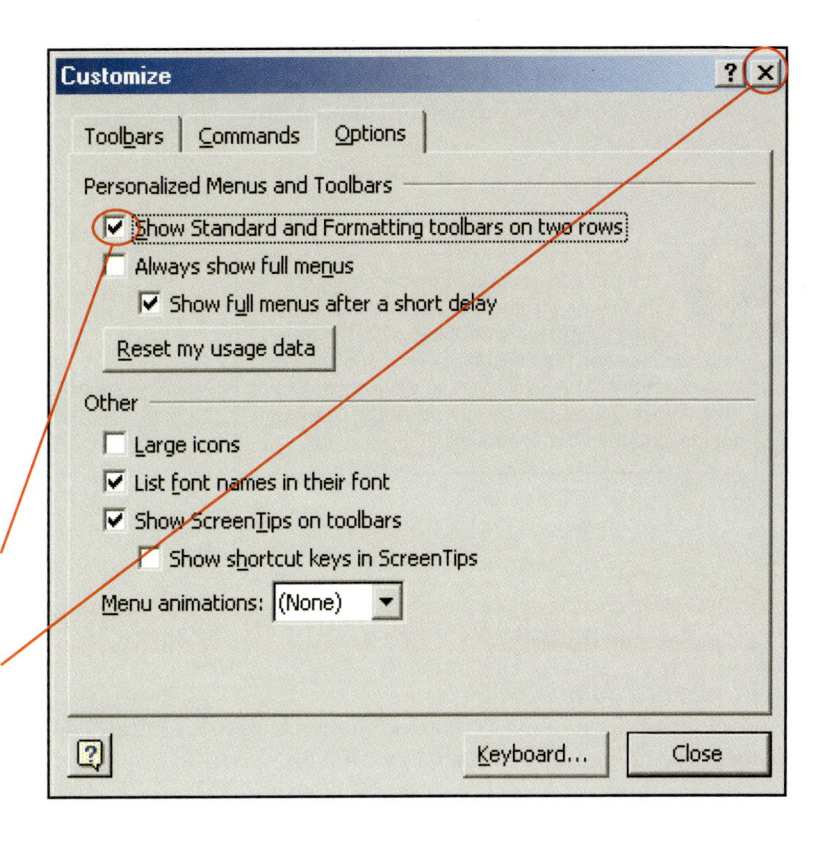

8 Click the **Close** button in the dialog box to close it.

Notice that you now have two rows of toolbars. Also, notice that some buttons on the toolbar have arrows on the right side, which are referred to as down arrows or list arrows.

Click the down arrow on the **Font Size** button on the Formatting toolbar and release the mouse button.

A drop-down list displays, showing some of the available font sizes. There is also a vertical scroll bar to the right of the drop-down list. Try scrolling up and down to see the different font sizes available to use.

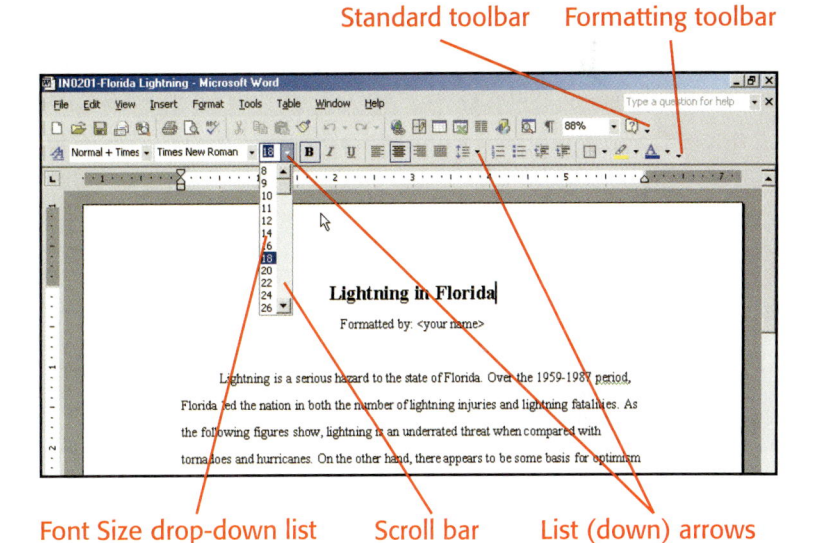

Standard toolbar   Formatting toolbar

Font Size drop-down list   Scroll bar   List (down) arrows

> **QUICK TIP**
>
> If you are using an operating system newer than Windows 95, you can grab the bar on the left edge of the Formatting toolbar and move it up to the Standard toolbar row or down to a row of its own if both toolbars are in one row. If you are using Windows Me or Windows 2000, you can also move back and forth between one row and two rows by clicking the down arrow at the right end of either the Standard or Formatting toolbars and selecting Show Buttons on One Row or Show Buttons on Two Rows from the drop-down list.

Task 4   Using Menus and Toolbars   CE   **15**

9 Click anywhere in the document to close the Font Size list. Leave the document open for the next task.

> **QUICK TIP**
> You can add or remove toolbars by right-clicking on any toolbar. This activates a shortcut menu that displays all of the available toolbars and the Customize option. Scroll down and select the toolbar you want to turn on or off and click it once. To test this, try turning on the Drawing toolbar and then turn it back off.

Task 5
PRINTING A DOCUMENT USING THE TOOLBAR BUTTON AND THE MENU

Why would I do this?

You will print documents for many different reasons—as draft copies for proofing, as final documents and handouts, or even for overhead transparencies. There are two different printing levels with most Office applications. The easiest way to print is to simply click the Print button. This sends a complete document to the printer. The problem with using the Print button is that it gives you little control over the process. You can also print using the Print command from the File menu. This gives you much more control and enables you to print specific pages or ranges of information. It also enables you to specify a printer and set the page layout.

In this task, you print the document you've been working on in this lesson using both the Print button and the menu command.

1 With the **IN0201-Florida Lightning** document still active, make sure your printer is turned on, and then click the **Print** button on the Standard toolbar.

The entire document is sent to the printer.

Print button

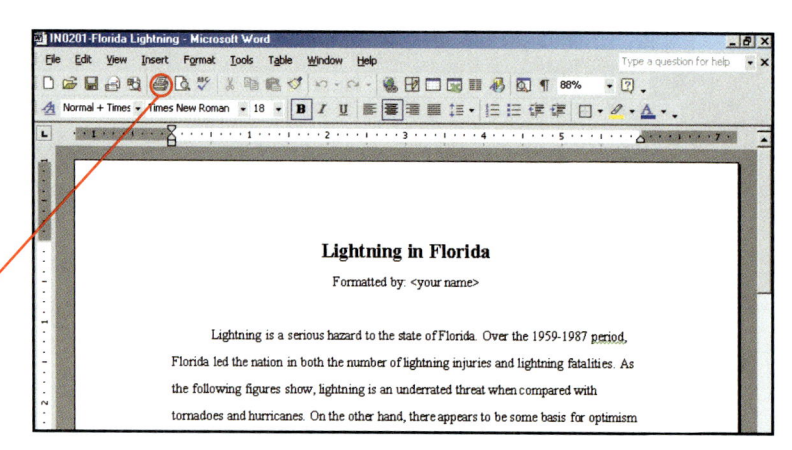

> **CAUTION**
> If the document does not print, it could mean that your printer is not turned on or is not connected properly. Check your connections and try again. If this does not work, you will need to make sure the correct printer is chosen in the Print dialog box, which you open in step 2. If there are several printers available, ask your instructor or lab administrator which printer you should use.

CE   Lesson 2   Using Common Elements in Office

2 Choose **File**, **Print** from the menu.

The Print dialog box displays. This dialog box enables you to choose a printer, specify the number of copies to be printed, select specific pages to print, and choose from several other important options.

Click here to select another printer

Current page option

Enter pages to print

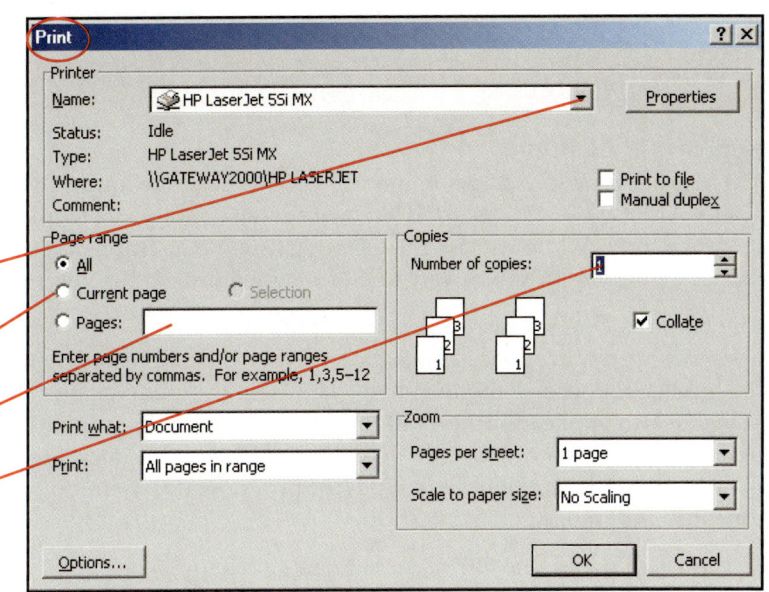

Specify the number of copies

3 Click the **Current page** option in the **Page range** section.

The page you print may not be the page showing on the screen. The program will print whichever page contains the insertion point.

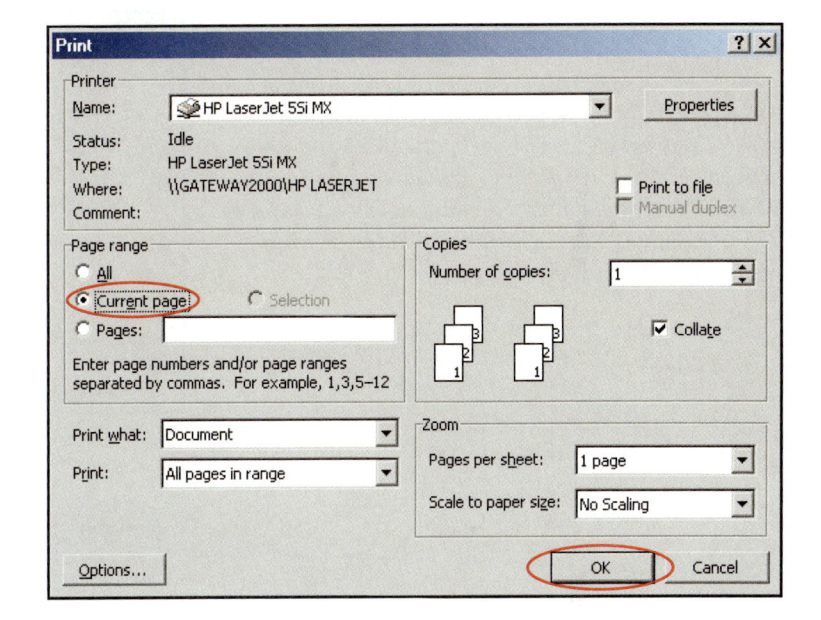

4 Click **OK** to print the current page.

The dialog box closes and the page containing the insertion point is printed. Leave the document open for the next task.

Task 5   Printing a Document Using the Toolbar Button and the Menu

Task 6
USING THE OFFICE ASSISTANT TO GET HELP

Why would I do this?

There are several ways to get help with your questions in any of the Office programs. The **Office Assistant** is a program that enables you to ask questions in sentence form. When you ask the Office Assistant a question, a series of related topics are displayed. You choose one of the topics to get further information.

The help that you see is specific to the application that you are using. If you are using several applications at once, be sure to access Microsoft Help from within the application where you need help. The Help program enables you to learn as you use an application. You will find that using an Office application is an ongoing learning process, and Microsoft Help can be an integral part of that process. Sometimes when you use a Help program, it is useful to print the topic for future reference.

In this task, you use the Office Assistant to get Help.

1 Select **Help**, **Show the Office Assistant** from the menu.

The Office Assistant displays on the screen. You can move it by dragging it to a new location. You can also activate the Office Assistant by clicking the **Microsoft Word Help** *button on the Standard toolbar. (Note: The name of this button changes depending on which application is running.)*

Office Assistant

IN DEPTH

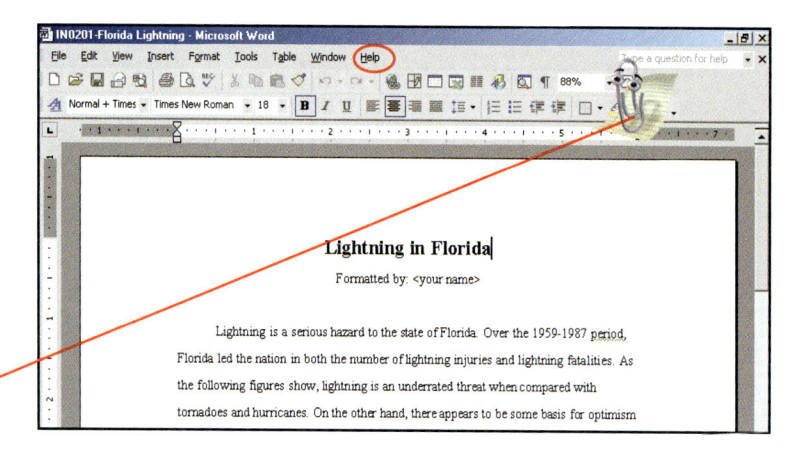

Occasionally, when you are typing a document or trying to perform a procedure, the Office Assistant will appear, even though you haven't selected it. Don't worry—the Office Assistant is just trying to be helpful. Read through the comment, and if it looks like it might be helpful, follow the on-screen instructions. If you do not want this Help, you can simply close the Help window. If you do not like these hints appearing on your screen, click the Office Assistant O̲ptions button and turn off the check boxes in the **Show tips about** section of the O̲ptions page.

2 To get help on a topic, click once on the Office Assistant.

A small dialog box displays, asking you what you would like to do.

Type your question here

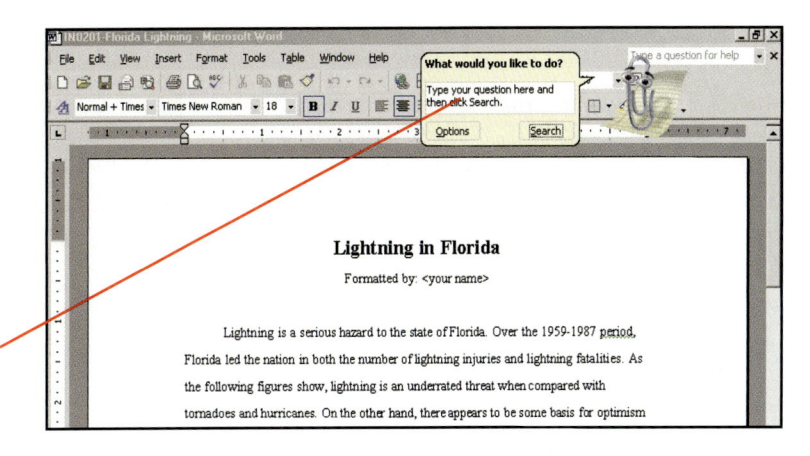

3 In the box, type **How do I center text**.

The Office Assistant looks for keywords in your question and tries to suggest answers. Notice that you do not have to add a question mark to your question.

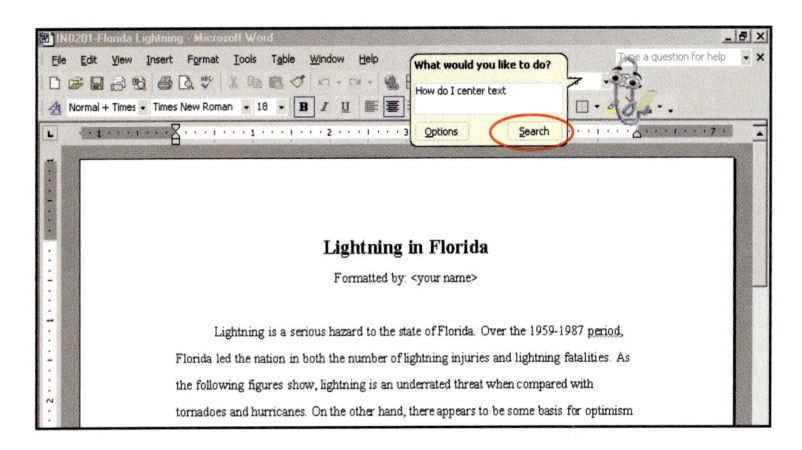

> **QUICK TIP**
> If you start to use the Office Assistant and change your mind, you can remove the dialog box from the screen by clicking anywhere in the document outside of the dialog box.

4 Click the **Search** button.

*The Office Assistant looks for topics that match the keywords it found in your question. Topics that have the most matches are listed first. Other possible matches are displayed if you click the **See more** button.*

A list of possible topics is displayed

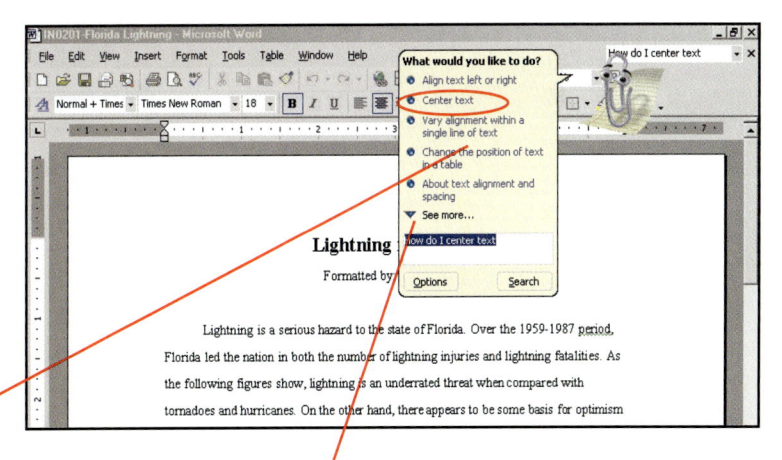

See more button

Task 6   Using the Office Assistant to Get Help   CE

5 Click the button for the **Center text** topic.

A Help window displays and covers part of your document. Notice that some of the text is in blue. This means that more help is available if you click the blue word or phrase. You can use the vertical scroll bar to move down the Help window. (Note: If your Help pane is wider than the one shown, you can skip step 6.)

Show button

A Help window explains the topic you select

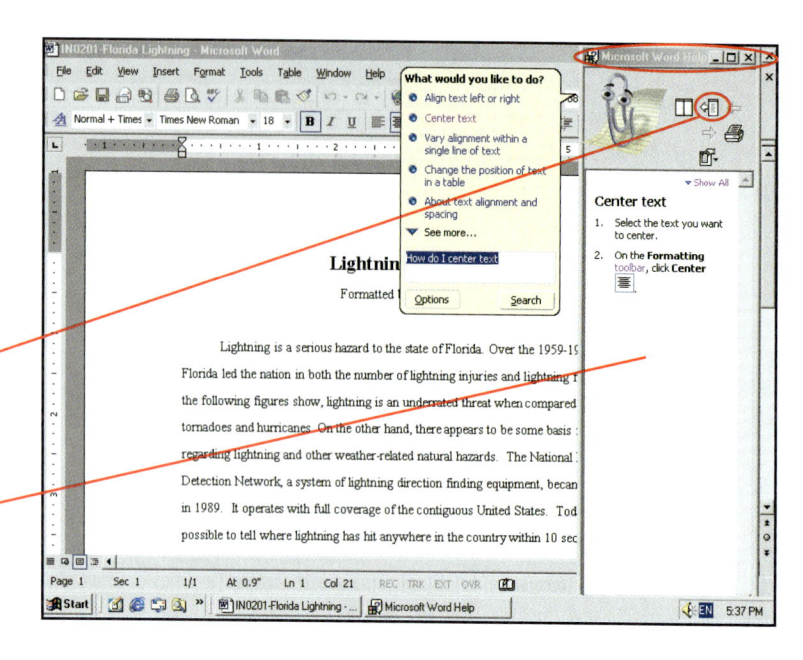

6 Click the **Show** button, if necessary.

The Help window expands to include different types of help. The text box in the Index tab may be used to enter a word and see if it matches a predefined topic, whereas the Contents tab lists chapters and topics. The Answer Wizard tab works just like the Office Assistant—you type in a question, and the wizard displays a list of related topics. To move between these features, simply click the tabs at the top of the window. The Show button changes to the Hide button. If you click the Hide button, the additional Help area is removed from the screen.

Hide button

Tabs for different Help options

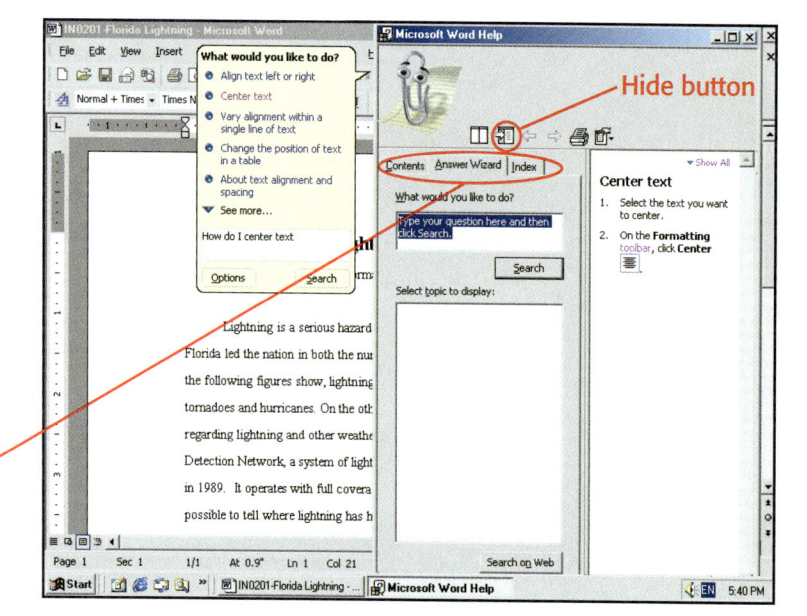

7 Click the **Contents** tab and double-click **Document Fundamentals**.

A number of topics are displayed. To get help, keep double-clicking on the appropriate topics until you see a group of icons with question marks. You can single-click these topics and read the Help topic, or follow the links for more help.

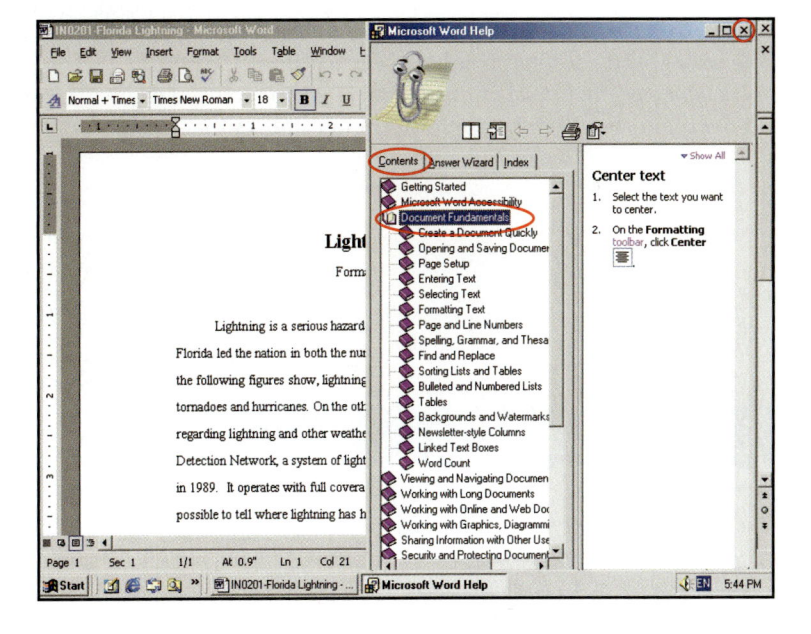

8 Click the **Close** button to close the Help window.

The Help window closes, and the Office Assistant remains on your screen.

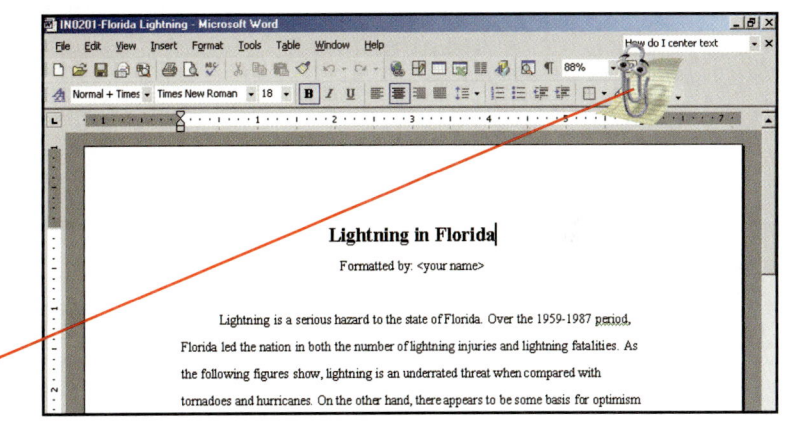

Office Assistant is still active

9 Right-click on the Office Assistant and choose **Hide** from the shortcut menu.

The Office Assistant is removed from the screen.

Click the **Close Window** button to close the document, and then click the **Close** button to exit Word.

IN DEPTH

Some people do not like to have the Office Assistant on the screen at all. If you open an application and see it on your screen, you can hide the Office Assistant by choosing **H**elp, Hide the **O**ffice Assistant. To turn it off completely, click once on the Office Assistant and click the **O**ptions button. Click the check box for the **U**se the Office Assistant option at the top of the dialog box.

Task 6 Using the Office Assistant to Get Help   CE   **21**

The exercises that follow are designed for you to review and use what you have learned in this lesson. You also have the opportunity to practice your skills and then expand on them by applying them to new situations.

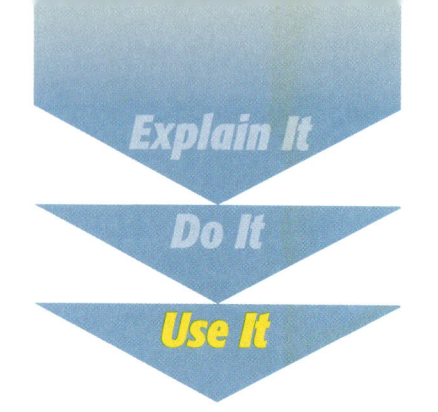

COMPREHENSION

Comprehension exercises are designed to check your memory and understanding of the basic concepts in this lesson. You distinguish between true and false statements, identify new screen elements, and match terms with related statements. If you are uncertain of the correct answer, refer to the task number following each item (for example, T4 refers to Task 4), and review that task until you are confident you can provide a correct response.

TRUE-FALSE

Circle either T or F.

T F **1.** To start an Office program, you need to close any other Office program that is running at the time. **(T3)**

T F **2.** You can activate the menu by pressing Ctrl. **(T4)**

T F **3.** One way to turn toolbars on or off is to right-click anywhere in the toolbar area and click on one of the toolbar choices. **(T4)**

T F **4.** Using **File**, **Print** from the menu gives you more control over printing than using the **Print** button. **(T5)**

T F **5.** You can type in questions in sentence form when you use the Office Assistant. **(T5)**

T F **6.** When you see blue text in a Help window, it means that more help is available by clicking on the text. **(T6)**

MATCHING QUESTIONS

A. **Open** button
B. **Show** button
C. Double-click the file name
D. **Hide** button
E. Right-click, select **Hide**
F. **Save** button

Match the following statements to the word or phrase that is the best match from the list. Write the letter of the matching word or phrase in the space provided next to the number.

1. ____ Button used in the Help window to access Contents and Index features **(T6)**

2. ____ Button used in the Help window so you can no longer see the Contents and Index features **(T6)**

3. ____ Button used to locate and open an existing file **(T2)**

4. ____ Button used to preserve the changes you have made to a document **(T2)**

5. ____ Procedure to remove the Office Assistant from your screen **(T6)**

6. ____ Opens a file from within Windows Explorer **(T2)**

IDENTIFYING PARTS OF THE SCREEN

Refer to the figure and identify the numbered parts of the screen. Write the letter of the correct label in the space next to the number.

1. _____
2. _____
3. _____
4. _____
5. _____
6. _____
7. _____
8. _____
9. _____
10. _____

A. Office Assistant (T6)

B. File name (T2)

C. Used to open drop-down list (T4)

D. Menu bar (T4)

E. Toolbars (T4)

F. Insertion point (T2)

G. **Save** button (T2)

H. **Open** button (T3)

I. **Print** button (T5)

J. Pointer (T4)

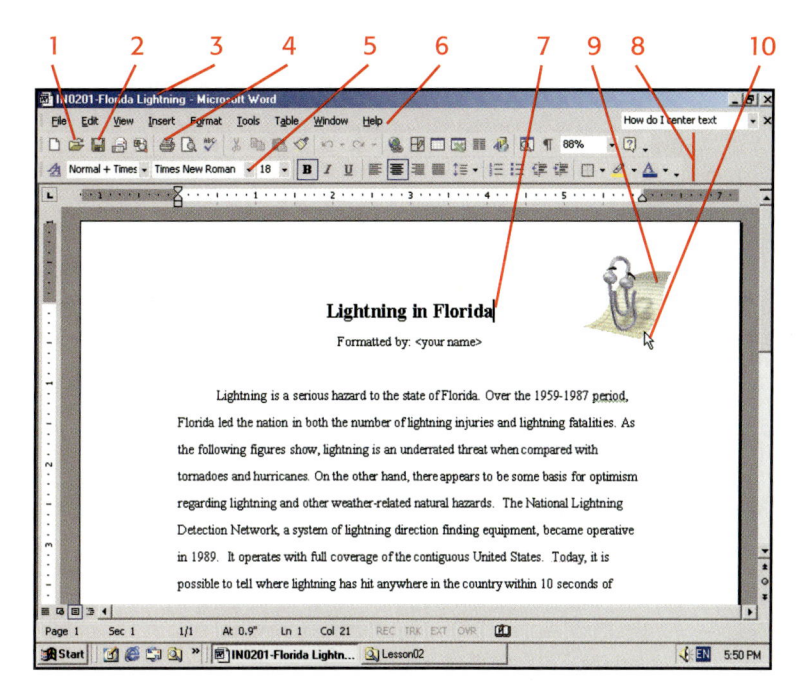

Comprehension CE

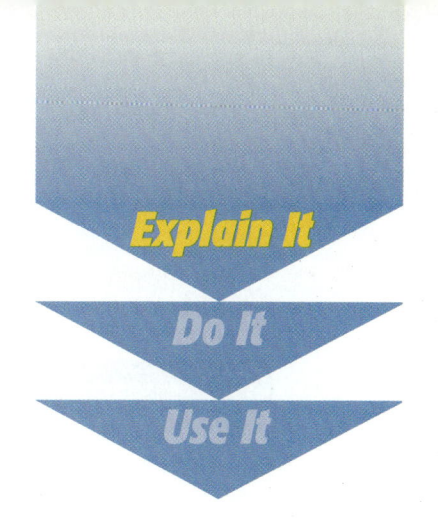

Lesson 1

Explain It
Do It
Use It

Learning the Basics of Excel

Task 1   Navigating a Workbook
Task 2   Selecting Individual Cells
Task 3   Entering Text and Numbers into Cells
Task 4   Fixing Simple Typing Errors
Task 5   Summing a Column of Numbers
Task 6   Saving a Workbook, Printing and Closing a Worksheet

INTRODUCTION

Spreadsheets are used for a variety of information that benefits from being displayed in a grid of columns and rows. Traditionally, spreadsheets have been used for financial information, but they can also be used for schedules, inventories, simple lists, and other information.

This lesson is designed to provide you with the basic skills that you need to create a simple spreadsheet, print it, and save it. In Excel, spreadsheets are called worksheets. A workbook may contain several worksheets.

In this lesson, you learn the basic skills necessary to create and print a useful worksheet. You will create a worksheet showing the May sales for the Armstrong Pool, Spa, and Sauna Company.

VISUAL SUMMARY

When you have completed this lesson, you will have created a worksheet that looks like this:

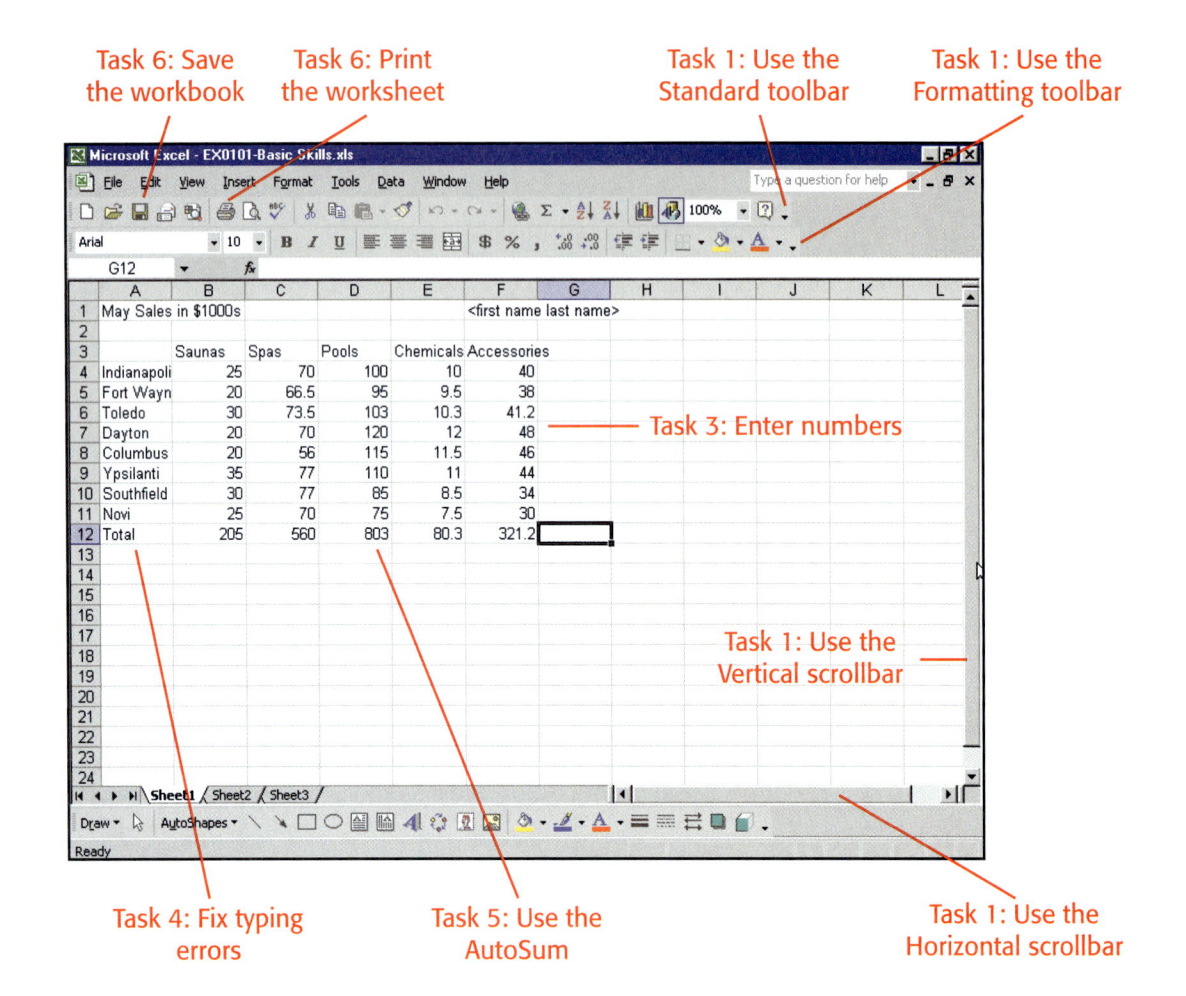

Task 6: Save the workbook
Task 6: Print the worksheet
Task 1: Use the Standard toolbar
Task 1: Use the Formatting toolbar
Task 3: Enter numbers
Task 1: Use the Vertical scrollbar
Task 4: Fix typing errors
Task 5: Use the AutoSum
Task 1: Use the Horizontal scrollbar

	A	B	C	D	E	F
1	May Sales in $1000s					<first name last name>
2						
3		Saunas	Spas	Pools	Chemicals	Accessories
4	Indianapoli	25	70	100	10	40
5	Fort Wayn	20	66.5	95	9.5	38
6	Toledo	30	73.5	103	10.3	41.2
7	Dayton	20	70	120	12	48
8	Columbus	20	56	115	11.5	46
9	Ypsilanti	35	77	110	11	44
10	Southfield	30	77	85	8.5	34
11	Novi	25	70	75	7.5	30
12	Total	205	560	803	80.3	321.2

EXC Lesson 1 Learning the Basics of Excel

Task 1
NAVIGATING A WORKBOOK

Why would I do this?
To understand how to use Excel, you first need to have a basic understanding of how Excel is structured. An Excel file is a *workbook* that consists of several *worksheets* identified by tabs at the bottom of the window. Each of these worksheets is divided into rows and columns; their intersections form a grid of cells. There are many more rows and columns available than will show in the window. To work in Excel, you need to know how to navigate in a worksheet to see different rows and columns.

In this task, you will learn how to select a *sheet* and scroll it to display additional rows and columns.

1 Start Excel.

The program displays a set of three empty worksheets by default. The sheets are designated with tabs near the bottom of the window.

Move the pointer to the tab labeled **Sheet2** at the bottom of the window. Click on the tab.

A second empty sheet is displayed.

Click the **Sheet1** tab to return to the default sheet. Notice the *task pane* on the right side of the screen.

The task pane is used for various functions such as opening previously created workbooks or creating new workbooks from existing ones. The workbooks and templates displayed on your screen will differ from those shown in the figure.

> **CAUTION**
> If the task pane is not displayed on your screen, you can display it by choosing **View, Task Pane** from the menu.

> **IN DEPTH**
> A feature introduced in Office 2000 places the two most commonly used toolbars, **Standard** and **Formatting**, on the same line. The buttons showing on that line change depending on recent use. To provide a consistent set of instructional images, we have disabled this feature. If the toolbars on your screen do not match the figures shown, see the introduction to this book for a description of how to disable this feature.

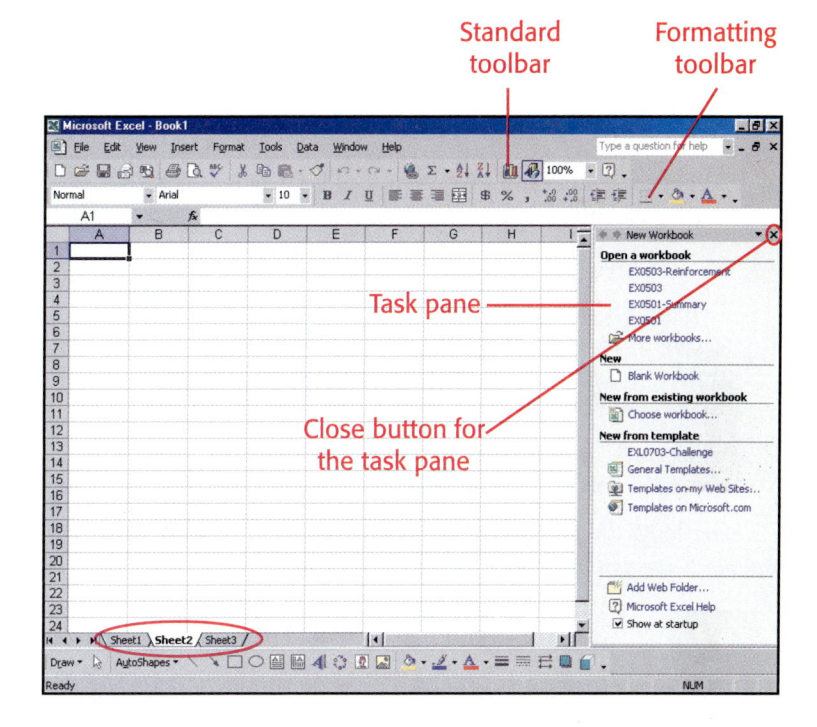

Task 1 Navigating a Workbook EXC 3

2 Click the **Close** button on the task pane to close it.

The task pane closes, and the worksheet window expands to display more columns.

Click once on the down arrow at the bottom of the *vertical scrollbar*.

Row 1 disappears, and a previously hidden row appears at the bottom of the screen. The vertical scrollbar may be used to scroll through the rows of the worksheet.

Row 1 is off the screen

Vertical scrollbar

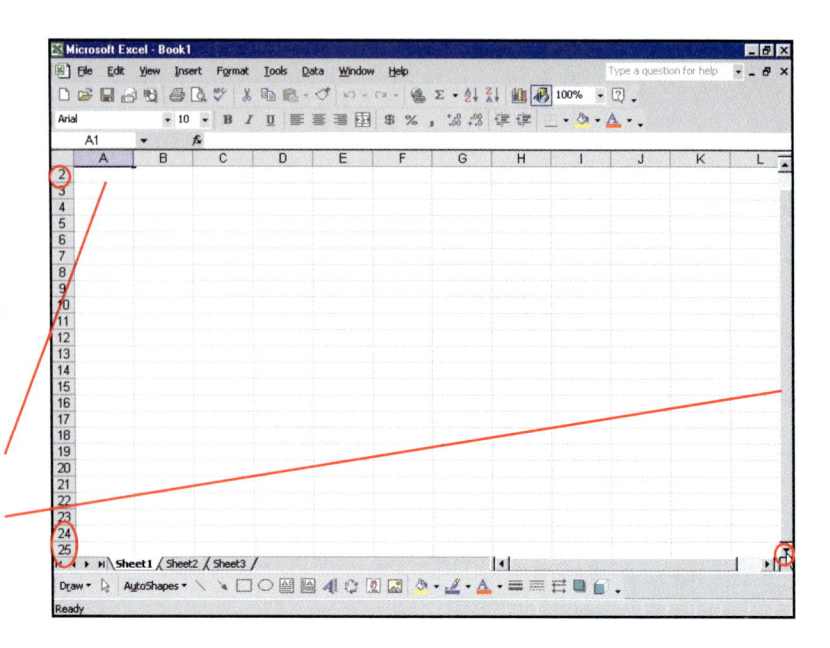

3 Click the same down arrow and hold down the mouse button.

The rows will scroll by rapidly.

Release the mouse button. Click the up arrow at the top of the vertical scrollbar and hold down the button until row 1 appears. Release the button.

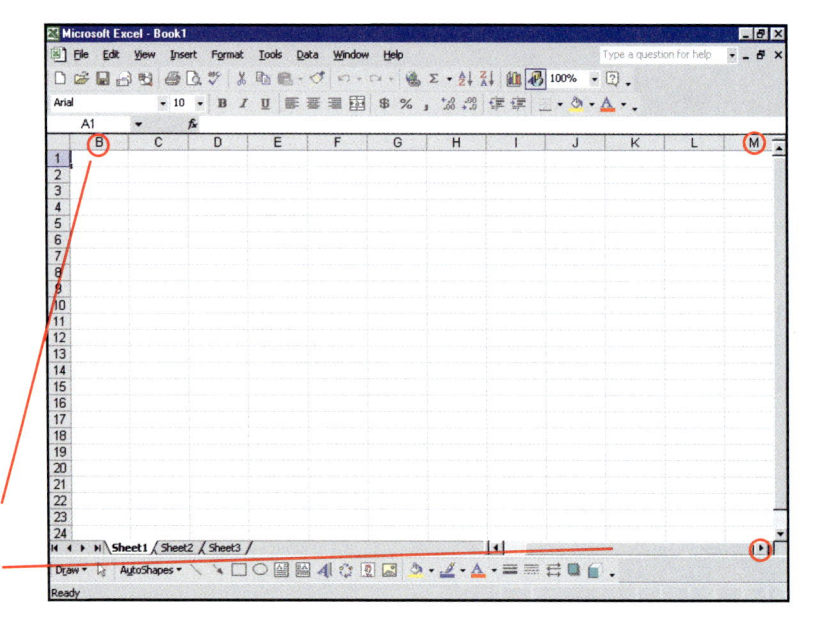

Click once on the right arrow on the *horizontal scrollbar*.

Column A will scroll off the screen, and the next column to the right will appear.

Column A is off the screen

Horizontal scrollbar

4 EXC Lesson 1 Learning the Basics of Excel

4 Click once on the left arrow on the horizontal scrollbar.

The sheet scrolls to the right and column A will reappear.

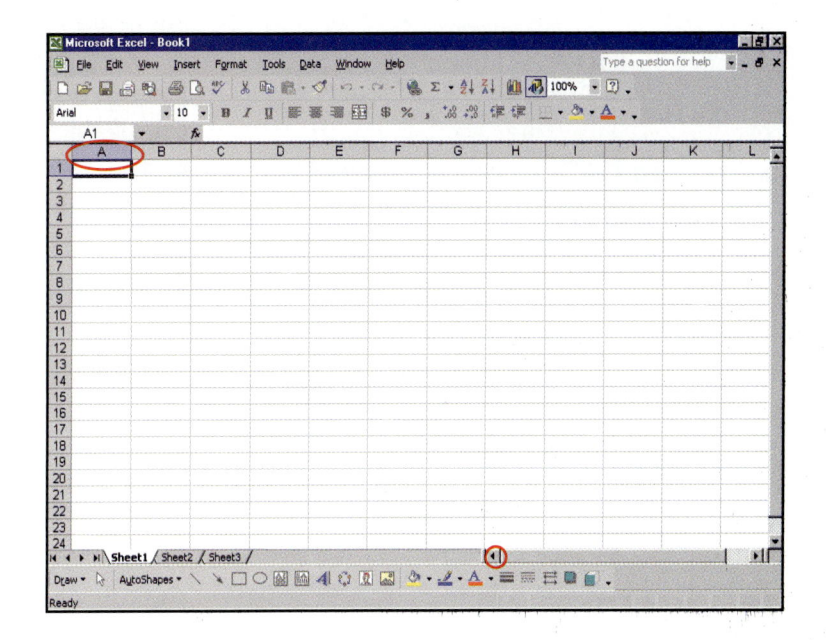

Task 2
SELECTING INDIVIDUAL CELLS

Why would I do this?
You must select a *cell* before you can enter text, numbers, or formulas. A cell is a bounded area that is identified by a column letter and a row number. If a cell is selected, it will have a dark border around it. Selecting cells is one of the most commonly used procedures in Excel and there are several ways to do this.

In this task, you learn how to select cells using the mouse, `Tab`, `Enter`, and the arrow keys.

1 Use the mouse to move the pointer to the cell that is in column **B** and row **2** (this cell is referred to as cell B2).

Notice that the cell selection does not move with the pointer.

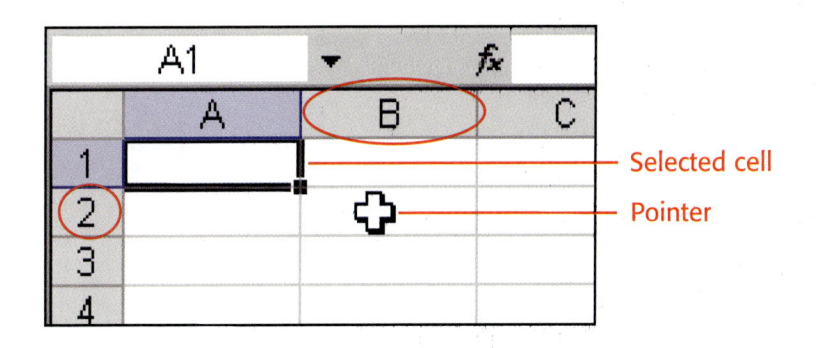

— Selected cell
— Pointer

CAUTION

Moving the pointer to a cell does not select it. If you start typing without actually moving the selection, your text or number will be placed in whatever cell is currently selected.

Task 2   Selecting Individual Cells   EXC   5

2 Click the left mouse button.

Notice that the border of the cell on which you clicked changes to a darker line. The **column heading** *and* **row heading** *are highlighted, and the address of the cell (B2) appears in the Name box.*

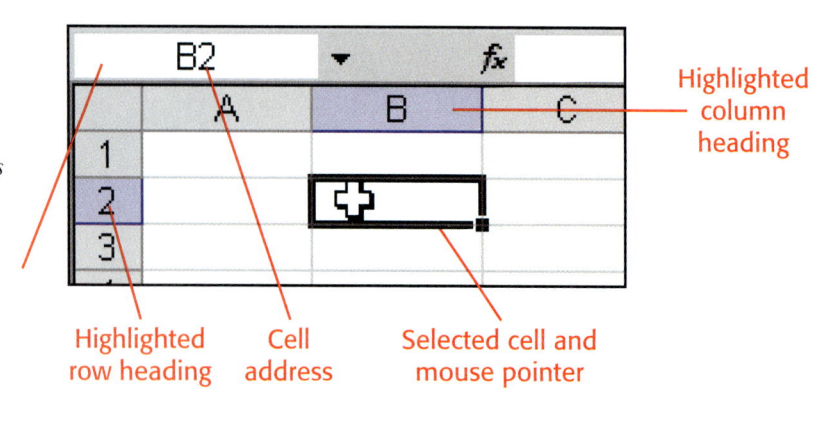

Name box

Highlighted column heading

Highlighted row heading

Cell address

Selected cell and mouse pointer

3 Press the up arrow on your keyboard once.

Notice that the selection moves to cell B1.

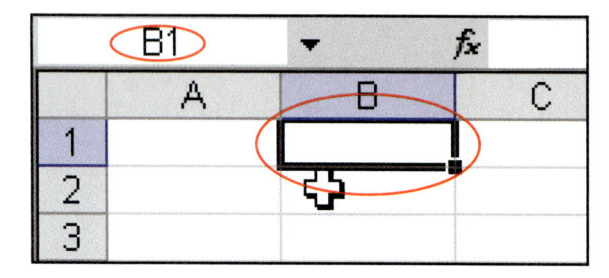

4 Press ↵Enter.

The selection moves downward one row to cell B2. This method of moving the selection is useful when you are entering columns of numbers.

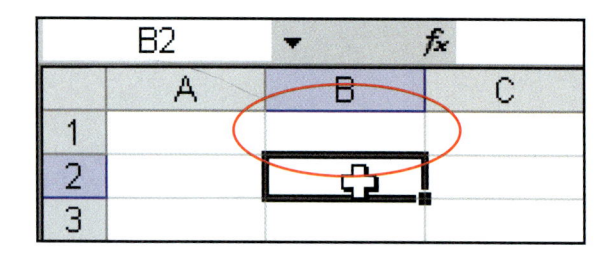

5 Press Tab three times.

The selection begins at cell B2 and moves one cell to the right each time you press this key. This method is useful when you are typing a series of numbers in a row of cells.

Press ↵Enter.

This time the selection moves to cell B3. When you enter numbers in a row of cells using Tab, ↵Enter *will return to the start of the next row of cells.*

6   EXC   Lesson 1   Learning the Basics of Excel

6 Press `Tab` three times.

The selection moves three cells to the right.

Hold `Shift` and press `Tab`.

The selection moves one cell to the left.

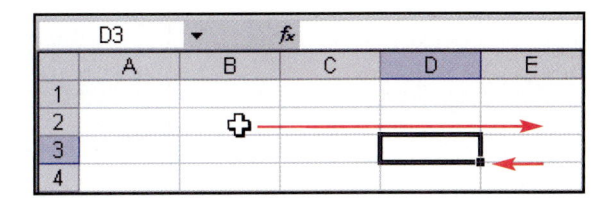

> **IN DEPTH**
> Notice that most `Tab` keys have two arrows on the key to indicate that it can be used to move the selection to the left or right depending on whether or not the `Shift` key is also pressed.

Task 3
ENTERING TEXT AND NUMBERS INTO CELLS

Why would I do this?

Before you start to enter words and numbers into a worksheet, it is a good idea to plan for the future. It is easier to copy formulas, chart data, and transfer tables of data into Word or Access if the data and its labels are organized correctly. If you plan to gather the same data each week or quarter, consider using a separate, identical worksheet for each time period. Place labels in cells at the top of a column or at the left of a row of data. Do not use empty cells or cells with dashes to separate sections of a table. Visual cues such as these should be signaled with borders or shading. Summaries are most useful if they are presented on their own sheet the same way that year-end summaries of quarterly data are treated.

Text is entered into cells to provide labels and other information for users of the sheet. Numbers are used in calculations and formulas. Usually, a cell contains text or numbers, but not both. Once the numbers have been entered into the cells, you can manipulate the numbers, perform calculations, and use the numbers to visually portray a trend by creating a chart. If numbers are used as labels or mixed with text, as in a street address, they are treated as text.

In this task, you learn how to enter text and numbers into cells.

1 Move the pointer to cell **A1** and click the left mouse button to select the cell.

Task 3 Entering Text and Numbers into Cells EXC 7

2 Type the phrase **Sales in May in $1000s** and press ⏎Enter.

The selection moves to cell A2.

> **IN DEPTH**
> The direction that the selection moves when you press ⏎Enter can be changed. The setting is found by using the menu bar. Choose Tools, Options, click the Edit tab, select **Move selection after Enter**, select a Direction, and click OK.

3 Select cell **A3**.

This will be the upper-left corner of the table of data. It is left blank. You will enter the table one row at a time by using Tab to move across and ⏎Enter to begin the second row.

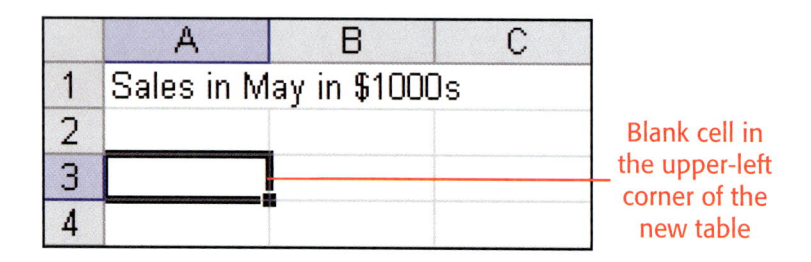

Blank cell in the upper-left corner of the new table

> **IN DEPTH**
> This cell is not used in this table, but you start here so that the selection will return to this column when you press ⏎Enter at the end of the row of cells.

4 Press Tab.

This moves the selection to cell B3.

Type **Saunas** and press Tab.

The first column heading is now in cell B3.

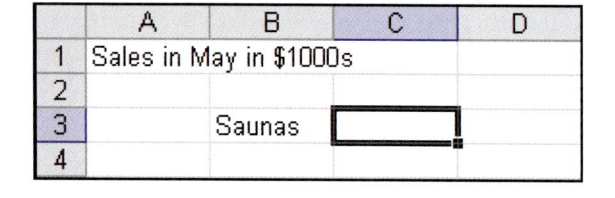

5 Type **Spas** and press Tab. Repeat this process to enter **Pools** and **Chemicals** in cells **D3** and **E3**.

If the word is wider than the cell, do not be concerned at this time. You will learn how to adjust column widths in a later task.

Type **Accessories** in cell **F3**, then press ⏎Enter instead of Tab.

The selection automatically returns to cell A4 to start the next row.

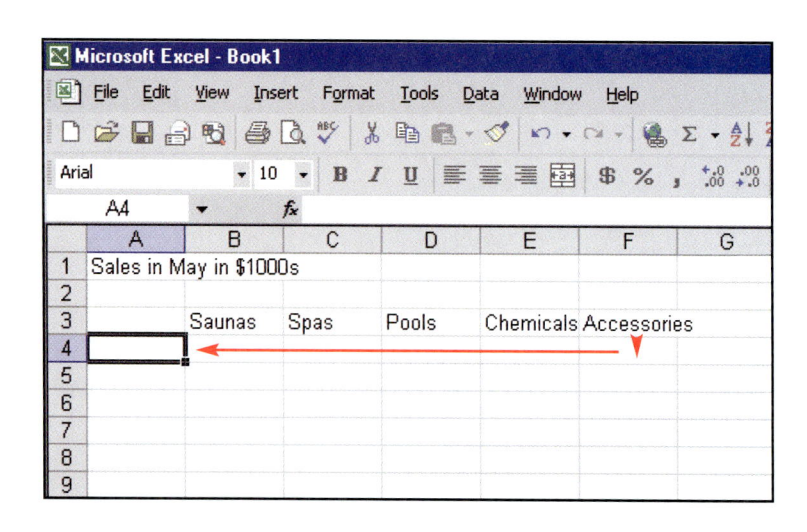

8 EXC **Lesson 1** Learning the Basics of Excel

6 Type **Indianapolis** in cell **A4** and press `Tab`.

Refer to the figure and use this method to fill out the table with the following sales figures for May:

	Saunas	Spas	Pools	Chemicals	Accessories
Indianapolis	25	70	100	10	40
Fort Wayne	20	66.5	95	9.5	38
Toledo	30	73.5	103	10.3	41.2
Dayton	20	70	120	12	48
Columbus	20	56	115	11.5	46
Ypsilanti	35	77	110	11	44
Southfield	30	77	85	8.5	34
Novi	25	70	75	7.5	30

> **CAUTION**
> When you use `Tab` to enter values in adjacent cells, Excel remembers the starting point of the series and returns to that column when you press `Enter`. Interrupting the pattern, for instance to correct an error, sets a new starting point. Therefore, if you make mistakes entering the text or the numbers, leave them for now. You will learn how to fix mistakes in the next task.

7 Select cell **F1** and type your last name. Press `Enter`.

If your name is too long to fit in the cell, enter it anyway. You will learn how to deal with this formatting problem in a later lesson.

Type your own name

Task 4
FIXING SIMPLE TYPING ERRORS

Why would I do this?
It is possible to make mistakes when entering data. Also, information may change and need to be adjusted. The power of using an electronic spreadsheet is in the ability to easily change information and have formulas recalculated automatically.

In this task, you learn how to edit the contents of the cells.

1 Select cell **A12** and type the incorrectly spelled word **Totle** in the cell. Do not press the ↵Enter or Tab key yet.

Notice that a vertical line marks the position where text is entered. This line is called the ***insertion point***.

The vertical line is the insertion point

2 Press ←Backspace twice.

The insertion point moves to the left, erasing the last two letters.

> **IN DEPTH**
>
> You can move the insertion point within the text by using the right and left arrow keys on the keyboard. ←Backspace deletes characters to the left of the insertion point, and Del deletes characters to the right of the insertion point.

3 Type **al** and press Tab.

EXC Lesson 1 Learning the Basics of Excel

4 To replace an entire entry, just type over it. Select cell **A1**, type **May Sales in $1000s** and press ⏎Enter.

The previous entry is replaced.

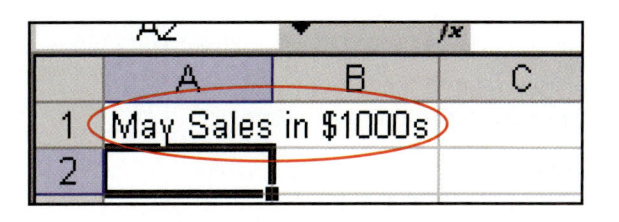

5 Click the **Undo** button on the Standard toolbar.

The Undo button reverses the previous action.

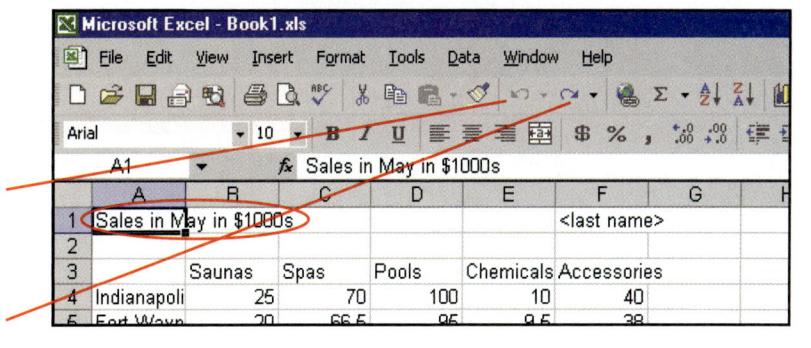

Undo button

Redo button

6 Click the **Redo** button.

*The cell changes back to **May Sales in $1000s**.*

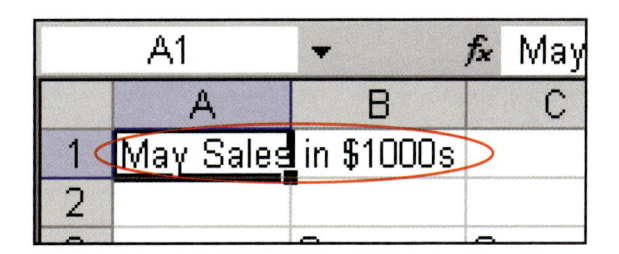

CAUTION If you are using the feature that places the Standard and Formatting toolbars on the same line, you may not see the Redo button if it has not been used recently. If that is the case, locate the Toolbar Options button for the Standard toolbar and click on it to display the rest of the buttons on the Standard toolbar. Do not use the Toolbar Options button at the far right. That one refers to the additional buttons on the Formatting toolbar.

7 Move the pointer to cell **F1**. Double-click the left mouse button to place the insertion point in the text within the cell.

Double-clicking on a cell allows you to edit the contents of a cell.

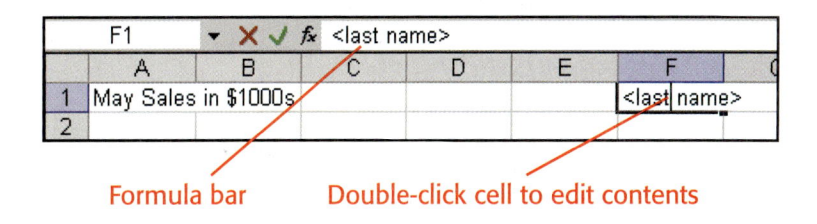

Formula bar   Double-click cell to edit contents

CAUTION You may have trouble double-clicking. The most common problem with double-clicking is caused by moving the mouse slightly between clicks. Rest the heel of your hand on the table so the mouse is less likely to roll. This may take a little practice. If double-clicking is frustrating you, click the cell once and the contents will appear in the **Formula bar**. Click once on the text in the Formula bar and edit it.

Task 4   Fixing Simple Typing Errors   EXC

8 Use the left arrow on the keyboard to position the insertion point to the left of your last name. Type your first name and a space.

Press `Enter` to finish.

Add your first name

Task 5
SUMMING A COLUMN OF NUMBERS

Why would I do this?
The purpose of most worksheets is to make **calculations** based on the data you have entered. The simplest and most commonly used calculation is the sum calculation. It is used so often, in fact, that Excel has a built-in AutoSum button.

In this task, you learn how to sum columns of numbers using AutoSum.

1 Select cell **B12**.

Click the **AutoSum** button located in the Standard toolbar.

Several things happen. A formula, =SUM(B4:B11), appears in cell B12 and in the Formula bar. Also, a moving dashed line called a **marquee** *surrounds the group of cells being summed.*

AutoSum button
Marquee

> **IN DEPTH**
> The program will guess which range of cells you wish to include in the formula. If the guess is incorrect, you may click-and-drag to select a different range of cells.

2 Press `Tab` to accept the formula and enter the result into the cell.

The sum is the total number of sauna sales in the various locations.

> **IN DEPTH**
> Excel guesses which group of numbers you want to sum. If it is not the correct group, you can edit the formula just as you edit text. In the formula above, B4:B11 refers to all of the cells in a rectangle that starts with B4 and ends with B11. If you wanted to add up a different range of cells, you would edit the formula and put in different cell addresses. You will learn more about such formulas in later lessons.

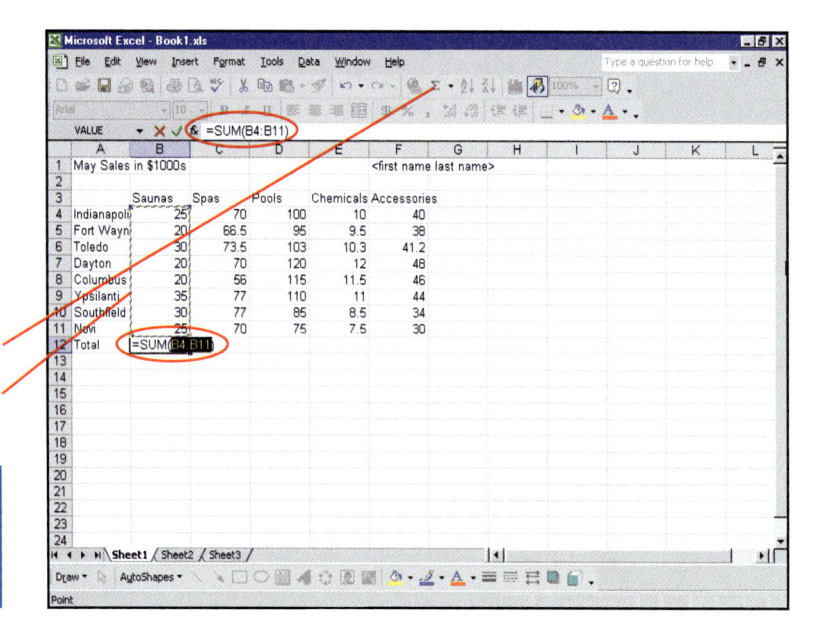

12 EXC Lesson 1 Learning the Basics of Excel

3 Repeat this process for each of the remaining columns.

The formula may be accepted by using ⏎Enter or Tab⇆.

	A	B	C	D	E	F	G
1	May Sales in $1000s					<first name last name>	
2							
3		Saunas	Spas	Pools	Chemicals	Accessories	
4	Indianapoli	25	70	100	10	40	
5	Fort Wayn	20	66.5	95	9.5	38	
6	Toledo	30	73.5	103	10.3	41.2	
7	Dayton	20	70	120	12	48	
8	Columbus	20	56	115	11.5	46	
9	Ypsilanti	35	77	110	11	44	
10	Southfield	30	77	85	8.5	34	
11	Novi	25	70	75	7.5	30	
12	Total	205	560	803	80.3	321.2	
13							
14							

Task 6
SAVING A WORKBOOK, PRINTING AND CLOSING A WORKSHEET

Why would I do this?
A computer has a short-term memory that forgets what it was doing when the power is turned off or interrupted. In order to record your spreadsheet for later use, you will need to make a more permanent copy of it. One way to do this is to save a copy magnetically on a disk.

Even in an age of digital communications, there are still advantages to recording data on paper. A paper copy is lightweight, portable, and compatible with older storage systems. It is often easier to review several pages of data simultaneously and share the information with others who do not have a computer.

In this task, you will learn how to print a worksheet and save the workbook on disk. In addition, you will learn how to close a workbook and exit Excel.

1 Click the **Save** button on the Standard toolbar.

The Save As dialog box appears with a suggested filename already highlighted in the File name box.

> **IN DEPTH**
> The conventions of this book assume that the file extensions for **registered programs** have been hidden. If this is not the case in your computer setup, you will see an .xls extension added to your Excel filenames. File extensions can be turned on or off in Windows Explorer under View, Folder Options.

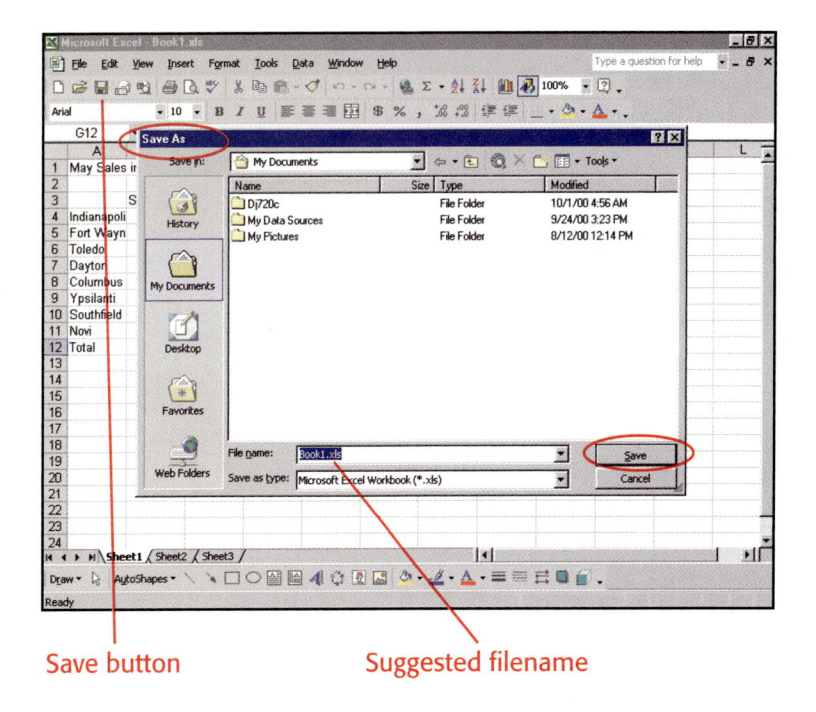

Save button   Suggested filename

Task 6   Saving a Workbook, Printing and Closing a Worksheet   EXC   13

❷ Type **EX0101-Basic Skills**. Do not press ⏎Enter yet.

This action replaces the highlighted text in the File name box.

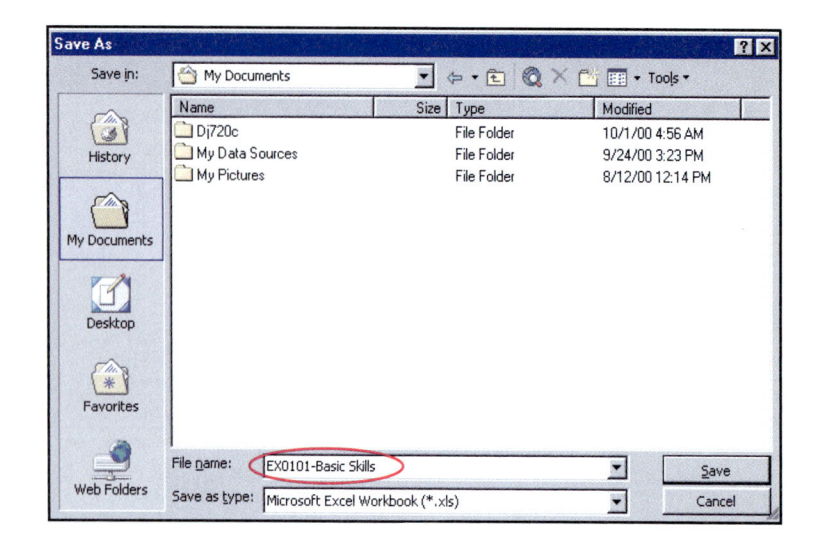

> **CAUTION**
>
> A dialog box has buttons in it that you can click on to produce certain actions. Often, one of the buttons is indicated as the default choice by a darker and thicker border. In this case, the Save button is the default. If you press the ⏎Enter key after typing in the name of the file, it will save the file in whatever folder or disk is currently selected. If you do this by mistake, click File, Save As. This will open the Save As dialog box, and you can now select the folder where this file should be saved.

❸ Place a 3½" floppy disk in drive A.

Ask your instructor for assistance if necessary.

Click the down arrow at the right side of the **Save in** box.

A diagram of your computer's disk drives will appear.

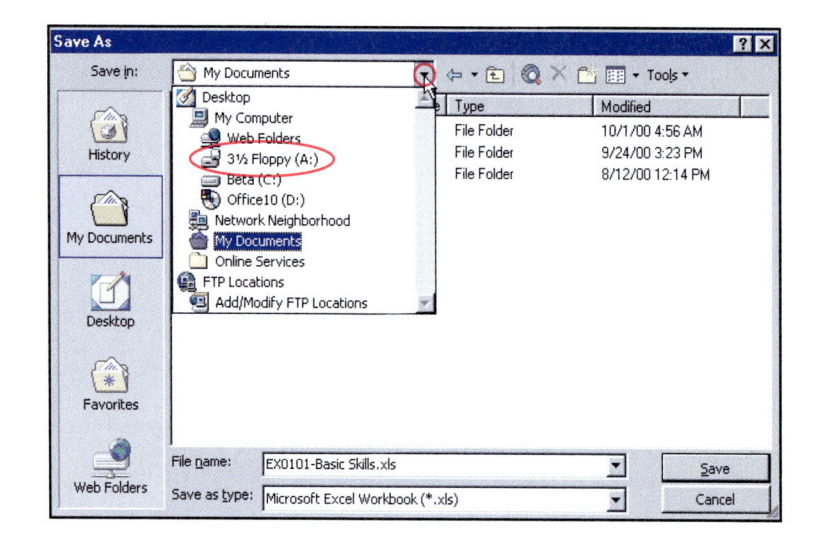

4 Click the **3½" Floppy (A:)** drive.

If your class is using another disk drive, follow your instructor's directions.

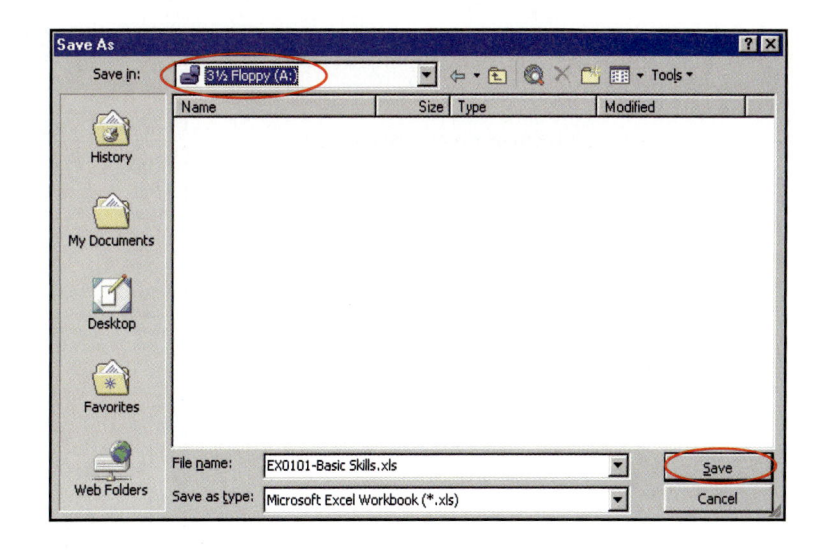

5 Click the **Create New Folder** button.

The New Folder dialog box is displayed.

Type **Excel Exercises** in the **Name** box.

A new folder will be created on the floppy disk.

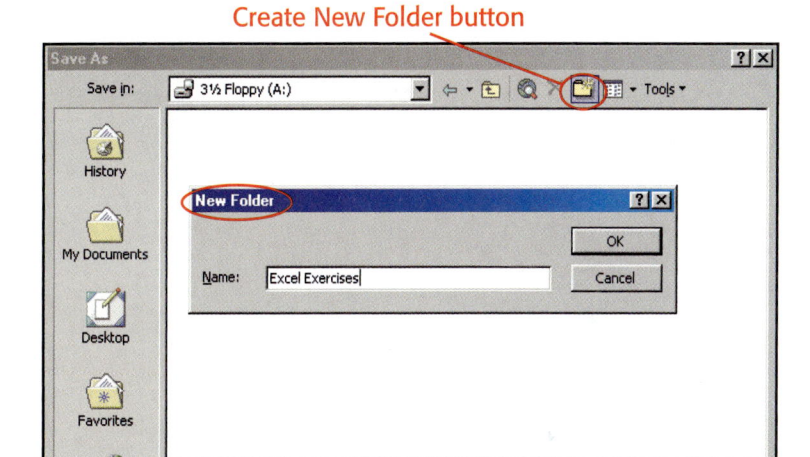

6 Click **OK**.

The folder is created on the floppy disk, and its name is displayed in the Save in box.

Click **Save**.

A copy of the workbook is saved on your floppy disk in the new folder. The pointer turns into an hourglass while the file is being saved, and an indicator displays in the status bar.

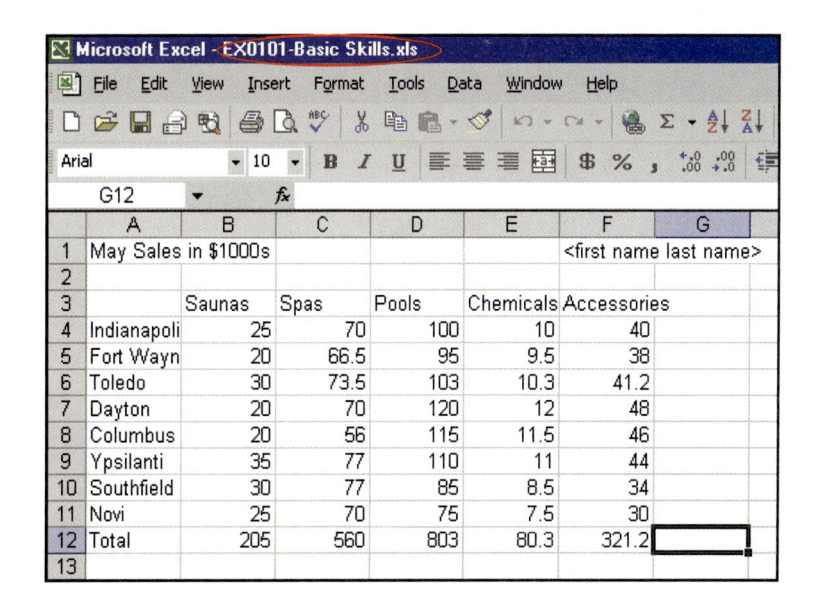

Task 6   Saving a Workbook, Printing and Closing a Worksheet   EXC   15

7 Check to make sure that your printer is connected and turned on.

Click the **Print** button on the Standard toolbar.

The current worksheet is sent to the printer.

Move the pointer onto the **Close Window** button on the menu bar.

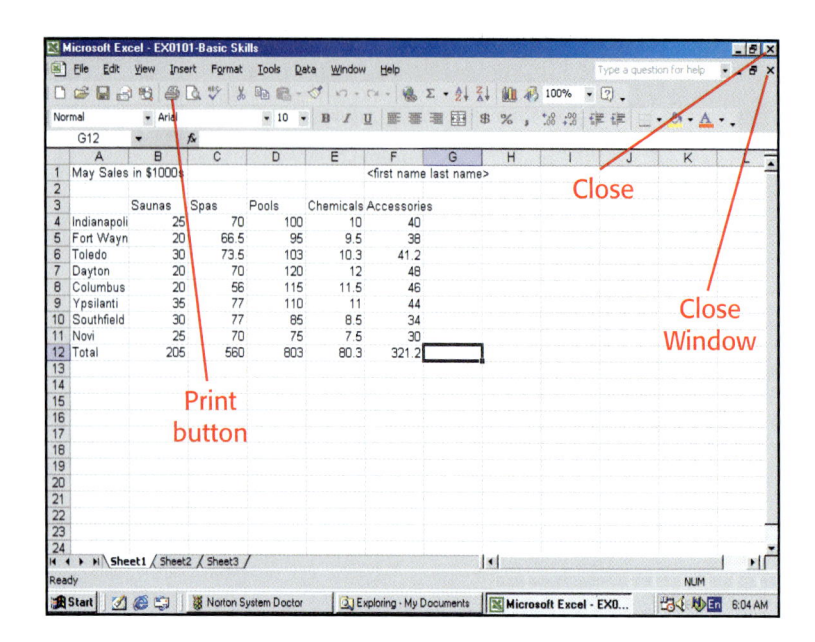

> ⚠ **CAUTION**
> If you click the **Close** button on the title bar, the Excel program will close along with any open workbooks. This is not a big problem since you will not lose your work. Simply launch Excel again if you had intended to leave it open.

8 Click the **Close Window** button on the menu bar.

The workbook closes, but Excel stays open. If you have made any changes to the workbook since the last time it was saved, you will be prompted to save it.

Click the **Close** button on the Excel title bar.

The Excel program closes.

EXC   Lesson 1   Learning the Basics of Excel

The exercises that follow are designed for you to review and use what you have learned in this lesson. You also have the opportunity to practice your skills and then expand on them by applying them to new situations.

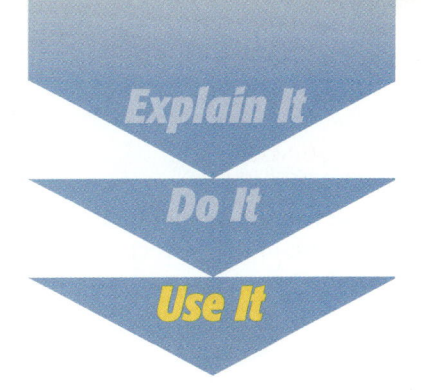

COMPREHENSION

Comprehension exercises are designed to check your memory and understanding of the basic concepts in this lesson. You distinguish between true and false statements, identify new screen elements, and match terms with related statements. If you are uncertain of the correct answer, refer to the task number following each item (for example, T4 refers to Task 4), and review that task until you are confident you can provide a correct response.

TRUE-FALSE

Circle either T or F.

T F 1. A workbook and a worksheet are the same thing. The words may be used interchangeably. **(T1)**

T F 2. The vertical scrollbar and its arrows can be used to rapidly scroll through the sheet or to scroll one row at a time. **(T1)**

T F 3. A cell in column C and row 2 would be referred to as cell 2C. **(T2)**

T F 4. A selected cell has a darker border than the other cells. **(T2)**

T F 5. When you press ⏎Enter, the selection will always move to the cell below it. This is a basic feature of Excel that cannot be changed. **(T3)**

T F 6. Clicking on the AutoSum button will place a formula in the currently selected cell that will automatically add up the nearest row or column of numbers. **(T5)**

MATCHING QUESTIONS

A. D3 **D.** Save
B. Button with an X in it **E.** AutoSum button
C. ⏎Enter **F.** Tab

Match the following statements to the word or phrase that is the best match from the list. Write the letter of the matching word or phrase in the space provided next to the number.

1. ____ Automatically adds up the numbers in nearby cells **(T5)**

2. ____ May be the Close button or the Close Window button **(T6)**

3. ____ Button that looks like a 3½" floppy disk **(T6)**

4. ____ The cell in row 3, column D **(T2)**

5. ____ May be used to finish the process of placing a number or text into a cell and move downward to the next cell **(T2)**

6. ____ May be used to move the selection to the right **(T2)**

IDENTIFYING PARTS OF THE EXCEL SCREEN

Refer to the figure and identify the numbered parts of the screen. Write the letter of the correct label in the space next to the number.

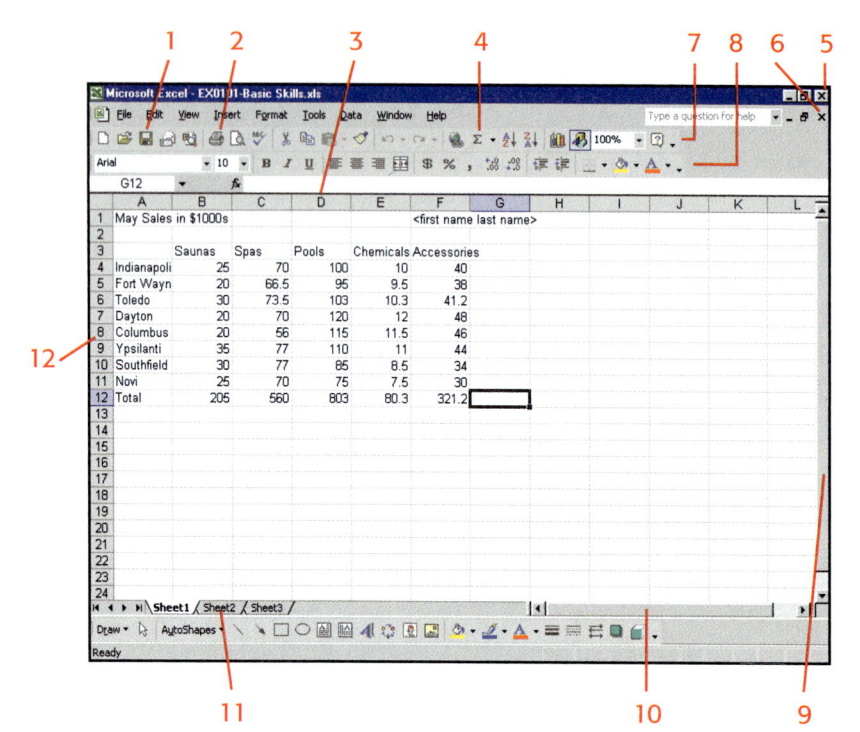

1. _____
2. _____
3. _____
4. _____
5. _____
6. _____
7. _____
8. _____
9. _____
10. _____
11. _____
12. _____

A. Tabs to identify sheets (T1)

B. Column heading (T2)

C. Row heading (T2)

D. Vertical scrollbar (T1)

E. Horizontal scrollbar (T1)

F. Save button (T6)

G. Print button (T6)

H. Close button for Excel (T6)

I. Close Window button for the workbook (T6)

J. AutoSum button (T5)

K. Standard toolbar (T1)

L. Formatting toolbar (T1)

18   EXC   Lesson 1   Learning the Basics of Excel

REINFORCEMENT

Reinforcement exercises are designed to reinforce the skills you have learned by applying them to new situations. Detailed instructions are provided along with a figure, where appropriate, to illustrate the result. The reinforcement exercises that follow should be completed sequentially. Leave the file open at the end of each exercise for use in the next exercise until you are specifically directed to close it.

In these exercises you create a worksheet for the utitlity bills for the Armstrong Pool, Spa, and Sauna Company stores.

R1—Creating a Worksheet to Show Utility Bills

1. Launch Excel and enter **January** in cell **A1**.
2. Enter your name in cell **F1**.
3. Select cell **A3** and press Tab. Enter the following data in the cells as shown in the figure:

	GAS	WATER	ELECTRIC	PHONE
Indianapolis	165	55	250	120
Fort Wayne	100	35	225	67
Toledo	150	45	215	125
Dayton	125	60	185	150
Columbus	150	75	170	85
Ypsilanti	220	85	285	300
Southfield	118	55	125	110
Novi	125	45	156	130

4. Use the **AutoSum** button at the bottom of each column.
5. Click the **Print** button to print the worksheet.
6. Save the workbook on your disk. Use **EX0102-Reinforcement** for its name. Leave the workbook open for use in the next exercise.

R2—Entering Data in Another Sheet

1. Click the **Sheet2** tab to select the second sheet of the **EX0102-Reinforcement** workbook.
2. Enter **February** in cell **A1**.
3. Place your name in cell **E1**.
4. Enter the following text and numbers as shown in the figure:

	GAS	WATER	ELECTRIC	PHONE
Indianapolis	175	55	230	110
Fort Wayne	120	30	245	90
Toledo	160	40	225	135
Dayton	155	65	195	140
Columbus	170	70	190	95
Ypsilanti	190	80	305	290
Southfield	98	65	145	120
Novi	105	50	170	110

5. Use the **AutoSum** button to calculate the sum of each column of numbers.
6. Print the sheet. Click the **Save** button on the Standard toolbar to save your changes. (You will not need to give it a name again. It will automatically update the existing file on your disk.) Leave the workbook open for use in the next exercise.

R3—Editing a Worksheet

1. Click the **Sheet1** tab to select Sheet1.
2. Edit cell **B4** to read **2400** and press ↵Enter. (If you have used the AutoSum button correctly, the sum of column B will be automatically updated.)
3. Click the **Save** button to save the change.
4. Print **Sheet1**. Leave the workbook open for the next exercise.

	A	B	C	D	E	F	G
1	January					<student name>	
2							
3		Gas	Water	Electric	Phone		
4	Indianapo	2400	55	250	120		
5	Fort Way	100	35	225	67		
6	Toledo	150	45	215	125		
7	Dayton	125	60	185	150		
8	Columbus	150	75	170	85		
9	Ypsilanti	220	85	285	300		
10	Southfield	118	55	125	110		
11	Novi	125	45	156	130		
12		3388	455	1611	1087		
13							

R4—Closing and Exiting Excel

1. Click the **Close Window** button to close the workbook. (If you have any unsaved work, the program will always prompt you to save your changes before it closes the workbook.)
2. Click the **Close** button to close the Excel program.

CHALLENGE

Challenge exercises are designed to test your ability to apply your skills to new situations with less-detailed instructions. These exercises also challenge you to expand your repertoire of skills by using commands that are similar to those you have already learned. The desired outcome is clearly defined, but you have more freedom to choose the steps needed to achieve the required result.

The following exercises use separate sheets in the same workbook. The exercises are not sequential and do not depend on each other.

C1—Calculating Trip Expenses

Your boss tells you to prepare for a short trip to Chicago and provide a detailed estimate of the cost.

Goal: Create a worksheet to itemize the expenses of a two-day trip to Chicago.

1. Launch Excel. Select **Sheet1**, if necessary, and place your name in cell **A1**.
2. Type the following expense categories in column **A** in cells **A3** through **A6**: **Air Fare**, **Rental Car**, **Hotel for Two Nights**, and **Food**.
3. Enter dollar values for these expenses in column **B** in cells **B3** through **B6**. Estimate the values, they do not have to be exact.
4. Use the **AutoSum** button in cell **B7** to add up the expenses.

	A	B
1	\<Your Name\>	
2		
3	Air Fare	110
4	Rental Car	85
5	Hotel for T\>	185
6	Food	80
7		460
8		

5. Save the workbook as **EX0103-Challenge**.
6. Print **Sheet1** if your instructor requires printouts. Leave this file open for use in the next Challenge exercise.

C2—Summarizing the Expenses of Conducting a Survey

Social scientists often write grant proposals in which they must estimate the cost of a project.

Goal: Create a worksheet to summarize the cost of preparing and conducting a survey.

Use the workbook **EX0103-Challenge**, which was created in the previous exercise. If you did not do exercise C1, start Excel and use a blank workbook.

1. Select **Sheet2** and place your name in cell **A1**.
2. Type the following expense categories in cells **A3** through **A8**: **Writing**, **Validating**, **Printing**, **Telephone**, **Callers**, and **Analysis**.

	A	B
1	\<Your Name\>	
2		
3	Writing	1500
4	Validating	3000
5	Printing	150
6	Telephone	300
7	Callers	1000
8	Analysis	500
9		6450

3. Enter dollar values for these expenses in cells **B3** through **B8**. Estimate the values; they do not have to be exact.
4. Use the **AutoSum** button in cell **B9** to add up the expenses.
5. Save the workbook. Name it **EX0103-Challenge**, if necessary.
6. Print **Sheet2** if your instructor requires printouts. Leave this file open for use in the next Challenge exercise.

C3—Tracking the Operating Costs of Alternative Fuel Vehicles

Schools and cities across the nation are using alternative fuel vehicles. In this exercise you track the consumption of bifuel automobiles that use compressed natural gas (CNG) or gasoline.

Goal: Create a worksheet to summarize the cost of fuel for a fleet of five bifuel vehicles.

Use the workbook **EX0103-Challenge**, which was created in the first challenge exercise. If you did not do exercise C1, start Excel and use a blank workbook.

1. Select **Sheet3** and place your name in cell **A1**. Select **A2** and type *September*.

2. Type the following column headings in cells **A4** through **C4**: *License*, *CNG*, and *Gasoline*.

	A	B	C	D
1	\<Your Name\>			
2	September			
3				
4	License	CNG	Gasoline	
5	35AGFI	85	15	
6	3698FA	60	30	
7	ACF345	120	50	
8	D90CFJ	35	65	
9	Total	300	160	460

3. Refer to the figure and the table below to fill out the fuel consumption. Units used for CNG are equivalent in energy to one gallon of gasoline.

LICENSE	CNG	GASOLINE
35AGFI	85	15
3698FA	60	30
ACF345	120	50
D90CFJ	35	65

4. Use the *AutoSum* button in cells **B9** and **C9** to add up each type of fuel used.

5. Use the AutoSum function in cell **D9** to calculate a grand total.

6. Save the workbook. Name it **EX0103-Challenge**, if necessary.

7. Print **Sheet3** if your instructor requires printouts. Close the workbook. Close Excel.

C4—Using Prewritten Spreadsheet Templates

When you use the menu option for opening a new workbook, you have the opportunity to create a new workbook that is based upon one of several prewritten workbook templates that have been set up to accomplish specific tasks.

Goal: Modify a prewritten workbook.

1. Start Excel. Choose *View*, *task pane* and choose **General Templates** from the **New from template** section.

2. Click the **Spreadsheet Solutions** tab, choose **Expense Statement**, and click *OK*.

3. Fill in the worksheet with numbers of your choosing. Add your name.

4. Save the workbook as **EX0104-Expense Statement**.

5. Print the worksheet if your instructor requires it. Close the workbook.

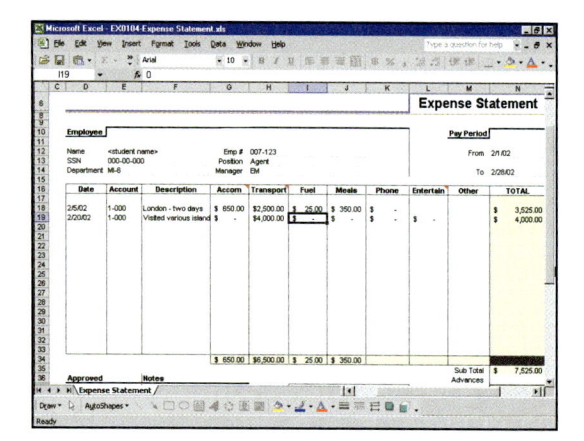

ON YOUR OWN

Create a worksheet to balance your checkbook. Criteria for grading will be:

1. Demonstration of mastery of Excel skills that were taught in this lesson.

Some examples of features that students have learned to use in previous classes to enhance their personal checkbook worksheet are:

- Entering text and numbers in separate cells
- Using negative numbers for checks and withdrawals and positive numbers for deposits
- Using the summation formula to add up the deposits, checks, and withdrawals to determine the balance
- Including a column for the date of the transaction
- Including a column for check number
- Including a column for a description of the deposit, withdrawal, or check
- Placing the description column last, so long text entries have room to overlap cells to the right
- Using the first row to show the starting balance

2. Identify yourself. Place your name in a cell that is clearly visible.

3. To complete the project Save your file on your own disk. Name it **EX0105-Checkbook**.

- Check with your instructor to determine if the project should be submitted in electronic or printed form. If necessary, print out a copy of the worksheet to hand in.

Lesson 2

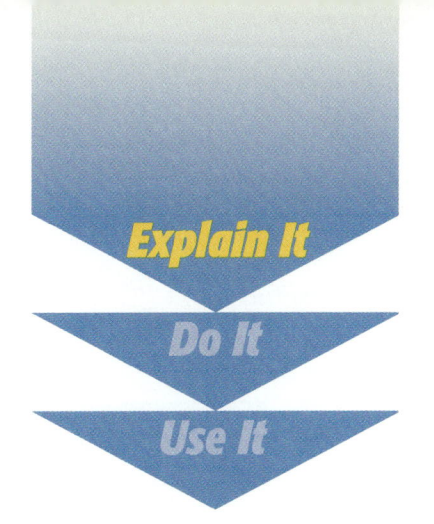

Formatting the Worksheet

Task 1   Selecting Groups of Cells
Task 2   Formatting Large Numbers, Currency, Decimal Places, and Dates
Task 3   Adjusting Columns and Cells for Long Text or Numbers
Task 4   Aligning Text in a Cell
Task 5   Changing the Font, Size, and Emphasis of Text
Task 6   Adding Lines, Borders, Colors, and Shading

INTRODUCTION

A variety of formatting techniques can be used to improve the appearance of a worksheet. Formatting your worksheet can also make it easier to read. This is especially important for worksheets that are used by others.

In this lesson, you learn how to work with existing worksheets to improve their appearance, make them easier to read, and give them a professional look. You will be working with the utility bills for the branch locations of the Armstrong Pool, Spa, and Sauna Company, the company you worked with in Lesson 1.

VISUAL SUMMARY

When you have completed this entire lesson, you will have a worksheet that looks like this:

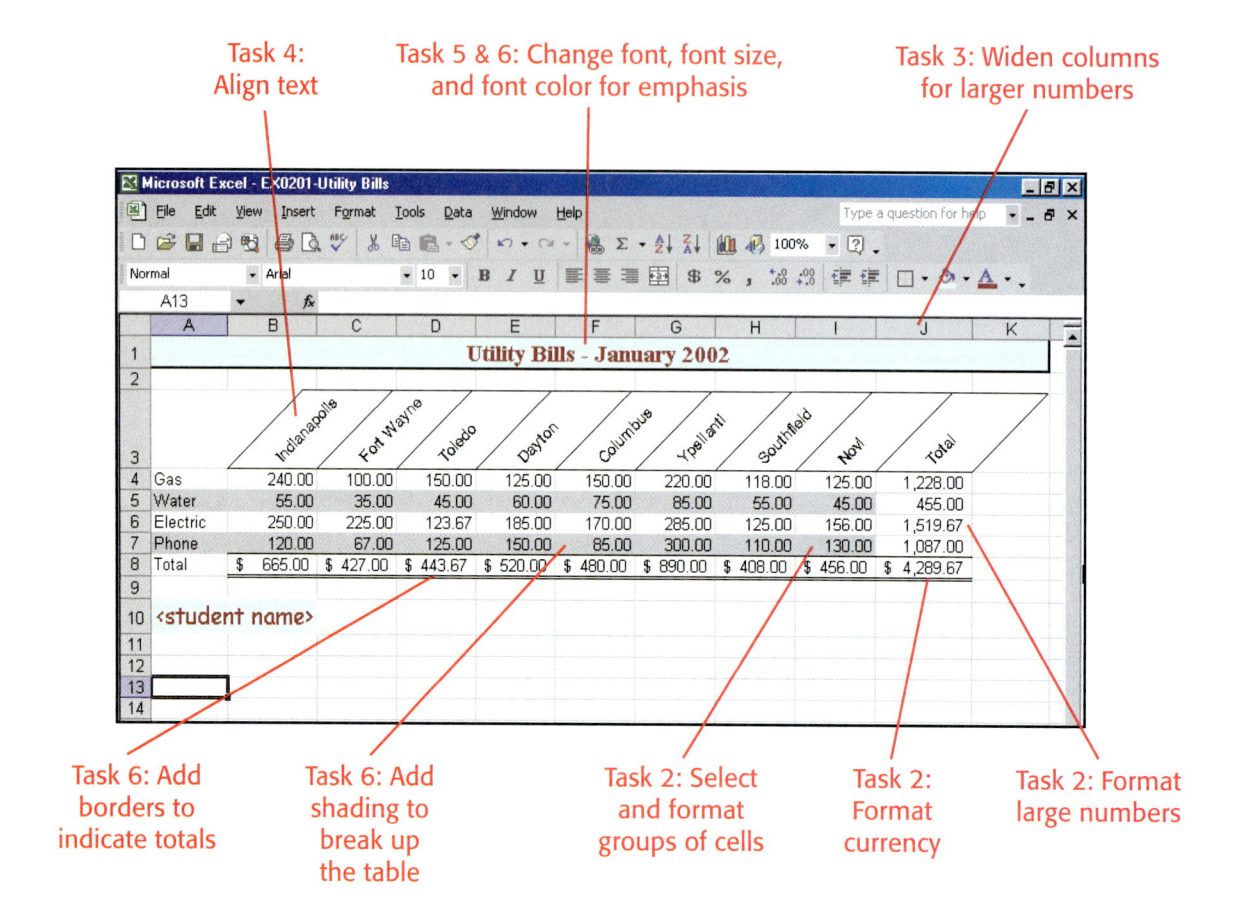

Task 4: Align text

Task 5 & 6: Change font, font size, and font color for emphasis

Task 3: Widen columns for larger numbers

Task 6: Add borders to indicate totals

Task 6: Add shading to break up the table

Task 2: Select and format groups of cells

Task 2: Format currency

Task 2: Format large numbers

EXC Lesson 2 Formatting the Worksheet

Task 1
SELECTING GROUPS OF CELLS

Why would I do this?
To change the formatting of a cell, it must be selected. It is common to want to change the formatting of groups of cells, so it is preferable to select the entire group and format all of them at the same time. You can select the entire sheet, an entire row or column, a rectangle of cells, or unconnected groups of cells. By selecting the entire group of cells, you help ensure that the same formatting is applied to all of them.

In this task, you learn different techniques for selecting a group of cells.

1 Launch Excel and click the **Open** button.

The Open dialog box is displayed.

Click the down arrow next to the **Look in** box, find **EX0201** in the **Student** folder, and open it.

This worksheet summarizes the Armstrong Pool, Spa, and Sauna Company utility bills by city.

Save the file as **EX0201-Utility Bills** on your floppy disk.

The new file name appears in the title bar.

Click the **Select All** button in the upper-left corner of the sheet.

The entire worksheet is selected.

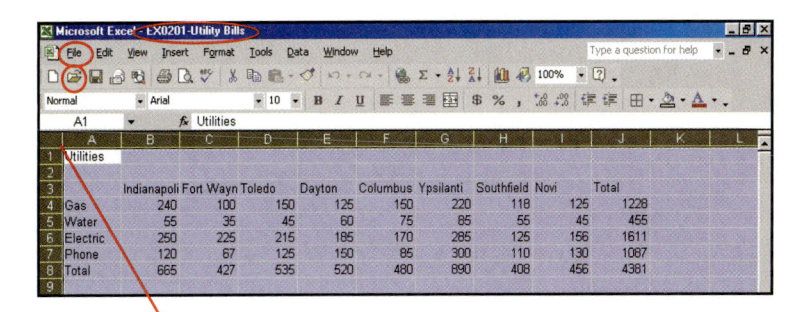

2 Click the heading of column **J**.

The entire column of totals is selected.

> **CAUTION**
> All of the cells in the row, including those that are not visible, are selected. Be careful when you select an entire sheet, row, or column. You may make unwanted changes to cells that are not on the screen.

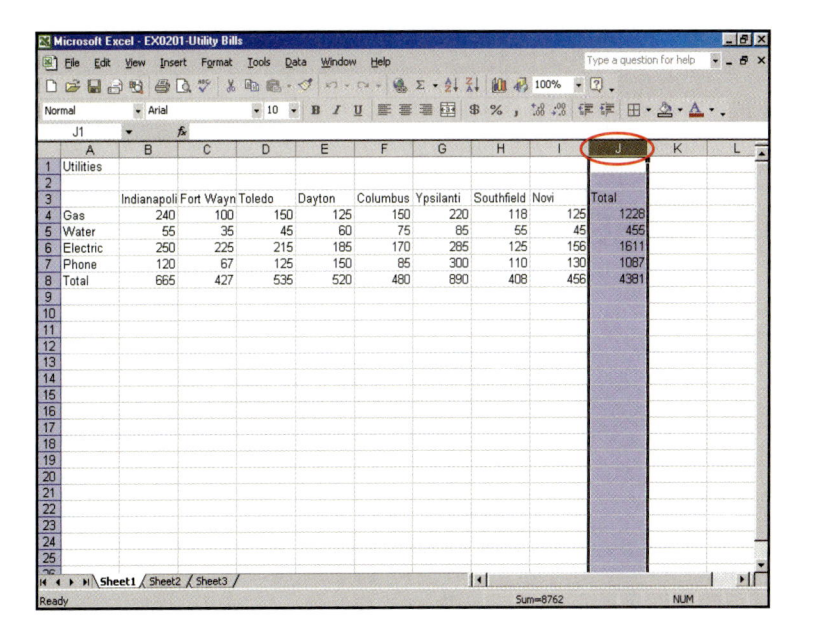

Task 1   Selecting Groups of Cells   EXC   27

3 Click the header for row **5**.

The entire row pertaining to water bills is selected. Notice that the first cell of the group is always the opposite highlight of the rest of the selected cells. This indicates that it is the active cell and its contents are displayed in the formula bar. It is still one of the selected group.

4 Position the pointer over cell **B4**. Click-and-drag a rectangular selection area to cell **I7** and then release the mouse button.

This selects the actual bills.

> **CAUTION:** The letters **I** and **O** may be easily confused with numbers, especially if the text font is Arial. Cell I7 refers to the cell in column I and row 7.

5 Select cells **B3** through **B7** and release the mouse button.

Selecting two groups of cells that are not next to each other is a two-step process.

> Hold down Ctrl and select cells **E3** through **E7**. Release the mouse button and Ctrl.

Both sets of cells are selected. This is a useful skill that can be applied in a later lesson when you chart content of cells that are not next to each other.

6 Click cell **B1** to select it. Use the vertical scrollbar to scroll down so that you can see cell **B60**.

> Hold down Shift and click cell **B60**.

*This selects all of the cells between **B1** and **B60**.*

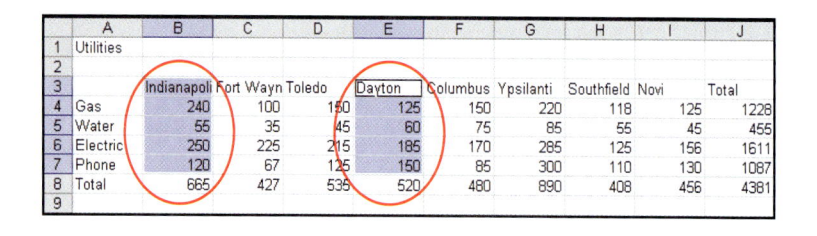

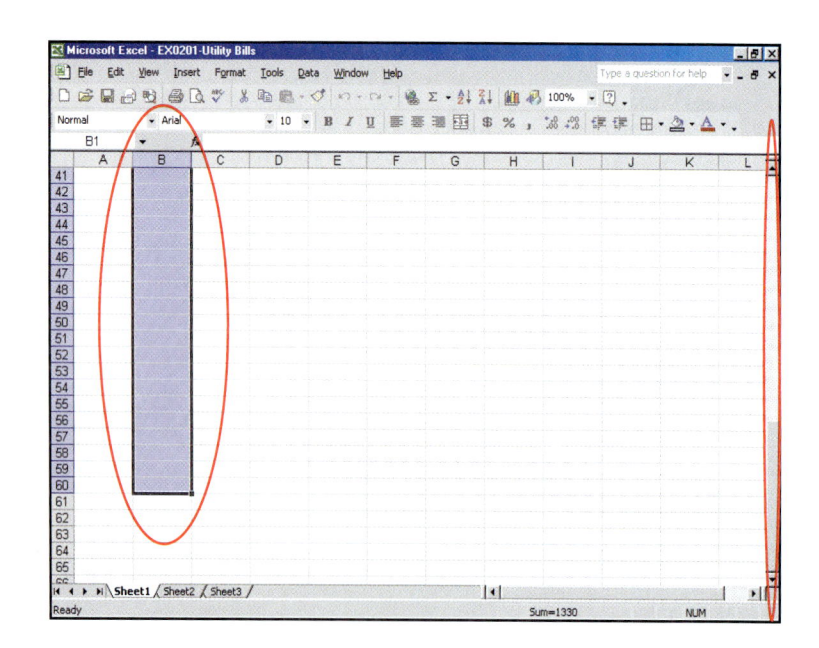

28   EXC   Lesson 2   Formatting the Worksheet

7 Scroll back to the top of the sheet.

This method is useful when selecting a group of cells that are so far apart that you have to use the scrollbar to find the other end of the group.

> **QUICK TIP**
> If you want to select a long range of cells without taking your hands off the keyboard, hold down the ⇧Shift key, and then use the arrow keys on the keyboard to select the range.

Task 2
FORMATTING LARGE NUMBERS, CURRENCY, DECIMAL PLACES, AND DATES

Why would I do this?
Most numbers greater than 999 should have commas inserted to make them easier to read. In some cases, numbers represent money and should have commas and dollar signs. Many numbers have decimal components and you have to decide how many decimal places to display. Excel allows you to format numbers the way you want them to be displayed. You also need to know how to handle dates.

In this task, you learn how to apply different types of numerical formats.

1 Select the cells from **B4** through **J7** and click the **Comma Style** button.

Notice the totals in column J are displayed with comma where needed and two decimal places are displayed by default.

Comma Style button

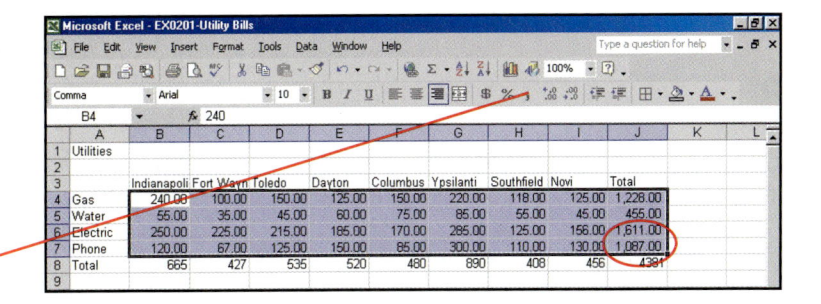

2 Select cells from **B8** through **J8** and click the **Currency Style** button.

A dollar sign is added to the left side of the cell, and commas are inserted in numbers that are greater than 999. Leave this range selected for the next step.

Currency Style button

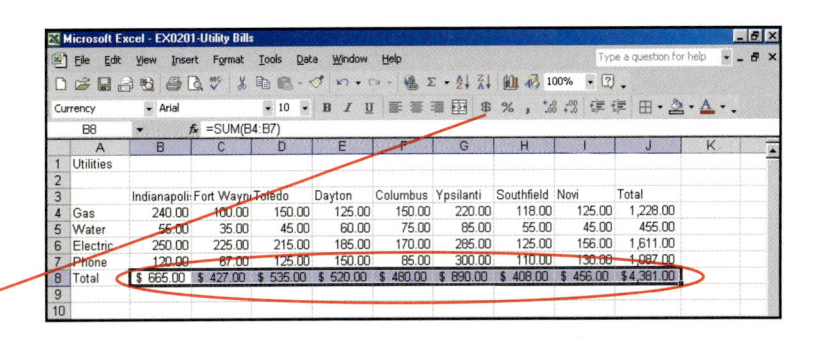

3 Click once on the **Decrease Decimal** button.

Notice that the numbers are displayed with one less decimal place.

Decrease Decimal button

> **IN DEPTH**
> The display of a number in a cell may be rounded off; however, Excel shows the full number in the formula bar and uses it in calculations. If the number that needs to be rounded ends in a 5, Excel rounds up. Numbers 0 through 4 are rounded down, and numbers 5 through 9 are rounded up.

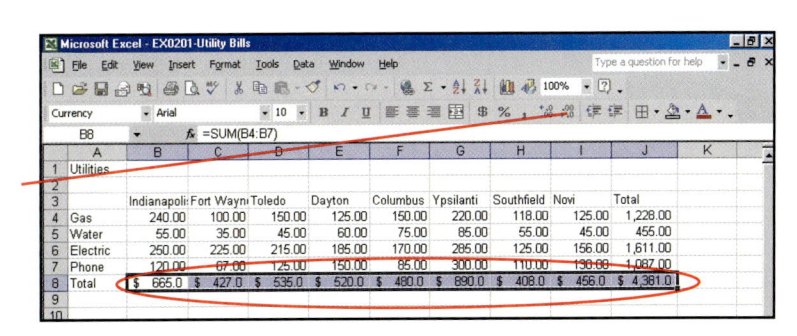

Task 2 Formatting Large Numbers, Currency, Decimal Places, and Dates EXC 29

4 Click the **Increase Decimal** button once.

The cells display two decimal places.

CAUTION
Rounding the display does not change the actual number in the cell or any cell that depends upon it. If you use the Decrease Decimal button to change the display so that it does not show all of the decimal places, cells containing totals or other values calculated using those numbers may appear to be incorrect.

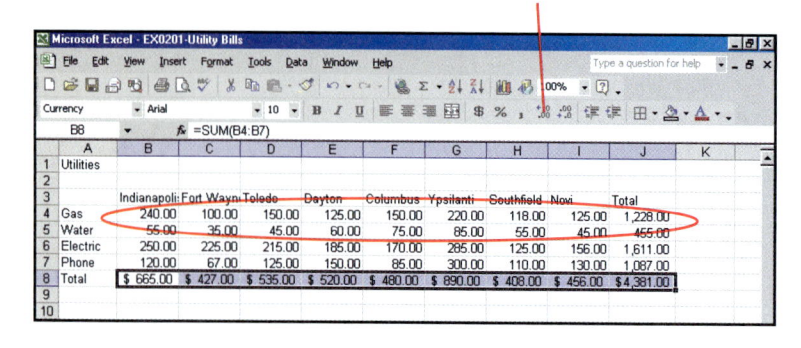

5 Select cell **A15**, type **1/30/02**, and press **Enter**.

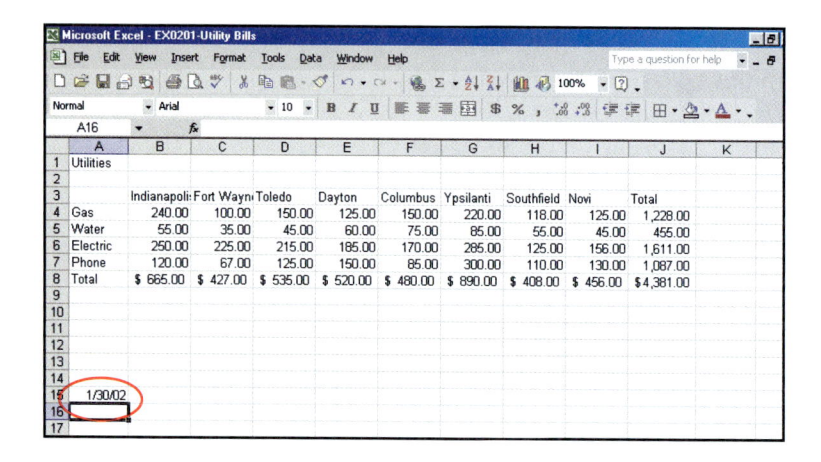

6 Select cell **A15** again. Choose **Format** from the menu, and then choose **Cells**.

The Format Cells dialog box is displayed.

Click the **Number** tab if necessary.

Click **Date** in the **Category** box if necessary. Scroll down the list of options and click the example **Mar-01** in the **Type** box.

This selection will display the month and year.

QUICK TIP
Commonly used menu items can be accessed quickly by clicking on an object using the right mouse button. A shortcut menu opens containing options that are relevant to the object. At step 6, you could have right-clicked cell A15 and chosen Format Cells from the shortcut menu.

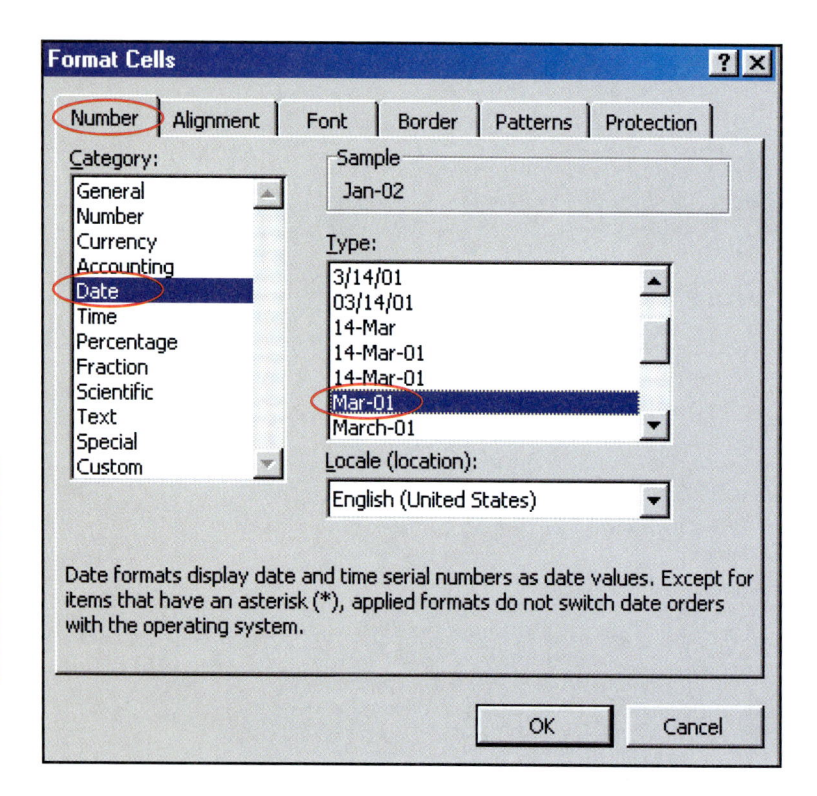

30 EXC Lesson 2 Formatting the Worksheet

7 Click **OK**.

The date now shows just the month and year. Notice that the actual content of the cell is displayed in the formula bar and that the program converted *02* to *2002*.

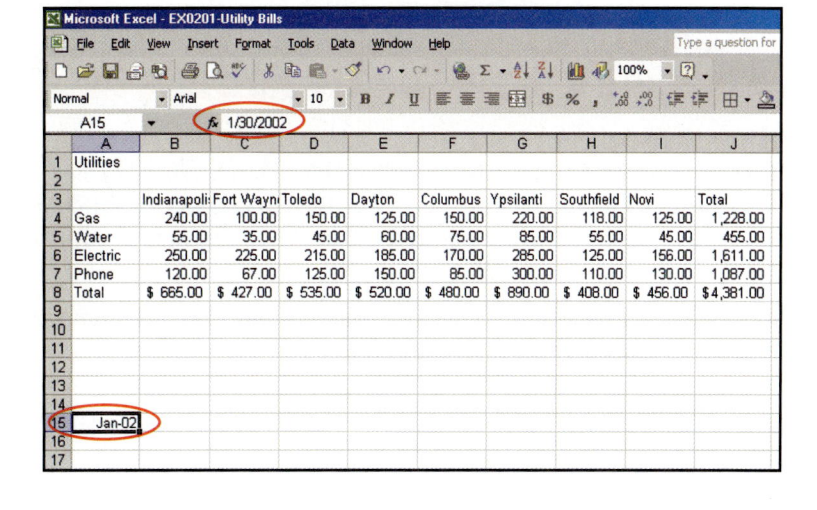

8 With cell **A15** still selected, choose **Edit**, **Clear**, **Formats** from the menu.

The number *37286* appears.

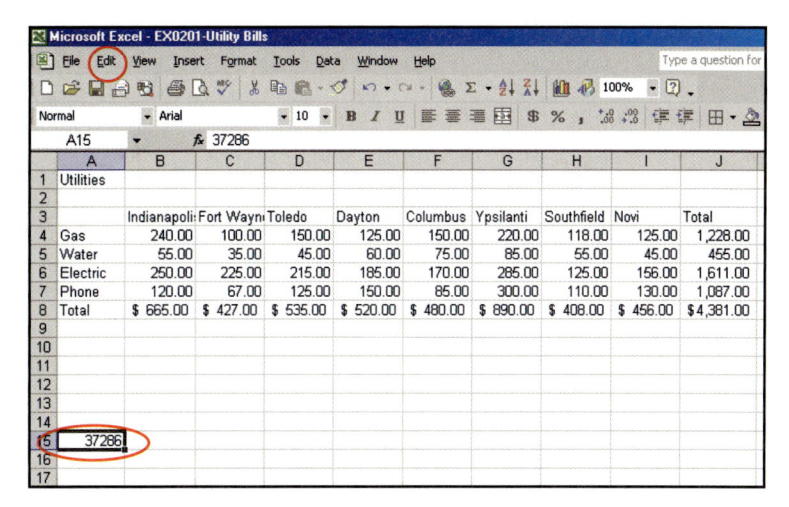

> Excel thinks of dates in terms of the number of days from a fixed date in the past. When you remove the formatting from the cell, it displays the number that it is actually using. This makes it possible to subtract one date from another to determine the number of days between two dates. The number that Excel uses for the date is the number of days since the year 1900—that is what is displayed when you remove all the formatting.

9 With cell **A15** selected, choose **Edit**, **Clear**, **All**.

The date is removed as well as the formatting.

Task 2   Formatting Large Numbers, Currency, Decimal Places, and Dates   EXC   31

Task 3
ADJUSTING COLUMNS AND CELLS FOR LONG TEXT OR NUMBERS

Why would I do this?
Text and numbers entered into a cell are often longer than the cell width. If the cell to the right contains an entry, the text in the left cell is cut off. If a number is too long to fit conveniently, but has fewer than eleven digits, Excel displays a string of # signs.

In this task, you learn how to change column widths to accommodate entries and center titles across several columns.

1 Select cell **B3**.

Notice that city's name is cut off. You can see the full name in the formula bar.

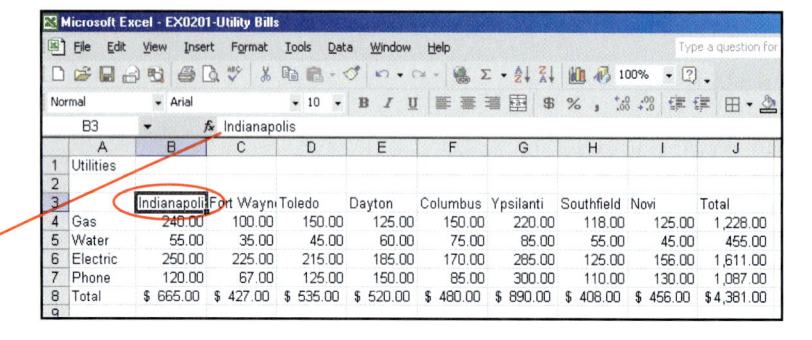

2 Move the pointer to the line that separates the headings for columns **B** and **C**.

The mouse pointer turns into a double-sided black arrow.

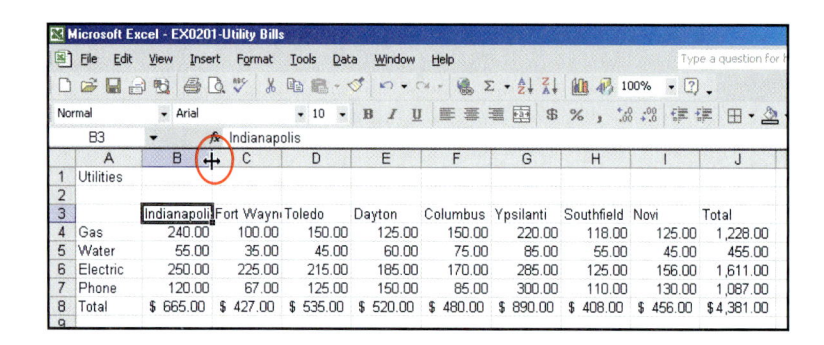

3 Double-click.

The width of the column automatically adjusts to fit the longest word in any of the cells in column B.

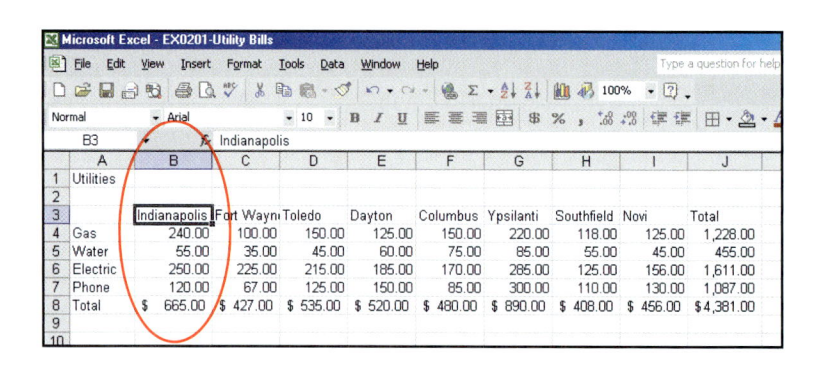

> **IN DEPTH**
> You can adjust the width of a column or the height of a row by clicking and dragging the boundary between two headings. If you click-and-drag across several headings to select them together, you can adjust the width or height of all of them at the same time.

32   EXC   Lesson 2   Formatting the Worksheet

4 Select cell **A1** and type **Utility Bills - January 2002**. Press ⏎Enter.

Notice that the text overlaps the cells to the right because they are empty. If cell B1 had any content, the display of cell A1 would be cut off.

5 Select cells **A1** through **K1**. Click the **Merge and Center** button.

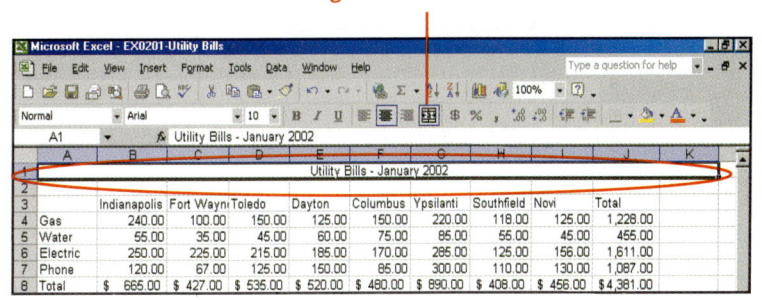

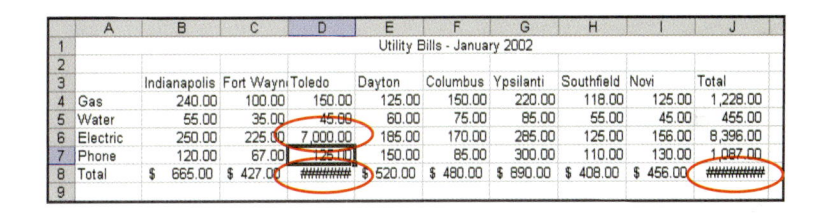

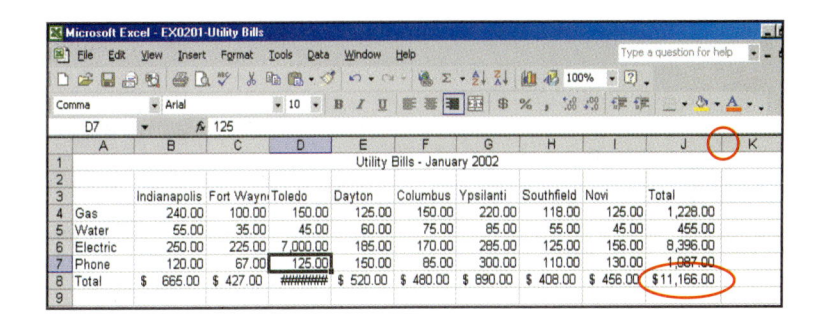

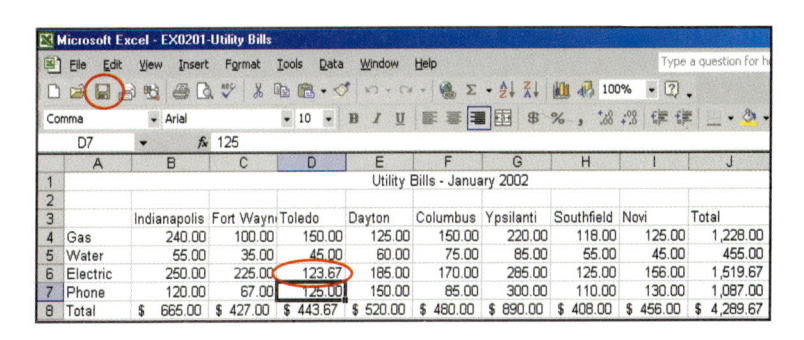

The selected cells display the text as if they were one cell, and the long title is centered. The text is centered across one more column than necessary to accommodate a change in the orientation of the cells that will be made in a later task.

> **IN DEPTH**
> To split cells that have been merged, select the cell and choose Format, Cells. Click the Alignment tab, and deselect the Merge cells box.

6 Select cell **D6**, type **7000**, and then press ⏎Enter.

Notice that the size of the totals in cells D8 and J8 exceeds the available cell space. A series of # signs is displayed in each.

7 Double-click the line between the headings for columns **J** and **K**.

The width of column J adjusts to display the larger number.

8 Select cell **D6**, type **123.67**, and then press ⏎Enter.

The entry is replaced with a more realistic number. Notice that column J did not revert to its narrower width.

Click the **Save** button to save the changes made up to this point.

Task 3   Adjusting Columns and Cells for Long Text or Numbers   EXC   **33**

Task 4
ALIGNING TEXT IN A CELL

Why would I do this?
If text is used to label a row or column, you may find that it looks better if the text is centered in or aligned with the right side of the cell. If the text used as a column label is much longer than the numbers in the column, you may want to increase the height of the row and wrap the text in the cell. Another way to handle long column labels is to slant the cells at an angle.

In this task, you learn how to wrap text onto several lines within a cell and align long text labels.

1 Select cells **B3** through **J3**. Choose **Format**, **Cells**.

The Format Cells dialog box appears.

Click the **Alignment** tab, if it is not already selected.

This dialog box may be used to control the alignment of text and numbers within cells.

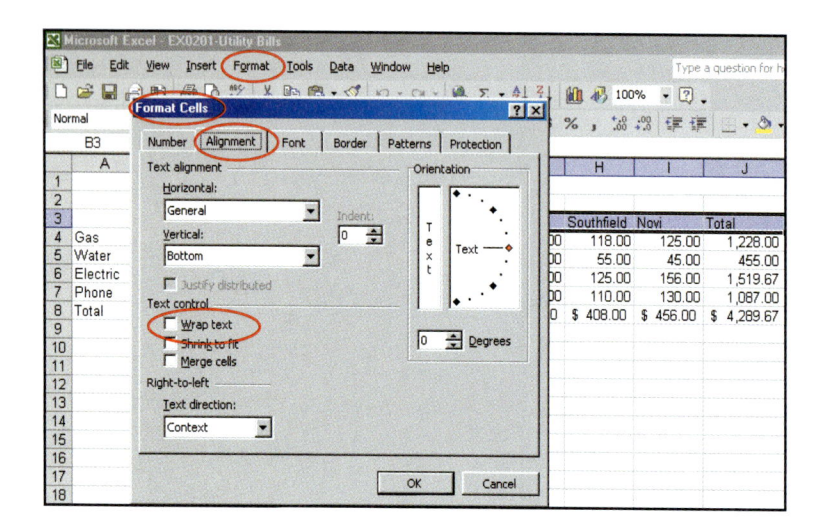

2 Click the **Wrap text** check box. Click **OK**.

The height of the row increases and the text wraps within the cells just as if it were a word processing document. In this example, the text in cell C3 wrapped to a second line.

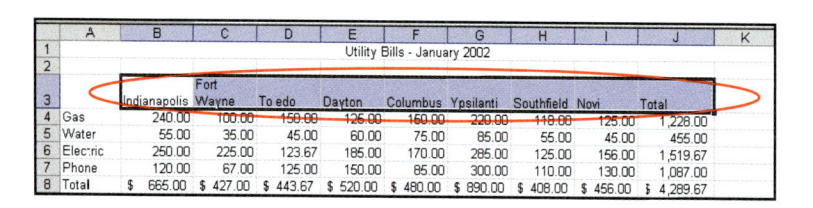

> ⚠ **CAUTION**
> Excel's word wrapping feature does not have an automatic hyphenation feature and is not as smart as a word processor when it comes to estimating where to break words. Check your work when you use the Wrap text feature.

3 Click the **Undo** button to remove the **Wrap text** feature.

There is another way to handle this type of column label.

Make sure that cells **B3** to **J3** are still selected and choose **Format**, **Cells** from the menu.

The Format Cells dialog box appears.

B3 to J3 still selected

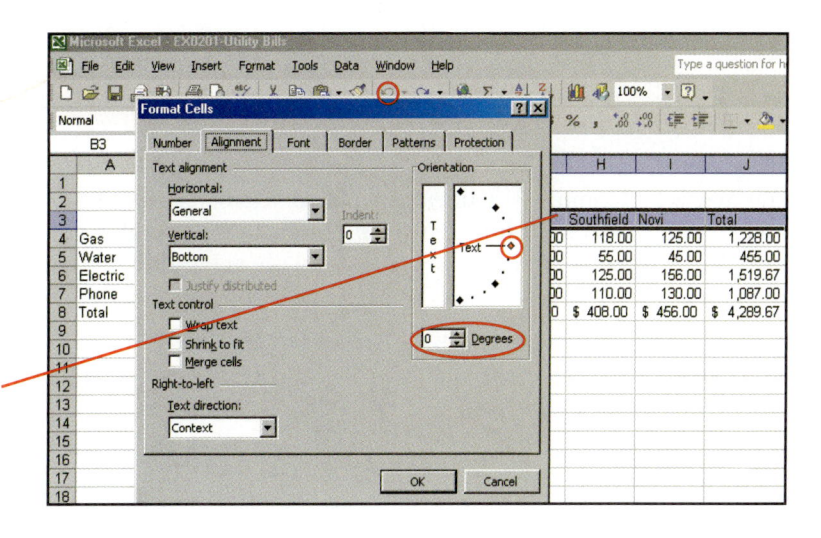

4 Click-and-drag the small red diamond in the **Orientation** window upward until the **Degrees** box reads **45**.

This will align the text at a 45-degree angle in the cell.

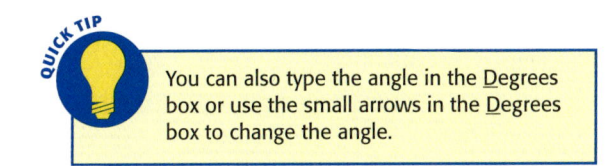

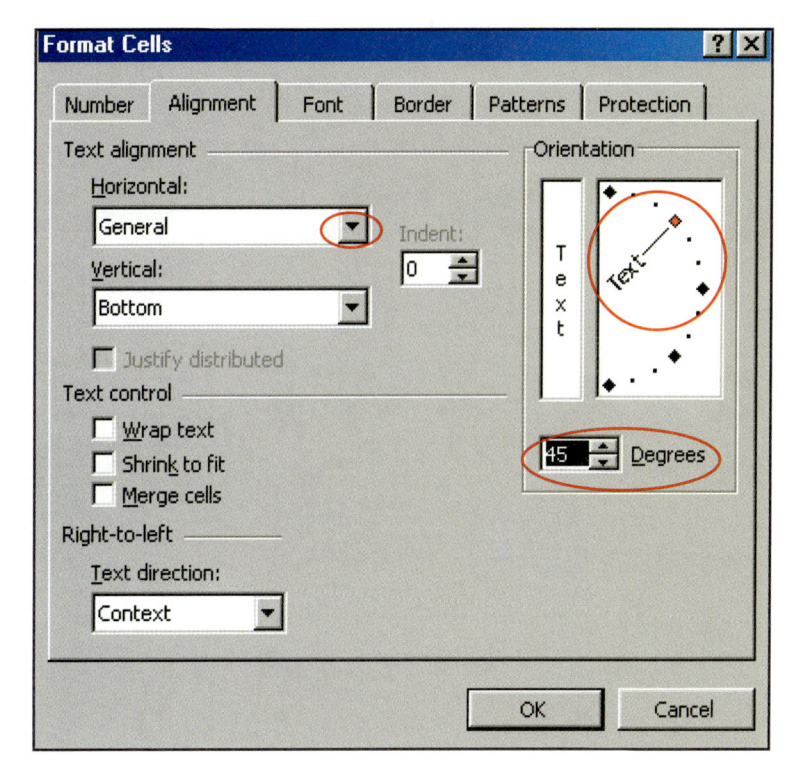

> **QUICK TIP**
> You can also type the angle in the Degrees box or use the small arrows in the Degrees box to change the angle.

5 Click the down arrow next to the **Horizontal** box. Click **Center**.

This centers the text in the cell.

Click **OK**.

The text in cells B3 to J3 is displayed at an angle.

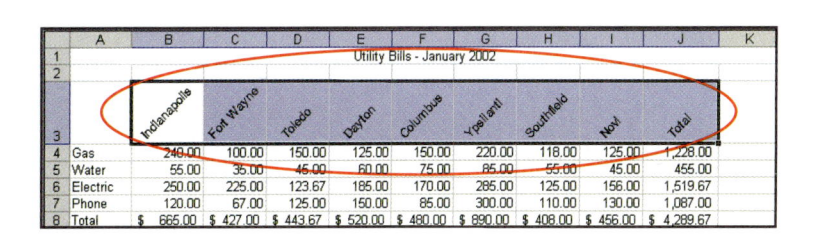

> **QUICK TIP**
> A faster way to change horizontal alignment is to use one of the three buttons on the Formatting toolbar: Align Left, Center, or Align Right.

Task 4   Aligning Text in a Cell   EXC   **35**

Task 5
CHANGING THE FONT, SIZE, AND EMPHASIS OF TEXT

Why would I do this?
You may want to emphasize titles and important words by making them larger and by using a different *font*. This helps improve the overall appearance of your worksheet. You can draw attention to key numbers by adding emphasis to those numbers.

In this task, you learn how to change the *point size* of a title and change a font from Arial to Times New Roman. You also add emphasis by using boldface or italicized versions of the font.

❶ Click anywhere on the title in the first row to select it. Click the down arrow next to the **Font** box. Scroll down and click **Times New Roman**.

The font of the title changes, and the height of the row increases to accomodate the larger text.

❷ Click the down arrow next to the **Font Size** box. Click **14**.

The title changes to 14 points.

❸ Click the **Bold** button.

The font, size, and emphasis have been changed to make the title stand out.

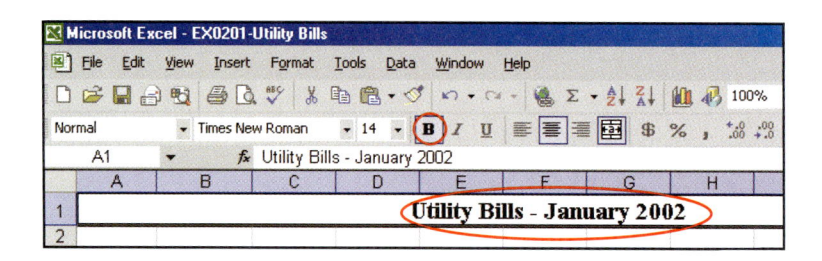

> **IN DEPTH**
> In addition to Bold, you also can change the emphasis of text or numbers by using the Underline or Italic buttons. Simply select the cells you want to change and click the appropriate button on the Formatting toolbar. Numerous other options may be found by using Format, Cells, and selecting the Font tab.

36   EXC   Lesson 2   Formatting the Worksheet

Task 6
ADDING LINES, BORDERS, COLORS, AND SHADING

Why would I do this?
Borders help emphasize important data, and also separate titles, subtotals, and totals. Colors and shading add emphasis and impact. They help draw the reader's attention and make the data easier to read.

In this task, you learn how to add borders and shading to various parts of the worksheet.

1 Make sure that the title is still selected from the previous task. Click the down arrow next to the **Borders** button.

A menu of borders is displayed.

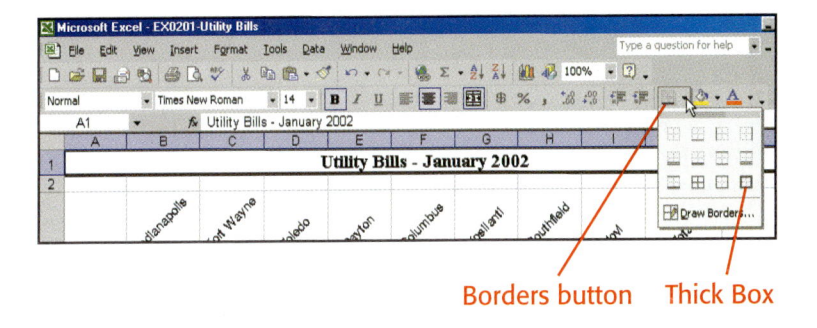

2 Click the **Thick Box Border** option at the right side of the bottom row.

The border that you select from the menu is applied to the selected cells.

Select cells **B3** to **J3**.

Click the down arrow next to the **Borders** button.

The cells with angled headings need borders to help identify the columns with which they are associated.

3 Click the **All Borders** option that is the second box from the left in the bottom row.

Borders are applied to all sides of the selected cells. Notice that the title in row 1 now appears to be centered due to the width of the angled headings.

Select cells **B8** through **J8**. Click the down arrow next to the **Borders** button.

The total of a column of numbers is usually indicated by a single top border and a double bottom border.

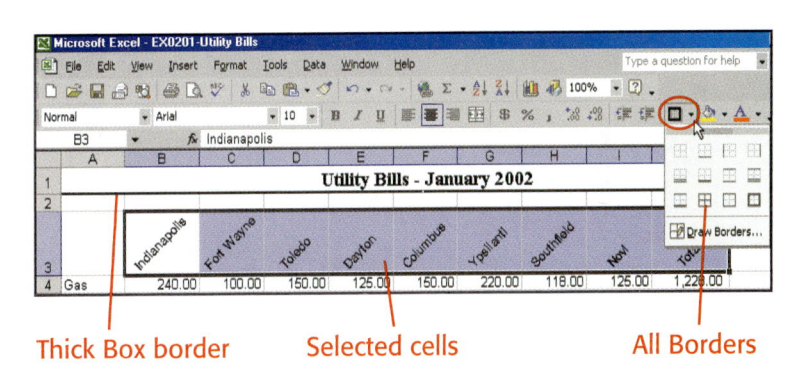

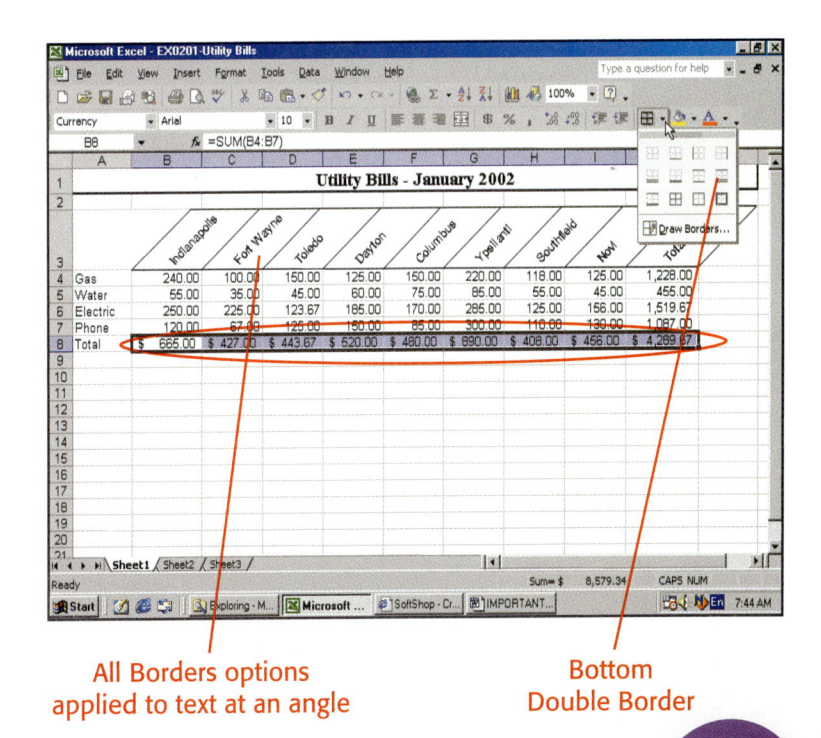

Task 6 Adding Lines, Borders, Colors, and Shading EXC

4 Click the **Top and Double Bottom Border** option that is fourth from the left in the second row.

The border is applied to indicate the totals.

Select cells **A5** through **I5** and cells **A7** through **I7** (remember to use Ctrl to select the second group of cells). Click the down arrow next to the **Fill Color** button.

It is easier to follow rows of data if some of the rows are shaded.

Fill Color button — Gray-25%

5 Click the **Gray-25%** button.

The selected cells are shaded. (To see the gray, deselect the shaded cells by clicking in any other cell.)

25% Gray fill color

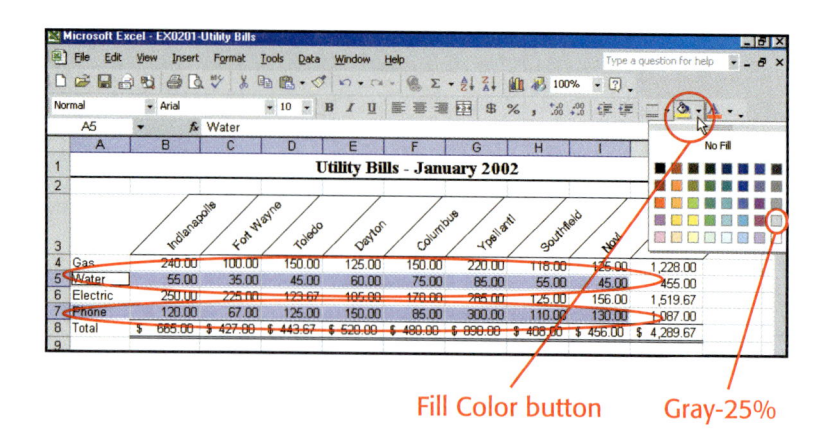

> **IN DEPTH**
> If you are unsure of the name of a color, allow the pointer to remain stationary on one of the colors for a few seconds and a ScreenTip displays the name.

6 Select the title again. Click the down arrow next to the **Fill Color** button and click the **Light Turquoise** option.

This changes the background (fill color) to a light turquoise color on the screen.

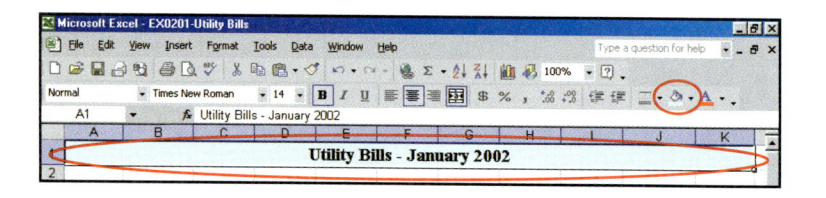

> **CAUTION**
> If you do not have a color printer, the program assigns different shades of gray to different colors. If you pick two colors for your text and background that are assigned to the same shade of gray, the printout is unreadable.

7 With the title still selected, click the down arrow next to the **Font Color** button.

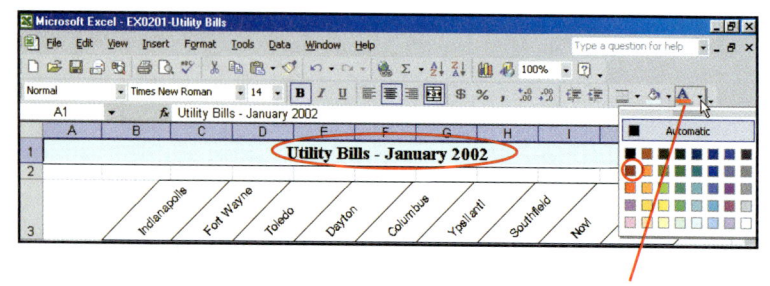

Font Color button

38 EXC Lesson 2 Formatting the Worksheet

8 Click the **Dark Red** option.

Select cell **A10,** type your name, and then press **Enter**. Change the font, font size, border, background color, and font color in cell **A10** to something you like. Merge across two or more cells if your name exceeds the current column width.

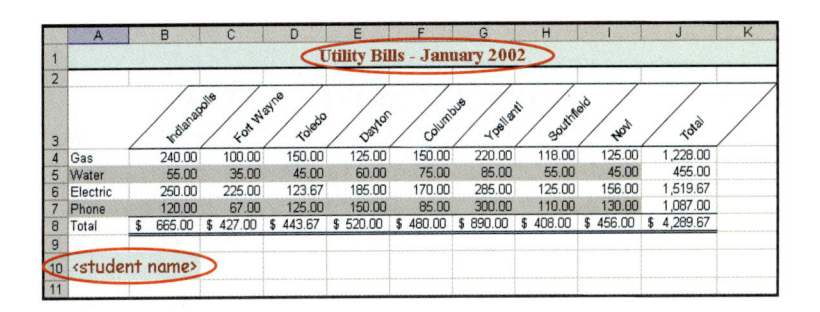

QUICK TIP

The Font Color, Fill Color, and Borders buttons on the Formatting toolbar display the most recent choice. If you want to use the type of emphasis that is displayed on the button, you can apply it by clicking once on the button without using the drop-down menu.

9 Click the **Print** button to print a copy of the worksheet.

Click the **Close Window** button to close the workbook.

A dialog box warns you that you have not saved the changes that you have made.

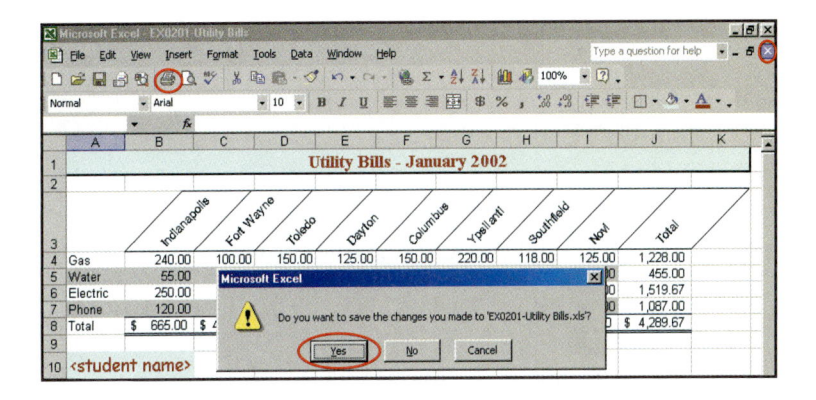

10 Click **Yes**.

The workbook closes, leaving the Excel program active.

Task 6 Adding Lines, Borders, Colors, and Shading

COMPREHENSION

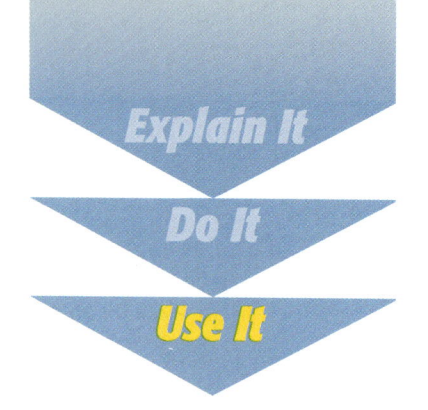

Comprehension exercises are designed to check your memory and understanding of the basic concepts in this lesson. You distinguish between true and false statements, identify new screen elements, and match terms with related statements. If you are uncertain of the correct answer, refer to the task number following each item (for example, T4 refers to Task 4), and review that task until you are confident you can provide a correct response.

TRUE-FALSE

Circle either T or F.

T F 1. If a number is too long to fit in a cell, it will extend into the cell to the right. **(T3)**

T F 2. You can select all of the cells in a row by clicking on the row heading. **(T1)**

T F 3. One way to handle long labels is to use the **Wrap text** option. **(T4)**

T F 4. A 16-point character is larger than an 8-point character. **(T5)**

T F 5. If you have a printer with only one color of ink, it does not matter what colors you choose for text and background. **(T6)**

T F 6. It is possible to print long column labels at an angle. **(T4)**

MATCHING QUESTIONS

A. Move pointer to the line between column headings and double-click

B. Ctrl

C. Click-and-drag the line between column headings

D. Wrap text

E. Merge and Center

F. Thick box

Match the following statements to the word or phrase that is the best match from the list. Write the letter of the matching word or phrase in the space provided next to the number.

1. ____ Text that is used as a title may occupy several cells using this feature **(T3)**

2. ____ Used to select a group of cells that is not touching the first group **(T1)**

3. ____ Method used to automatically adjust the width of a column to accommodate the widest cell entry **(T3)**

4. ____ Method used to manually change the width of a column **(T3)**

5. ____ Setting that forces long text entries to fit within the available column width by increasing the row height and displaying the text on several lines within the cell **(T4)**

6. ____ A border style **(T6)**

IDENTIFYING PARTS OF THE EXCEL SCREEN

Refer to the figure and identify the numbered parts of the screen. Write the letter of the correct label in the space next to the number.

1. _____
2. _____
3. _____
4. _____
5. _____
6. _____
7. _____
8. _____
9. _____
10. _____
11. _____
12. _____
13. _____
14. _____

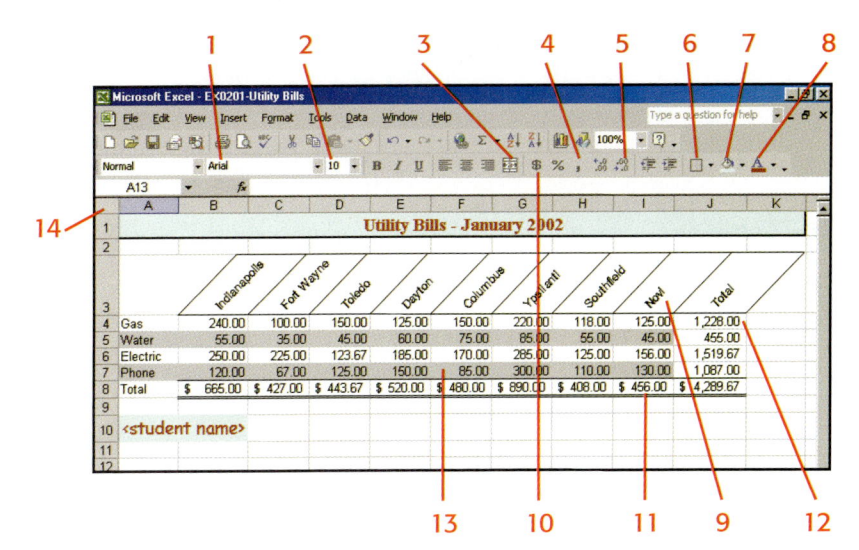

A. Text aligned at an angle (T4)

B. Cells displaying a gray fill color (T6)

C. **Select All** button (T1)

D. Example of Comma Style (T2)

E. **Currency Style** button (T2)

F. **Comma Style** button (T2)

G. **Decrease Decimal** button (T2)

H. **Merge and Center** button (T3)

I. **Borders** button (T6)

J. Font Size (T5)

K. Font name (T5)

L. **Fill Color** button (T6)

M. **Font Color** button (T6)

N. Cell with a top and double bottom border (T6)

Comprehension EXC

REINFORCEMENT

Reinforcement exercises are designed to reinforce the skills you have learned by applying them to a new situation. Detailed instructions are provided along with a figure, where appropriate, to illustrate the result. The reinforcement exercises that follow should be completed sequentially. Leave the workbook open at the end of each exercise for use in the next exercise until you are specifically directed to close it.

Open **EX0202** and save it as **EX0202-Reinforcement** on your disk for use in the following exercises.

You have been asked to compare two types of office cubicle dividers that are of different heights. A weighted average comparison method is used in your department to make such decisions, but the worksheet doesn't look good enough to distribute to members of the committee. Change the formatting as described in these exercises.

R1—Applying Formats to an Existing Worksheet

Format Sheet1 to match the figure. See the following steps for more detail.

1. Select **Sheet1**, if necessary.
2. Enter your name in cell **A19**.
3. Use the **Merge and Center** feature to center the main title across columns **A** through **F**. Center the subtitle **Four Feet High** across **C2** and **D2** and the subtitle **Six Feet High** across cells **E2** and **F2**.
4. Center and wrap the text in cells **B3** through **F3**.
5. Center data in all cells from **B4** through **F13**.
6. Select cells **C4** through **C13** and **E4** through **E13**. Choose a fill color of **Gray-25%**.
7. Select cells **A1**, **A4**, **A7**, **A11**, **A14**, **A15**, and **A16**. Make them **Bold**.
8. Select **D15** and **F15** and format the numbers to display currency with no decimals.
9. Select **D16** and **F16** and format the numbers to display only three decimal places.
10. Adjust the width of column **A** to display the full contents of cell **A16**, print the sheet, and save the workbook.

R2—Adding Border Lines and Colors

Add border lines and colors to match the figure. See the steps below for more information.

1. Select **Sheet2**. Enter your name in cell **F19**.
2. Place a **Thick Box** border around the title and the two ratio numbers in cells **D15** and **F15**.
3. Add a **Bottom Border** to cells **A3** through **F3**, **A6** through **F6**, and **A10** through **F10**.
4. Add a **Bottom Double Border** to the bottom of cells **D12** and **F12**.
5. Change the **Fill Color** of the title to **Turquoise** and change the **Font Color** to **Dark Red**.
6. Change the orientation of the column labels in cells **B2** through **F2** to a **45-degree** angle. Select the **All Borders** option that shows all lines. (Your text may wrap differently than is shown in the figure.)
7. Save the workbook. Leave the workbook open for use in the next exercise.

R3—Formatting a Worksheet

Format the sheet to match the figure. Make sure you change font size and style, merge and center, center text, fill color, align text, and add borders. Remember to adjust the columns to fit to the data. See the steps below for further details.

1. Select **Sheet3**. Enter your name in cell **A17**.

2. Merge and center the title in cell **A1** across cells **A1** through **L1**. Change its font to **Times New Roman**, **16** point, and make it **Bold**.

3. Select cells **A2** through **L2**. Format the cells to wrap text, centered, and display the text at a **45-degree** angle. Use the **All Borders** option (The text will not fit correctly.)

4. Drag the boundary between rows **2** and **3** to adjust the height. Select the column headers, **A** through **L**, and double-click on one of the boundaries between column headings to adjust all of the widths at once.

5. Apply a **Gray-25%** fill color to the cells **D2** through **D15**, **J2** through **J15**, and **L2** through **L15**.

6. Format cells **B4** through **B15** as currency.

7. Save and close the workbook.

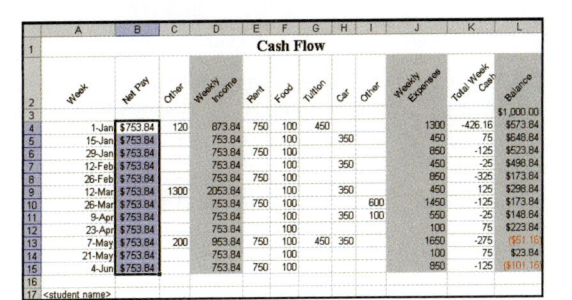

CHALLENGE

Challenge exercises are designed to test your ability to apply your skills to new situations with less detailed instruction. These exercises also challenge you to expand your repertoire of skills by using commands that are similar to those you have already learned. The desired outcome is clearly defined, but you have more freedom to choose the steps needed to achieve the required result.

The following exercises use separate sheets in the same workbook. The exercises are not sequential and do not depend on each other. Open **EX0203** and save it on your floppy disk as **EX0203-Challenge**.

C1—Using Formatting to Indicate Organization

If a table of data is to be distributed to other people, it is useful to use formatting tools so they can understand how the table is organized. In this example, several people in the office have been asked to evaluate and compare two room divider systems using a weighted scale.

Goal: Format the table to make it easier to identify the organization of the numbers.

Use the following guidelines:

1. Select **Sheet1**.
2. Center the text in cells **B2** through **F2**.
3. Use **Tools**, **Options**, **View** tab, **Gridlines** to turn off the gridlines on the screen.
4. Use **Borders** to add the lines shown.

5. Save the workbook. Leave this file open for use in the next Challenge exercise.

C2—Aligning Text Displayed at an Angle

When you display a column heading at a 45-degree angle, it is unclear which direction is indicated by the horizontal or vertical controls. You can determine how to align the text through a little trial-and-error.

Goal: Change the column headings to align at a 45-degree angle and add a border. Adjust the height of the row so that the text wraps as shown.

1. Select **Sheet2**. Select cells **B2** through **F2** and align the text at 45 degrees.
2. Use the **All Borders** option that looks like a window with four panes.
3. Drag the line between row headings 2 and 3 to adjust the height of the row so that none of the text wraps to more than two lines and no words are wrapped incorrectly.

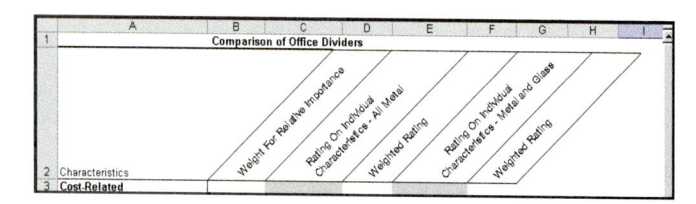

4. Save the workbook.

C3—Working with Two-Digit Dates

Representing the year in a date with only two digits creates problems because the computer is forced to guess the century in which it belongs. If you are using Excel to compute the age of elderly people, you may get incorrect answers if you subtract their birth dates from today's date.

Goal: Determine how to work with the century assumptions built into Excel 2002 so that you know when you must use four digits to represent the year in a date.

1. Select **Sheet3**. Place your name in cell **A1**. Enter today's date in cell **C3**.

2. In cell **B3**, type a date of birth from the 1920s such as **5/20/27**. Notice that the calculation in cell **D3** displays a negative number because it assumed you meant 2027 rather than 1927.

3. Type the date in cell **B3** again, but specify the year **1927**, using four digits. The formula in cell **D3** displays a positive number because the date in **B3** is earlier than today's date.

4. Try dates with different two-digit years in cell **B3** to determine which years are assumed to be from the 1900s and which years are assumed to be from the 2000s.

5. Write a directive in cell **A6** that instructs users when to use four digits for the year when entering numbers into Excel worksheets.

6. Widen column **A** to about four times its current width and format the text in cell **A6** to wrap.

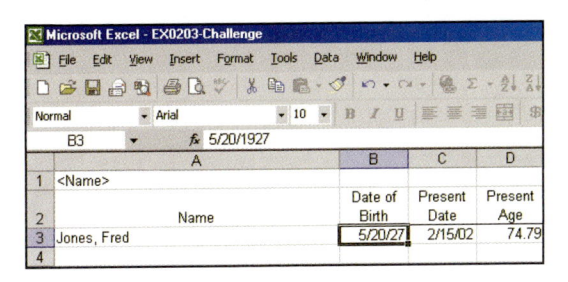

C4—Protecting Cells from Unintentional Change

The problem with using a lot of volunteers on a project is that there is little time to train them and the turnover is high. It is important to be able to prevent accidental mistakes.

The formula in cell D3 will be lost if someone accidentally enters a value in the cell. Similarly, you do not want others to change the column headings or message you have chosen. To prevent users from overwriting formulas or making unauthorized changes, you can limit the cells they can write in by unlocking particular cells and then protecting the rest of the sheet.

Goal: Unlock cells B3 and C3, and then protect the rest of the sheet so that users can only change values in cells B3 and C3.

Use the following guidelines:

1. Select **Sheet3**, if necessary. Select cells **B3** and **C3**. Choose **Format**, **Cells**, and the **Protection** tab. Deselect **Locked** and click OK.

2. Choose **Tools**, **Protection**, **Protect Sheet** to protect the sheet. Do not use a password. Click OK.

3. Try to make changes to any other part of the sheet and observe the error message.

4. Save the changes you have made. (You are going to use this workbook, Sheet 4, in the next exercise)

C5—Splitting Merged Cells and Moving Cells Using Click-and-Drag

Merged cells make good table titles and prevent truncation of the display when text is added to adjacent cells. The merged cells can cause problems when you are trying to work with one of the columns that is included in a merged cell. It is occasionally necessary to remove the merge-and-center formatting from a set of cells.

It is also useful to be able to move the contents of a cell more quickly than using the cut and paste options.

Goal: Remove the **Merge cells** format from the cells that contain the student name, and then move the name to another location using the click-and-drag method.

Use the following guidelines:

1. Select **Sheet4**. Click cell **A1** and enter your first and last name.

2. Select cell **A1** then choose **Format**, **Cells**, and the **Alignment** tab. Deselect **M**erge cells. Click **OK**.

3. Confirm that cell **A1** is still selected. Move the mouse pointer onto the edge of the cell where it turns into a four-headed pointer.

4. Click-and-drag the selected cell to **G5** and release the mouse button.

5. Save the changes you have made.

C6—Filtering a List

Many people use Excel as a database to record information about events, purchases, or transactions because they are not familiar with Access. Excel can perform basic sorting and filtering to help people find information.

The filter feature of Excel places a small down arrow at the top of each column of the table. The list box associated with the down arrow displays one of each type of data in the column. When you choose an item from the list, the table is displayed with rows that match the chosen item.

Goal: Filter the table of sales to show those made by the Jackson branch.

Use the following guidelines:

1. Select **Sheet4**, if necessary. Click on one of the branch names in column **E**. (You may select any cell of the contiguous data in the table.)

2. Choose **Data**, **Filter**, **AutoFilter**.

3. Click the down arrow at the top of the **Branch** column. Choose **Jackson** from the list.

4. Save the changes you have made. Close the workbook and close Excel.

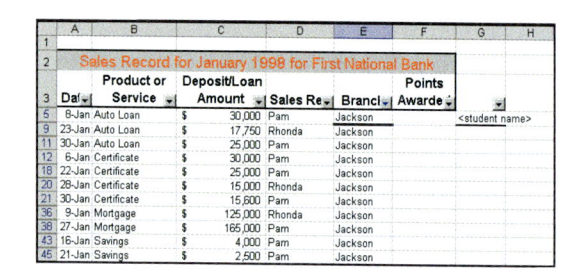

ON YOUR OWN

Create a worksheet to track expenses for a wedding, a holiday party, or some other event that would involve expenses from various sources. Format the worksheet to take advantage of the skills you have learned. Criteria for grading will be:

1. Demonstration of mastery of Excel skills that were taught in this lesson.

Some examples of features that students have learned to use in previous classes to enhance their expense worksheet are:
- Formatting currency to two decimal places
- Adjusting the width of columns or wrapping the text within cells to avoid overlap of adjacent cells by long text entries
- Using font size appropriately to identify column headings and titles
- Using color to emphasize an important aspect of the sheet
- Using borders to separate the sheet into sections

2. Identify yourself. Place your name in a cell that is clearly visible.

3. To complete the project:
    - Save your file on your own disk. Name it **EX0204-Event**.
    - Check with your instructor to determine if the project should be submitted in electronic or printed form. If necessary, print out a copy of the worksheet to hand in.

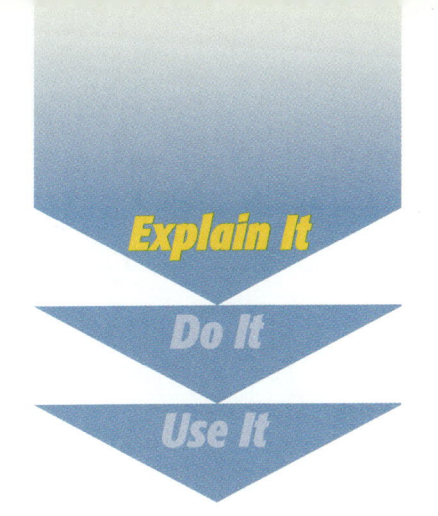

Lesson 3

Explain It
Do It
Use It

Using Formulas

Task 1 Adding, Subtracting, Multiplying, and Dividing Using Cell References and Numbers
Task 2 Using Formulas with More than One Cell Reference
Task 3 Combining Operations and Filling Cells with Formulas
Task 4 Filling Cells with Relative and Absolute Formulas
Task 5 Applying Basic Formulas to a Loan Repayment
Task 6 Using Built-In Financial Formulas

INTRODUCTION

Excel is at your command, whether you need to do basic arithmetic or advanced statistics. Once you set up a worksheet, you can change the numbers many times to see how those changes affect the "bottom line."

In this lesson, you work on three worksheets. The first worksheet shows you how to perform basic math calculations using Excel. The next worksheet shows you how to use the Fill function with a formula and how to use absolute and relative cell references. In the third worksheet, you learn how to use the Insert Function dialog box to calculate a monthly payment on a car or house loan. You also calculate the total amount you will pay for the loan.

VISUAL SUMMARY

By the time you have completed this entire lesson, you will have created three worksheets that look like these:

Task 4: Add your name to the custom header

Task 3: Combine formulas with operations

Task 4: Fill formulas with relative references

Task 4: Fill formulas with absolute references

Task 1: Add formulas with one cell reference

Task 2: Add formulas with two cell references

Worksheet 1 – Sample Numbers / Formula examples:

Sample Numbers:		
B	6	
3	12	

Cell and number:		Two cells		Combinations	
Addition:	=B3+5	Addition:	=B2+A3	Grouping - example o	=(A2+B2)/A3
Subtraction:	=B3-5	Subtraction:	=A2-A3	Grouping - example tv	=B3/(A3+B2)
Multiplication:	=A2*3	Multiplication:	=A2*A3	Relative	Filling: =A2 =A3
Division:	=A2/4	Division:	=B3/B2	Absolute	=$A$2 =$A$2

Worksheet 2 – D12 fx =D11*$B$2

	A	B	C	D	E	F
1			Calculation of Sales Commission			
2	Commission rate:	5%				
3						
4		Dave	Eric	Sally	Natasha	Siri
5	Monday	2,500	2,000	600	800	1,900
6	Tuesday	1,500	1,800	3,000	700	2,500
7	Wednesday	600	1,400	2,000	550	2,000
8	Thursday	1,900	1,500	1,900	3,000	900
9	Friday	1,000	1,900	1,400	700	800
10	Saturday	1,000	500	900	2,000	2,000
11		8,500	9,100	9,800	7,750	10,100
12		$ 425.00	$ 455.00	$ 490.00	$ 387.50	$ 505.00

Task 4: Fill formulas with relative references

Task 4: Fill formulas with a mix of relative and absolute references

---

Worksheet 3 – B6 fx =PMT(B3,B5,B1)

	A	B	C
1	Loan Amount (pv):	$ 10,000	
2	Annual Interest	7.50%	
3	Monthly Interest (rate)	0.625%	
4	Years to Pay Back	3	
5	Number of Payments (nper)	36	
6	Monthly Payment	($311.06)	
7	Total of All Payments	$ (11,198.24)	

Task 5: Use basic formulas

Task 6: Use a financial formula

EXC Lesson 3 Using Formulas

Task 1
ADDING, SUBTRACTING, MULTIPLYING, AND DIVIDING USING CELL REFERENCES AND NUMBERS

Why would I do this?
Worksheets have been used in paper form for years as a means of keeping track of financial data. The value of using an electronic worksheet program such as Excel is its ability to quickly make mathematical calculations. Before the era of computers, people were employed to calculate rows and columns of numbers for use in navigational charts or other types of computational charts. The job title for the people who performed these calculations was Computer. In today's world, electronic computers keep track of financial data and perform mathematical computations. Computers are faster and more accurate than people for these kinds of tasks.

When you use Excel to perform a mathematical operation, it needs to be done in a way that is similar to ordinary math, but with a few special rules. For example, all formulas must begin with an equal sign (=), and you use cell references or names in the formulas.

In this task, you practice applying the basic formula rules in Excel. The sheet you produce serves as a convenient reference for later use.

1 Open **EX0301** from the **Student** folder. Save it as **EX0301-Math** on your disk.

In the **Basic Operations** sheet, select cell **B7** and type **=B3+5** in the cell.

This formula adds the contents of cell B3 and the number 5.

Enter button on the formula bar

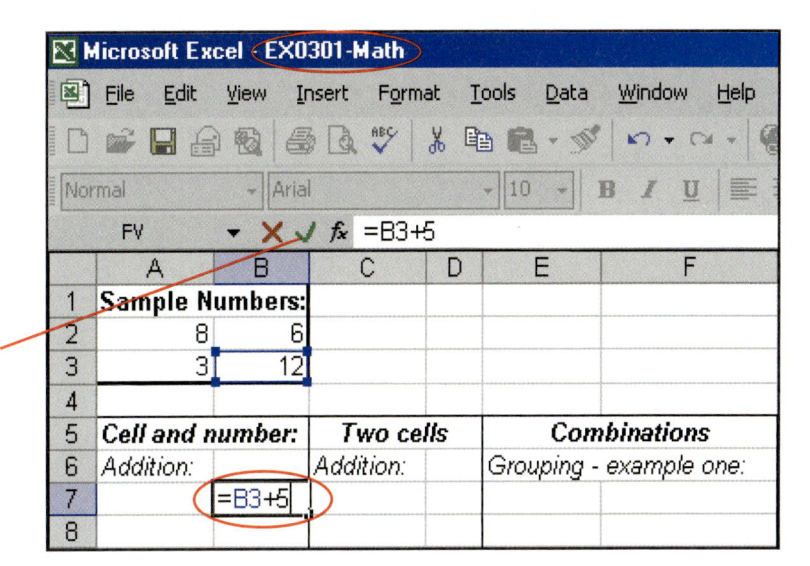

2 Click the **Enter** button on the formula bar.

Notice that cell B3 contains the number 12, and that cell B7 displays the result of adding 5 to the contents of B3.

IN DEPTH

You can enter a formula by pressing ⏎Enter or Tab⇥; however, the selection moves to another cell, and you have to move the selection back if you want to see the formula in the formula bar. If you click the Enter button on the formula bar, the selection does not move to another cell.

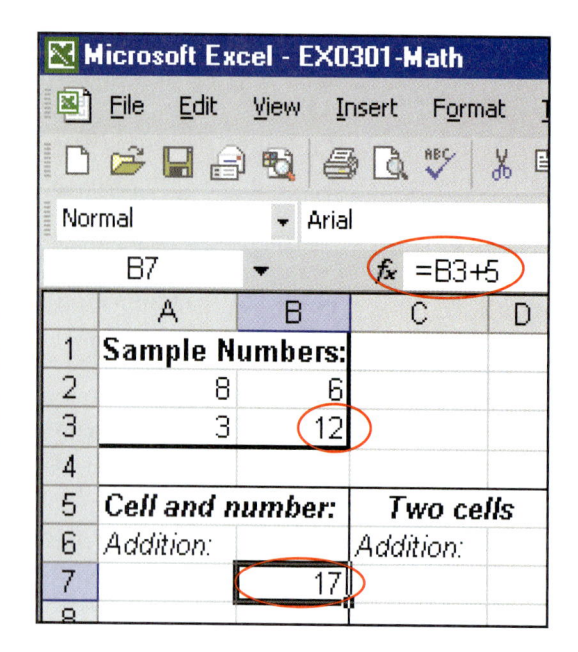

3 Select cell **B10** and type **=B3-5**.

Determine what you think the answer should be before you proceed. In this case, you subtract 5 from the contents of cell B3.

Click the **Enter** button on the formula bar.

If you anticipated a different answer, take the time to figure out why.

4 Select cell **B13**, type **=A2*3**, determine what you think the answer should be, and then click the **Enter** button on the formula bar.

Excel uses the asterisk to indicate multiplication.

5 Select cell **B16**, type **=A2/4**, anticipate the answer, and then click the **Enter** button on the formula bar.

Excel uses the slash to indicate division.

> **CAUTION**
> There are two slash keys. The forward slash (/) is used to indicate division in Excel formulas. If you use the backslash (\) by mistake, Excel displays #NAME? to indicate that it does not recognize your entry as a formula, but thinks it is a misspelled cell reference.

Task 2
USING FORMULAS WITH MORE THAN ONE CELL REFERENCE

Why would I do this?
When writing a *formula*, an equation used to calculate values in a cell, it is common to refer to numbers entered in more than one cell on your worksheet. For example, if you want to know the profit for your business, you subtract expenses from income. If you want to know the percent increase in sales, you use numbers entered for two different sales periods to make that calculation.

In this task, you learn to use numbers from more than one cell to make calculations.

1 Select cell **D7**, type **=A2+A3**, estimate the answer, and then click the **Enter** button on the formula bar.

In this case, the formula adds the numbers in cells A2 and A3.

> **QUICK TIP**
> After typing an equal sign to begin the formula, you can point to a cell and click to enter its name in the formula. You can then type the math symbol you want to use before you point and click on the next cell you want in the formula. When this method is used, a marquee outlines the cell that has been selected. This method is preferable if you are writing a formula and the cell you want is off the screen where you cannot see the cell reference.

Task 2 Using Formulas with More than One Cell Reference EXC 53

2 Select cell **D10**, type **=A2-A3,** estimate the answer, and then click the **Enter** button on the formula bar.

This formula tells the program to take the number in cell A2 and subtract the number in cell A3.

3 Select cell **D13**, type **=A2*A3**, determine what the answer should be if the numbers in these cells were multiplied together, and then click the **Enter** button on the formula bar.

In this case, you told the program to multiply the number in cell A2 by the number in cell A3.

4 Select cell **D16**, type **=B3/B2,** estimate the answer, and then click the **Enter** button on the formula bar.

In this case, you told the program to take the number in cell B3 and divide by the number in cell B2.

> **QUICK TIP**
>
> While you are editing a formula, buttons with a green check mark and a red X appear next to the formula on the formula bar. If you click the green check mark, the formula is entered but the selection does not move to another cell so you can still see the formula in the formula bar. If you click the red X, it takes you out of edit mode.

54 EXC Lesson 3 Using Formulas

5 Double-click on cell **D7**.

The formula is displayed in the cell and in the formula bar. The cell references, in the formula and the cells to which they refer, change to matching colors. An insertion mark is placed in the formula.

> **IN DEPTH**
>
> If you select a cell that contains a formula, you may edit the formula in the formula bar. You may click on the formula in the formula bar to place the insertion point in the formula and then edit it using the [+Backspace] and [Del] keys. You may also select parts of the formula to edit by clicking and dragging across parts of the formula to select them before typing a replacement.

6 Use the [+Backspace] and [Del] keys to edit the formula the way you would edit ordinary text. Change it to **=B2+A3**.

Click the **Enter** button on the formula bar to finish the change.

> **QUICK TIP**
>
> Cell references are not case sensitive. Excel interprets A2 the same as a2. When entering cell references, it is not necessary to capitalize the column reference letter.

Task 3
COMBINING OPERATIONS AND FILLING CELLS WITH FORMULAS

Why would I do this?

You may want to add the contents of several cells together and then divide by the contents of another cell. To do this, use parentheses to group operations together to make sure they are done first.

If the same formula is to be used in several cells, it may be filled into those cells using the *fill handle*. The fill handle is a small box at the lower-right corner of a selected cell that can be used to fill in a series of cells. Sometimes you want cell references to change to adapt to the new position they are in; for example, you may have a formula that totals the cells above it and wish to copy this formula across several cells. In each case, you want the formula to add up the column of cells directly above the formula. This is called a *relative reference*. In other cases, you want the cell reference to always refer to a specific cell. This is called an *absolute reference*.

In this task, you will learn how to group operations in a formula and how to fill cells with formulas using relative and absolute cell references.

Task 3 Combining Operations and Filling Cells with Formulas EXC

❶ Select cell **F7**, and then type **=(A2+B2)/A3**. Estimate what the result should be if you add the contents of cells A2 and B2 and then divide by the number in cell A3 (it is not a whole number). Click the **Enter** button on the formula bar to confirm your estimate.

Notice that the numbers in cells A2 and B2 (8 and 6) are added first and then divided by the number in cell A3 (3).

❷ Select cell **F10**, and then type **=B3/(A3+B2)**. Estimate what the answer will be if the number in cell B3 is divided by the sum of the numbers in cells A3 and B2. Click the **Enter** button on the formula bar to confirm your estimate.

❸ Select cell **F13**.

Look at the formula in the formula bar. It shows that the formula simply equals the value of cell A2.

EXC   Lesson 3   Using Formulas

4 Click-and-drag the fill handle down to cell **F14**. Release the mouse button.

Notice that cell F14 displays the number 3, which is the value in cell A3.

> **IN DEPTH**
> The Auto Fill Options button that appears next to the fill handle may be used to choose options for how to fill a selection. For example, you could choose to fill the formatting rather than the numbers or text.

Fill handle   Auto Fill Options

5 Select cell **F14**.

Notice that the formula equals the value in cell A3. The formulas in cells F13 and F14 both refer to a cell that is eleven rows up and five columns to the left.

> **IN DEPTH**
> When you fill a formula from one cell to another, Excel uses a relative cell reference. In this example, Excel used A3 to fill cell F14. Cell F14 is one position below F13, and cell A3 is one position below A2. Excel uses the relative position of the cell that is being referenced to determine the location of the next value to place in the new cell. This is the default method that Excel uses to fill a formula from one cell to another.

Task 3   Combining Operations and Filling Cells with Formulas

6 Select cell **F16**. Look at the formula in the formula bar.

In this case, a $ has been placed to the left of the column and row identifiers to indicate that the cell reference will not change when it is copied.

IN DEPTH

The dollar sign ($) that is used as a code to prevent the reference from changing has nothing to do with currency. It is a symbol that was used in the earliest spreadsheets for this purpose and has been used ever since. The dollar sign to the left of the column letter makes the column reference absolute and the dollar sign to the left of the row number makes the row reference absolute. It is possible to create mixes of absolute and relative references by using only one dollar sign.

7 Use the fill handle to fill this formula into cell **F17**.

Notice that F17 also displays the contents of cell A2.

Absolute reference to cell A2

Fill handle

58 EXC Lesson 3 Using Formulas

8 Select cell **F17**. Look at the formula in the formula bar.

Notice that it did not change when the formula was filled into the cell. This type of cell reference (with the $ sign) is called an absolute reference. Use an absolute reference when you want to ensure that the formula always refers to a specific cell.

9 Press Ctrl+` (the accent grave mark found on the key to the left of the 1 key).

The formulas for each cell and the Formula Auditing toolbar are displayed.

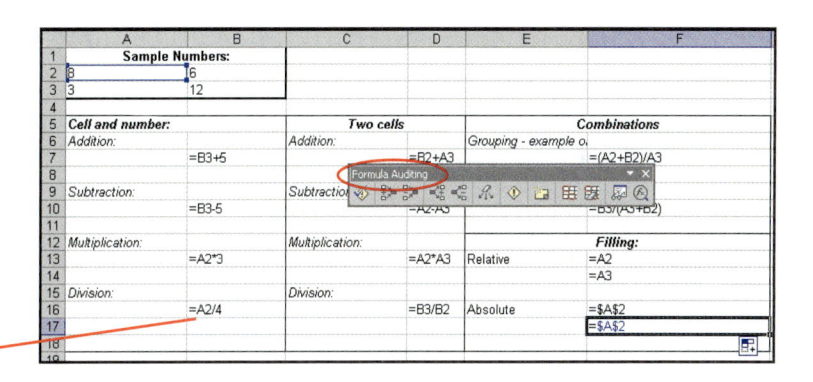

Cells display formulas

10 Choose **File**, **Page Setup**, **Header/Footer** tab, **Custom Header**. Add your name to the custom header **Center section**. Click **OK**.

Click **Print** to print the worksheet. Check the printer destination, and then click **OK**.

The printed worksheet displays a record of the formulas in your worksheet.

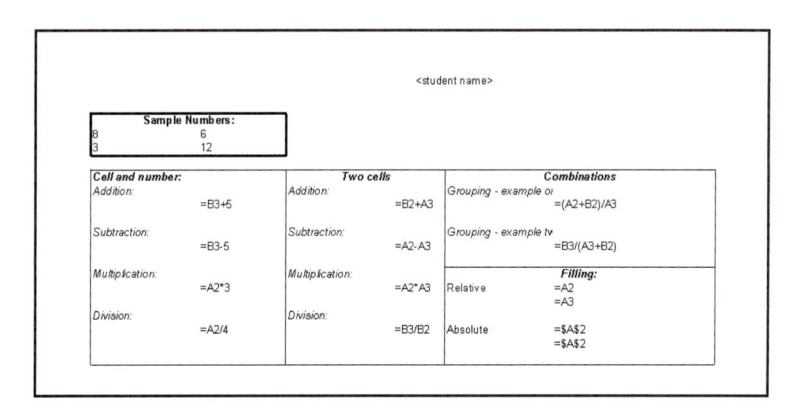

Task 3 Combining Operations and Filling Cells with Formulas   EXC   59

11 Press Ctrl+` to return the worksheet to the Normal view, showing the formula results.

Click the **Save** button to save your workbook.

Task 4
FILLING CELLS WITH RELATIVE AND ABSOLUTE FORMULAS

Why would I do this?
The ability to fill formulas into adjacent cells greatly increases the speed at which a worksheet can be created. Formulas or text can be filled into adjacent cells. The formulas are automatically revised to reflect the new locations.

In this task, you learn how to fill cells using formulas that include both relative and absolute references.

1 Click the **Commission** tab to switch to the **Commission** sheet and select cell **B11**, if necessary.

Notice that it contains a formula that adds the contents of cells B5 through B10, which are directly above B11.

> **IN DEPTH**
> Two cell references separated by a colon, such as B5:B10, indicate a rectangular-shaped group of cells where the two cells are at opposite corners of the block of cells.

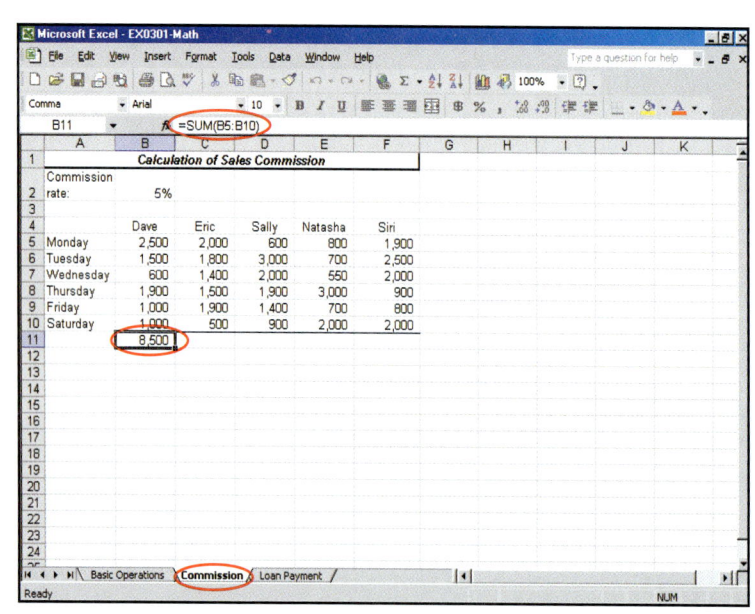

2 Drag the fill handle to the right to cell **F11** and release the mouse button.

The formula is filled into cells C11 through F11.

Fill handle

3 Click on cell **D11**.

You see that the formula changed to add the six cells in the column directly above cell D11. This shows how the use of the fill handle results in a relative reference.

4 Select cell **B12** and type **=B11*$B$2**, then click the **Enter** button on the formula bar.

This formula multiplies the sum of Dave's sales in cell B11 by the commission rate in cell B2. The reference to B11 is relative, and the reference to B2 is absolute.

Absolute reference to cell B2

Task 4 Filling Cells with Relative and Absolute Formulas   EXC   **61**

5 Drag the fill handle to the right to cell **F12** and release the mouse button.

The formula is filled into cells C12 through F12.

6 Click on cell **D12** and look at the formula bar.

The relative reference changed so that it refers to the sum of Sally's sales in cell D11, but the absolute reference to the commission rate in cell B2 did not change.

Relative cell reference changed

Absolute cell reference did not change

7 Choose **File**, **Page Setup**, **Header**/**Footer** tab, **Custom Header**. Add your name to the custom header **Left section**. Click **OK**.

Click Print to print the worksheet. Check the printer destination, and then click OK.

Save the workbook and leave it open for use in the next task.

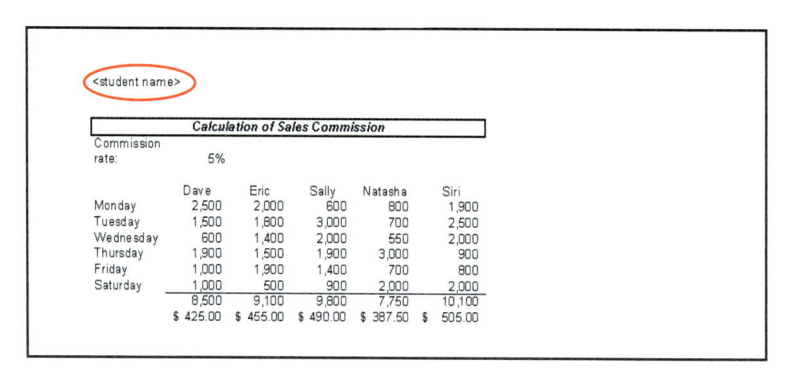

Task 5
APPLYING BASIC FORMULAS TO A LOAN REPAYMENT

Why would I do this?
When you borrow money for a car or a house, the loan repayment is based on several factors, such as interest rate, time to repay, and the loan amount. With Excel, you can set up a worksheet to calculate your monthly payments based on these factors, then change the value of the factors to match whatever loan terms you are quoted by a bank or other lender.

In this task, you learn how to set up a worksheet to calculate total monthly payments.

1 Click on the **Loan Payment** tab to switch to the **Loan Payment** sheet.

Notice that column A is used for labels and column B is used for formulas.

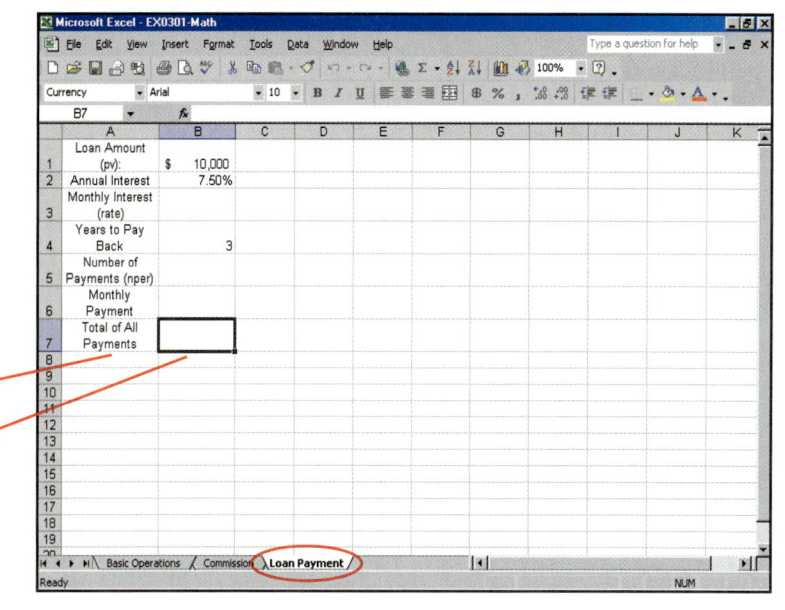

2 Select cell **B3,** type **=B2/12**, and click the **Enter** button on the formula bar.

This formula takes the annual interest rate in cell B2 and divides by 12 to calculate the monthly interest rate.

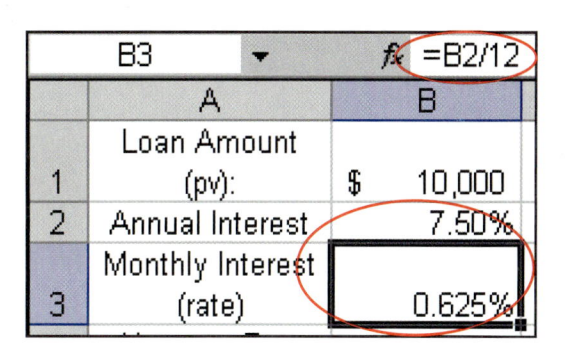

> **IN DEPTH**
> To calculate the monthly payment, the formula requires the number of months and the interest rate per month. Most loan interest rates are given as an Annual Percentage Rate, or **APR**. If the payment is made every month, the formula needs to use one-twelfth of the annual interest rate to calculate the interest cost per month.

Task 5   Applying Basic Formulas to a Loan Repayment   EXC   63

3 Select cell **B5**, type **=B4*12**, and then click the **Enter** button on the formula bar.

This formula calculates the number of months over which the loan is repaid.

4 Select cell **B7**, type **=B5*B6**, and then click the **Enter** button on the formula bar.

This formula multiplies the number of payments in cell B5 times the amount of the payment in B6. In this case, no number is displayed in the cell because cell B6 is still empty, and cell B7 has been formatted to show a dollar sign and a dash when the value is zero.

Leave the workbook open for the next task.

Task 6
USING BUILT-IN FINANCIAL FORMULAS

Why would I do this?
When you take out a loan, you usually rely on someone else to tell you how much the payment will be. In order to shop around for the best rate or terms, it is helpful to see the effect of different loan terms that may be quoted to you. In the previous task, the factors used to calculate a loan were outlined.

In this task, you learn how to use one of Excel's built-in financial formulas to calculate the monthly payment.

1 Select cell **B6**. Choose **Insert**, **Function** from the menu.

The Insert Function dialog box opens.

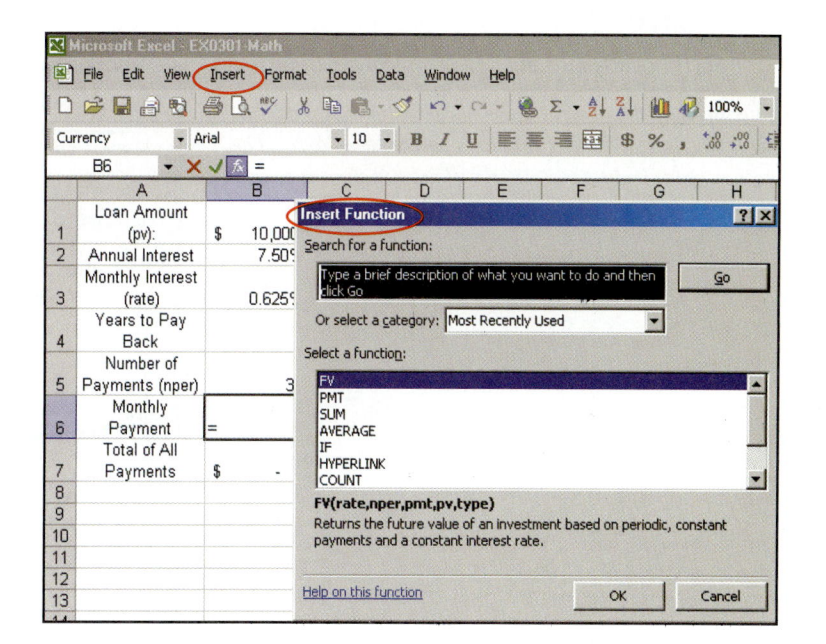

> The default category, Most Recently Used, displays a list of recently used functions in the box below. This list is different for each computer because it is based on recent use.

2 Click the down arrow to the right of the Or select a category box.

Categories of formulas are displayed.

Click **Financial**.

*A list of built-in financial formulas appears in the **Select a function** box.*

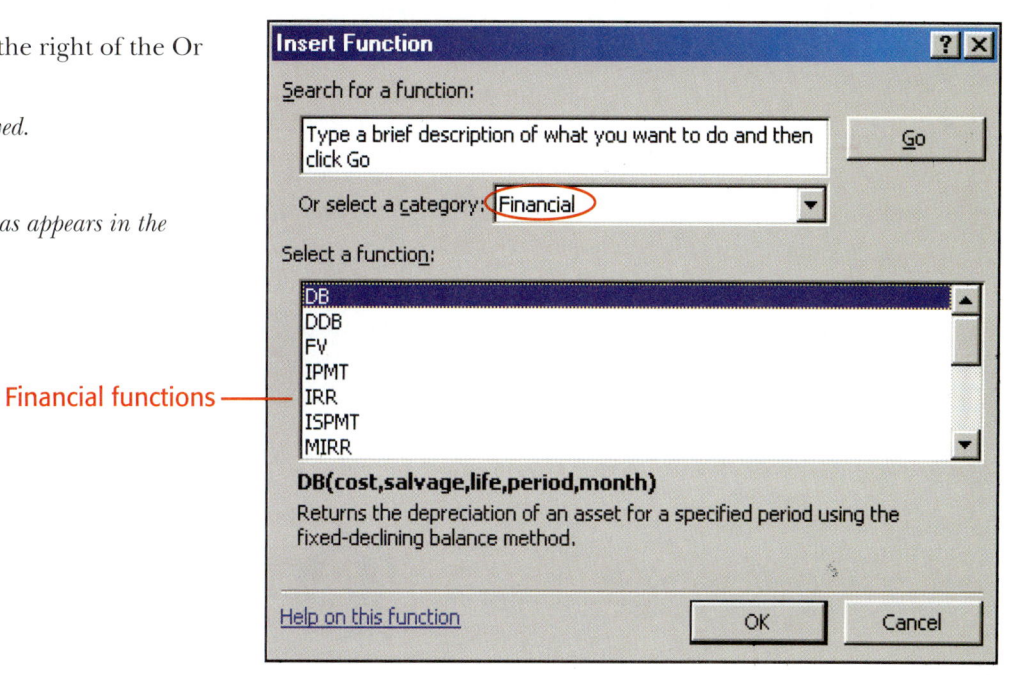

Financial functions

Task 6   Using Built-In Financial Formulas   EXC

③ Scroll down and click on the **PMT** function.

The name of the function, the values it requires, and a brief description of the function's use are displayed. The values are called **arguments**. *This function is used to calculate loan payments.*

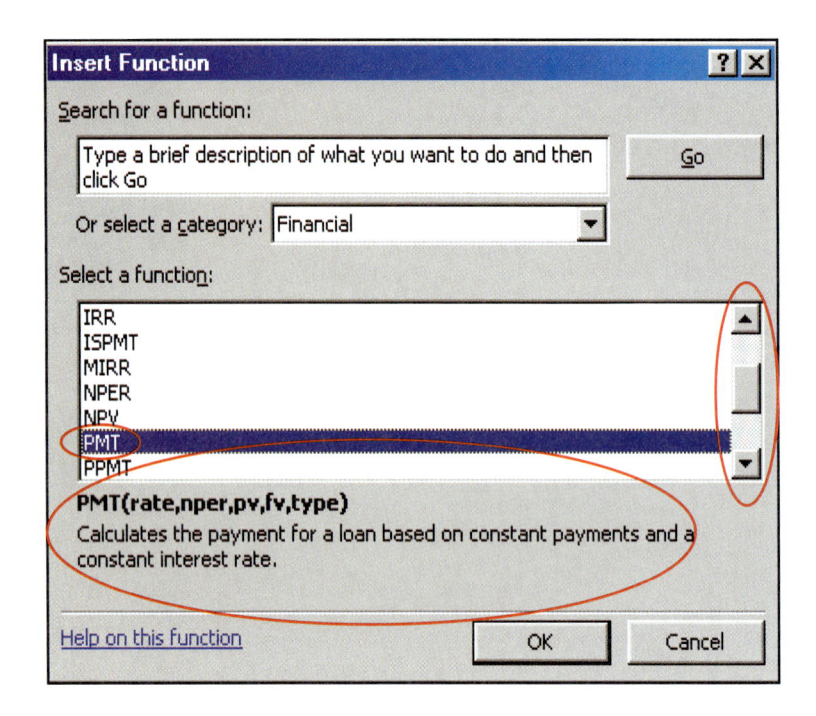

④ Click **OK**.

A wizard dialog box opens. You use the wizard to identify the cells that contain values, or arguments, that the PMT function requires. The first three arguments are required, and their names are in boldface type. The last two are optional, and their names are in normal type.

Required arguments

Optional arguments

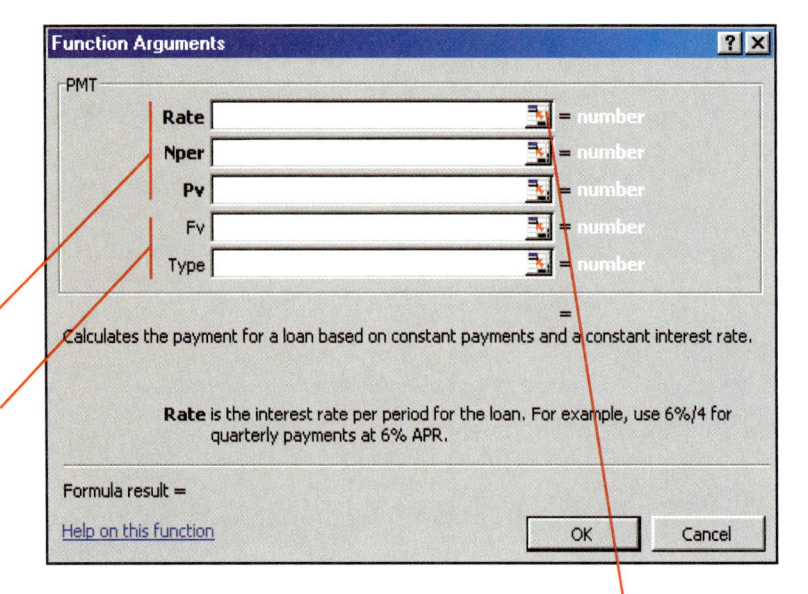

Collapse Dialog Box button

> **IN DEPTH**
>
> Wizards usually consist of a series of questions that guide you through the creation of a formula or a chart. Wizards are used in Excel to help with a number of different processes. These include a Help Wizard known as the Office Assistant, a Chart Wizard used for creating charts, and the wizards in Insert Function that help create complex formulas such as a payment formula. When you are working on a formula, you can click the equal sign on the formula bar to open the Formula Palette, which displays current information about the formula you are using.

EXC   Lesson 3   Using Formulas

5 Click the **Collapse Dialog Box** button at the right end of the **Rate** box.

The dialog box collapses to a single input box to make it easier to view the worksheet.

> **QUICK TIP**
> You can move back and forth between the worksheet and the dialog box. It is not necessary to collapse the dialog box if you can see the numbers you want to use.

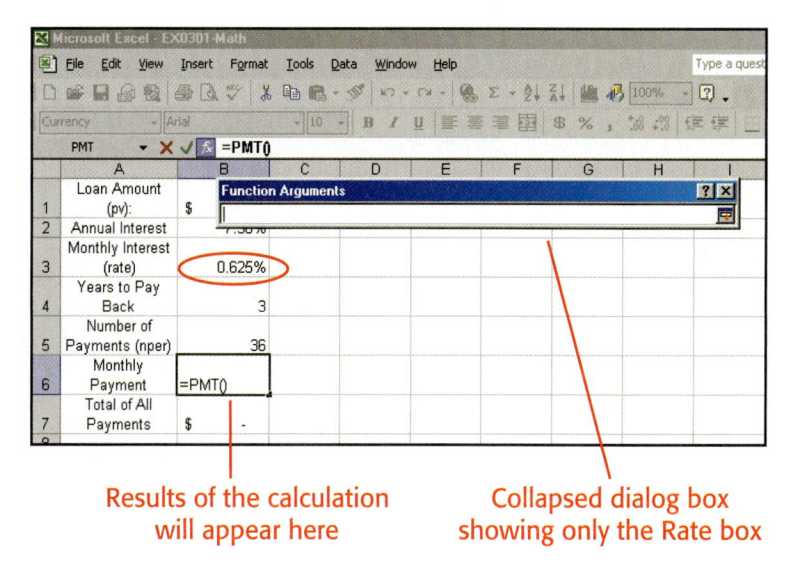

Results of the calculation will appear here

Collapsed dialog box showing only the Rate box

> **IN DEPTH**
> If the collapsed dialog box obscures the range of cells that you want to select, drag it to another location.

6 Click cell **B3**.

This cell reference is entered into the formula as the first argument.

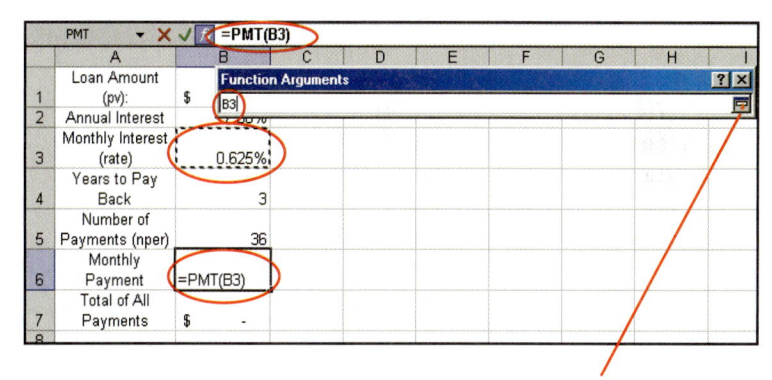

Expand Dialog Box button

7 Click the **Expand Dialog Box** button.

This action restores the dialog box. The cell reference is displayed in the Rate box.

Task 6   Using Built-In Financial Formulas   EXC   67

8 Press Tab to move to the **Nper** box.

The message at the bottom of the box explains that this is the total number of loan payments.

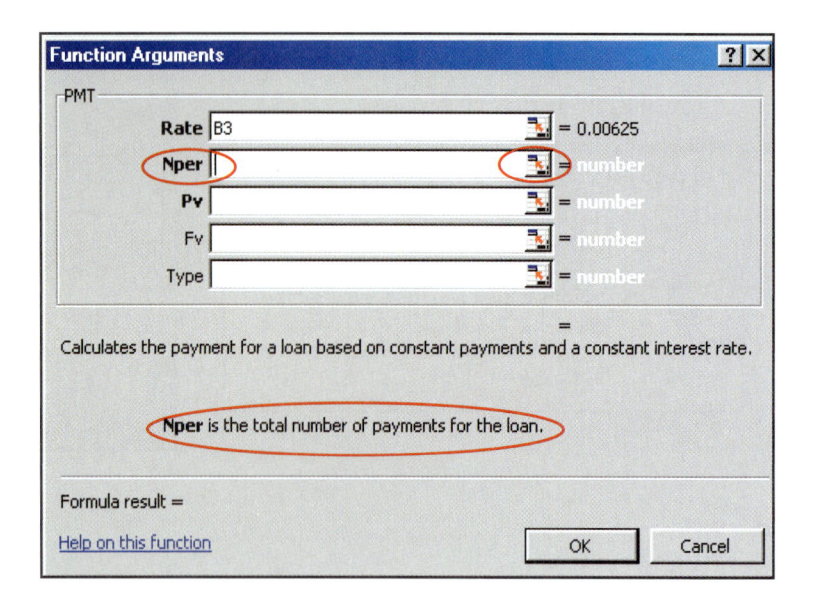

9 Click the **Collapse Dialog Box** button at the right side of the **Nper** box, click on cell **B5**, and then click the **Expand Dialog Box** button.

The reference to cell B5 is added as the second argument to the formula.

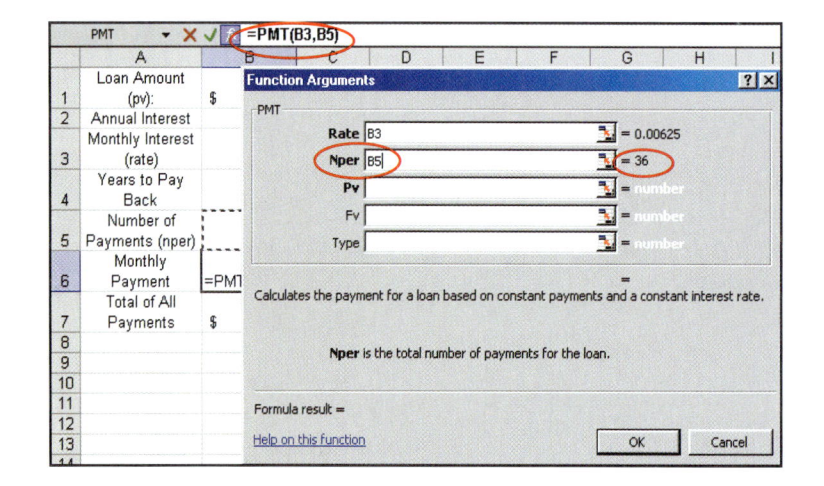

10 Press Tab to move to the **Pv** box.

This argument is used to identify the present value of the loan or the amount you want to borrow.

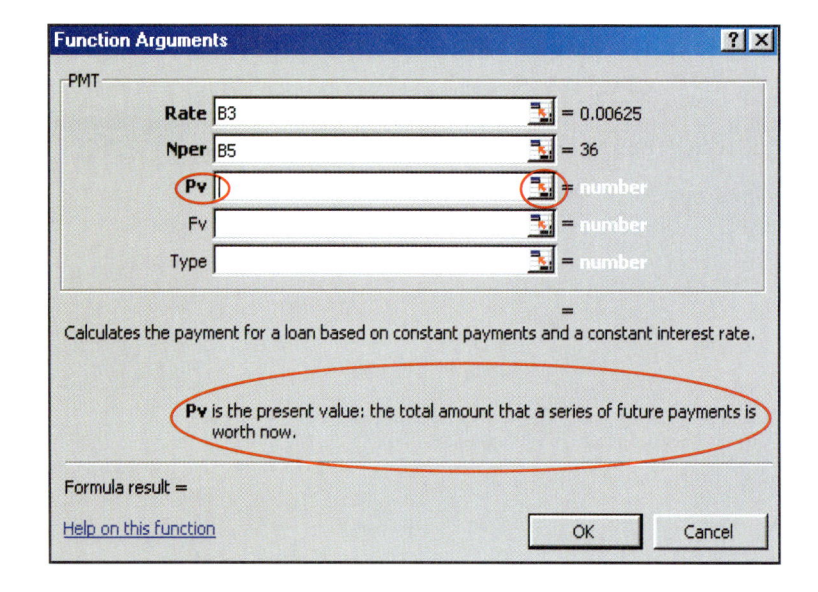

68   EXC   Lesson 3   Using Formulas

11 Click the **Collapse Dialog Box** button, click on cell **B1**, and click the **Expand Dialog Box** button.

The reference to cell B1 is added as the third argument to the formula. The formula now has enough information to calculate the payment. The result is displayed at the bottom of the dialog box.

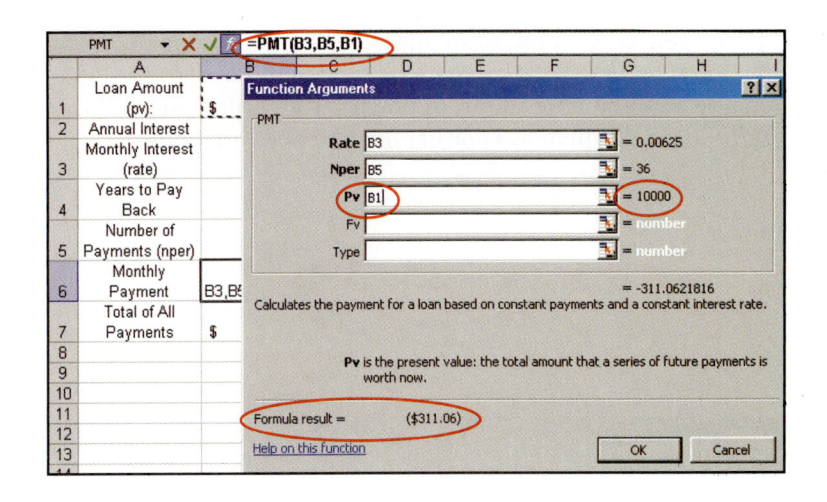

12 Click **OK**.

The calculated payment is displayed. The currency format that has been chosen for this cell displays negative numbers in red, enclosed by parentheses. (If the loan amount is entered as a positive number, the payment is negative.) Notice that cell B7 now shows the total amount of all payments.

13 Click the **Save** button on the toolbar, and then close the workbook.

Task 6   Using Built-In Financial Formulas   EXC

The exercises that follow are designed for you to review and use what you have learned in this lesson. You also have the opportunity to practice your skills and then expand on them by applying them to new situations.

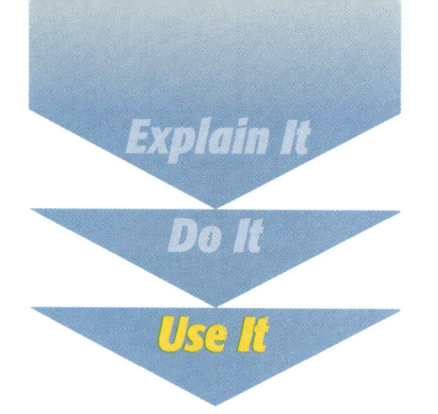

COMPREHENSION

Comprehension exercises are designed to check your memory and understanding of the basic concepts in this lesson. You distinguish between true and false statements, identify new screen elements, and match terms with related statements. If you are uncertain of the correct answer, refer to the task number following each item (for example, T4 refers to Task 4), and review that task until you are confident you can provide a correct response.

TRUE-FALSE

Circle either T or F.

T   F   1. You can only use one cell reference in a formula. **(T2)**

T   F   2. When you use the fill handle to copy a formula that sums a column, Excel assumes an absolute reference to the numbers in the original column. **(T3)**

T   F   3. To designate a cell reference as absolute, place a $ to the left of both the column and row identifiers. **(T4)**

T   F   4. The loan payment formula uses an annual interest rate and the number of years of the loan to calculate the monthly payment amount. **(T5)**

T   F   5. A relative reference is a cell reference that will change when the formula is copied, moved, or filled. **(T4)**

T   F   6. A quick way to format a cell to display currency is to use dollar signs in the name of the cell. **(T3)**

MATCHING QUESTIONS

A. Arguments   D. $B$3
B. ✓   E. /
C. Accent grave   F. =

Match the following statements to the word or phrase that is the best match from the list. Write the letter of the matching word or phrase in the space provided next to the number.

1. ____ Symbol used to represent division **(T1)**

2. ____ Term used for numbers or words that are used by a function to perform a calculation or operation **(T6)**

3. ____ **Enter** button on the formula bar **(T1)**

4. ____ Used to begin every formula **(T1)**

5. ____ Name of the character that is used with the Ctrl key to reveal the formulas in the cells (it resembles an apostrophe) **(T3)**

6. ____ An example of an absolute cell reference **(T4)**

IDENTIFYING PARTS OF THE EXCEL SCREEN

Refer to the figure and identify the numbered parts of the screen. Write the letter of the correct label in the space next to the number.

1. _____
2. _____
3. _____
4. _____
5. _____
6. _____
7. _____
8. _____
9. _____
10. _____

A. Optional argument (T6)

B. **Enter** button (T1)

C. Projected payment amount (T6)

D. Interest rate per loan period (T6)

E. Amount of money that is borrowed (T6)

F. Number of payments in a loan (T6)

G. **Collapse Dialog Box** button (T6)

H. Formula with arguments (T6)

I. Description of the selected argument (T6)

J. **Cancel** button (T2)

Comprehension   EXC   71

REINFORCEMENT

Reinforcement exercises are designed to reinforce the skills you have learned by applying them to new situations. Detailed instructions are provided along with a figure, where appropriate, to illustrate the result. The reinforcement exercises that follow should be completed sequentially. Leave the file open at the end of each exercise for use in the next exercise until you are specifically directed to close it.

Open **EX0302** and save it as **EX0302-Reinforcement** on your floppy disk for use in the following exercises.

R1—Using Basic Excel Formulas

Worksheets are very useful when calculating retail prices for items purchased at wholesale prices.

Modify the **Patio Furniture** worksheet to match the figure. See the steps below for more detail. (The sheet zoom is set at 80 percent to provide a full view of the worksheet.)

1. Click the **Patio Furniture** sheet tab, if necessary. Select cell **D3** and enter **=B3*C3** to calculate the total cost of each item.

2. Use the fill handle to copy the formula in **D3** to cells **D4** through **D9**. Format the values in cells **D3** through **D9** to be currency with no decimals. Reduce the column width as shown in the figure.

3. Select cell **F3** and enter **=B3*E3** to calculate the retail values.

4. Use the fill handle to copy the formula in **F3** to cells **F4** through **F9**. Format the values in cells **F3** through **F9** as currency with no decimals. Reduce the column width as shown in the figure.

5. Use the **AutoSum** button to place a SUM function in cells **D10** and **F10** to add the numbers in the column above.

6. To calculate the percent markup, select cell **G3** and enter **=(E3-C3)/C3**. Fill the formula to cells **G4** through **G9**. Format the values in this column as percentages with no decimals (use the **Percent Style** button on the Formatting toolbar).

7. To calculate the percent contribution, select cell **H3** and enter **=F3/$F$10**. Fill the formula to the other cells in the column. Format the values in this column as percentages with two decimals.

8. Place a top and double bottom border on cells **D10**, **F10**, and **H10**. Sum the column in cell **H10**.

9. Choose **File**, **Page Setup**, **Header/Footer** tab, **Custom Header**. Add your name to the custom header **Left section**. Click **OK**.

10. Click the **Page** tab and choose **Landscape** orientation. Click **Print Preview** and print the sheet if your instructor requires it.

11. Close Print Preview and use Ctrl+` to display the formulas. Narrow the columns and wrap the column headings so the worksheet will print on one page (see figure). Print the sheet showing the formulas.

12. Change the worksheet back to show the values rather than the formulas and save the workbook. Leave the workbook open for use in the next exercise.

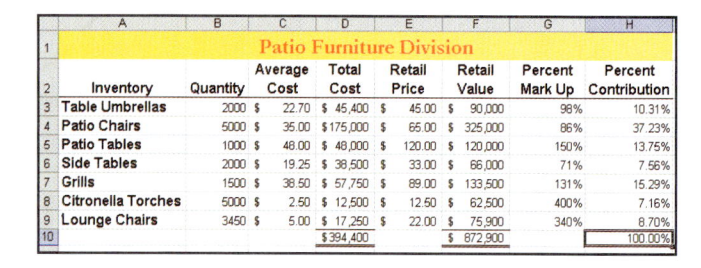

	A	B	C	D	E	F	G	H
1				Patio Furniture Division				
2	Inventory	Quantity	Average Cost	Total Cost	Retail Price	Retail Value	Percent Mark Up	Percent Contribution
3	Table Umbrellas	2000	$ 22.70	$ 45,400	$ 45.00	$ 90,000	98%	10.31%
4	Patio Chairs	5000	$ 35.00	$175,000	$ 65.00	$ 325,000	86%	37.23%
5	Patio Tables	1000	$ 48.00	$ 48,000	$ 120.00	$ 120,000	150%	13.75%
6	Side Tables	2000	$ 19.25	$ 38,500	$ 33.00	$ 66,000	71%	7.56%
7	Grills	1500	$ 38.50	$ 57,750	$ 89.00	$ 133,500	131%	15.29%
8	Citronella Torches	5000	$ 2.50	$ 12,500	$ 12.50	$ 62,500	400%	7.16%
9	Lounge Chairs	3450	$ 5.00	$ 17,250	$ 22.00	$ 75,900	340%	8.70%
10				$394,400		$ 872,900		100.00%

R2—Using Absolute and Relative References

Tracking employee salaries and taxes can be done using a worksheet.

Modify the **Computer Support** worksheet to match the figure. See the steps below for more detail.

1. Select the **Computer Support** sheet, select cell **B5**, and enter **=B3*$B$15**. Use the fill handle to copy the formula to the right to cell **G5**. With the cells still selected, use the **Comma Style** button to format the cells, if needed, then decrease the decimals to show no decimals.

2. Select cell **B6** and enter **=B3*.20**. Use the fill handle to copy the formula to the right to cell **G6**. Format row **6** the same as row **5**.

3. Select cell **B7** and enter **=B3*$B$16**. Use the fill handle to copy the formula to the right to cell **G7**. Format row **7** the same as rows **5** and **6**.

4. Select cell **B8**. Write a formula that will multiply the salaries by an absolute reference to the Medicare tax percent (refer to the **Fixed Percentages** table in the figure). Use the fill handle to copy the formula to the right to cells **C8** through **G8**. Use the same format for these cells.

5. Add a double bottom border to the figures in row **8** and sum the deductibles in each column in row **9**. Notice that the empty cell in row **4** prevents the AutoSum function from accidentally selecting the salaries in row **3**.

6. Calculate the net salary figures by writing a formula in cell **B11** that takes the salaries for the month and subtracts the deductibles for the month. Copy the formula to cells **C11** through **G11**.

7. Check the results of your formulas against the figure to be sure they are working properly. Change the state tax to **6%**. (Type **.06** or **6%**, not just the number 6.) The worksheet is recalculated.

8. Choose **File**, **Page Setup**, **Header/Footer** tab, **Custom Header**. Add your name to the custom header **Left section**. Click **OK**.

9. Change the page orientation to **Landscape**. Save and print your work.

R3—Calculating a House Payment and Amortization Schedule for a Five-Year Balloon Mortgage

In this exercise, you use the PMT function to calculate a house payment. Then you use Excel's ability to copy relative and absolute cell references to calculate a list of payments and balances for each month. You also learn how to use this table of payments to determine how much you would need to refinance if you select a common form of loan known as a five-year balloon mortgage.

Modify the **Mortgage** worksheet to match the figure. See the steps below for more detail.

1. Select the **Mortgage** sheet. Select cell **B5** and write a formula to determine the monthly interest rate. Format it as a percent showing three decimal places. =B4/12

2. Select cell **B7** and write a formula to determine the number of monthly payments over the term of the loan.

3. Select cell **B8** and use **Insert**, **Function** to insert the financial payment formula, **PMT**, for the mortgage. Select the appropriate arguments for the formula.

4. Select cells **D5** and **D6**. Use the fill handle to fill the date column for five years. The last date should be **1/1/07** in row **64**. Interest Pd = G4*B5

5. Select cells **E6** through **G6**. Drag these three cells to the bottom of the date column to complete the amortization schedule. Look in cell **G64**. If you need to refinance the home loan in five years, you will need to borrow **$118,559.67** (and pay closing costs again). Principle = -$B$8-F5

6. Change the Annual Percentage Rate (APR) to **8%**.

7. Add your name to the sheet header. Save the workbook and close it. Balance = G4-E5
Use fill handle to fill the dates + formula

CHALLENGE

Challenge exercises are designed to test your ability to apply your skills to new situations with less-detailed instructions. These exercises also challenge you to expand your repertoire of skills by using commands that are similar to those you have already learned. The desired outcome is clearly defined, but you have more freedom to choose the steps needed to achieve the required result.

Challenge exercises C1 through C5 use different worksheets in the workbook **EX0303-Challenge**. Open **EX0303** from the **Student** folder on your CD-ROM disc and save it as **EX0303-Challenge** on your floppy disk.

C1—Using Goal Seek to Find an Interest Rate

Sometimes you know what the answer needs to be, but you do not know how to get there. If you have a worksheet set up to calculate an answer based on one or more cells, you can use an Excel tool named Goal Seek that will try different numbers in the cell you select until the answer in another cell matches the value you set.

Goal: Use the Goal Seek tool to determine the annual interest rate that would produce a monthly payment of $600 if the loan amount and payment period remain unchanged.

Use the following guidelines:

1. In the **EX0303-Challenge** workbook, select the **Goal Seek (1)** sheet tab.

2. Select **Tools**, **Goal Seek** from the menu.

3. Use the Goal Seek dialog box to set cell **B6** to **600** by changing the annual interest rate in cell **B2**. The resulting Annual Interest Rate is approximately **7.02%**. (The display is limited to two decimal places, but the actual calculated answer is much more precise.)

4. Save the workbook and leave it open for use in the next exercise.

	A	B
1	Loan Amount	$ 90,000
2	Annual Interest Rate	7.02%
3	Monthly rate	0.585%
4	Years	30
5	Months	360
6	Payment	$ 600.00

C2—Using Goal Seek to Determine the Largest Loan Amount

When you buy a car, you may know how much you can afford to pay each month and you may know the interest rate that is charged for a car loan, but you do not know how much you can afford to borrow under those conditions. You can use Goal Seek to find out.

Goal: Determine how big a loan you can afford (Loan Amount) on a five-year car loan at an Annual Interest Rate of 8.5 percent if the most you can afford for a monthly car payment is $350.

Use the following guidelines:

1. In the **EX0303-Challenge** workbook, select the **Goal Seek (2)** sheet tab.

2. Use **Goal Seek** to find out what loan amount will yield a payment of **$350**. The sheet is protected so that you do not accidentally overwrite the formulas. The answers shown in the figure are rounded, but the actual values computed by the program are not.

3. Save the workbook. Leave the workbook open for use in the next exercise.

	A	B
1	Loan Amount	$ 17,059
2	Annual Interest Rate	8.50%
3	Monthly rate	0.708%
4	Years	5
5	Months	60
6	Payment	$ 350.00

C3—Calculating Percentage Increases or Decreases

Prices are often determined by marking up a wholesale price by a certain percentage. When those items go on sale, the price is reduced by a certain percentage.

In this exercise, you will see how formulas are used to increase or decrease a price by a given percentage. In general, if you want to increase a value by 40 percent, you multiply the value by (1+40%). If you want to decrease the price by 20 percent, you multiply by (1-20%). An example is provided to show how a merchant starts with a wholesale price for a pair of boots, increases the price by 40 percent to get the retail price, decreases the retail price by 20 percent for a sale, and then figures out the gross profit and percent profit.

Goal: Calculate percentage increases and decreases.

1. In the **EX0303-Challenge** workbook, select the **Percent** sheet.
2. Look at the formula in cell **C2**. Notice how the retail price for the boots was calculated by multiplying the wholesale price in cell **B2** by **(1+40%)**.
3. Enter a similar formula in cell **C3** that calculates a retail price for gloves at a **50%** increase over the wholesale price.
4. Observe the formula in cell **D2** to see how the sale price for boots was determined by multiplying the retail price by **(1-20%)**.
5. Enter a similar formula in cell **D3** to calculate the sale price for gloves if their price is reduced by **30%**.
6. Fill the formulas in cells **E2** and **F2** into cells **E3** and **F3**, respectively. The percent profit on the gloves will be **5%** if you have written the formulas correctly.
7. Enter similar formulas for the hats. Use an increase of **120%** to determine the retail price and then determine the sale price for a **50%** off sale. Fill the gross profit and percent profit formulas into cells **E4** and **F4**.
8. Check your work. All three items should have a positive profit. Save the workbook. Leave the workbook open for use in the next exercise.

	A	B	C	D	E	F
1	Item	Wholesale price	Retail Price	Sale Price	Gross Profit	Percent Profit
2	Boots	$ 22.35	$ 31.29	$ 25.03	$ 2.68	12%
3	Gloves	$ 12.35	$ 18.53	$ 12.97	$ 0.62	5%
4	Hats	$ 18.20	$ 40.04	$ 20.02	$ 1.82	10%

C4—Using Statistical Functions: Average, Median, Minimum, Maximum, and Standard Deviation

When we describe a set of numbers, such as the income of a certain group, we often use terms such as average or median. We can use Excel to compute these numbers and see how they describe a set of numbers. Average and median are two ways of describing where the "center" of a set of numbers is. They do not describe whether the numbers are all close to that central number or if they vary greatly. The statistic that describes this type of variation is the standard deviation. It is also useful to know the greatest and least values to see how far from the "center" the numbers can vary.

In this exercise, you look at the monthly rainfall in Buffalo and Seattle. The average for both is about the same, but looking at just one statistic does not tell the whole story.

Goal: Use Excel's statistical functions to compare the average, median, minimum, maximum, and standard deviation of rainfall.

1. In the **EX0303-Challenge** workbook, select the **Stats** sheet. Notice that both cities have almost the same total annual rainfall. Look at the rainfall for each month of the year—it is apparent that the rainfall in Seattle varies much more from month to month.
2. Insert the **AVERAGE** function in cell **B16** (it is one of the Statistics functions, as are all of the remaining functions you enter in this exercise).
3. The median of a set of numbers is the value that has as many values above it as below it. Insert the **MEDIAN** function in cell **B17**. Make sure the range of cells is restricted to **B3** through **B14**.
4. To see how much the numbers vary from the average, find the standard deviation of the rainfall. Use the **STDEVP** function in cell **B18**. If you add or subtract this amount from the average, the resulting range will contain roughly two-thirds of the values. The larger the standard deviation, the more the values differ from the average. Use cells **B3** through **B14** in the **STDEVP** formula; do not include the total in cell **B15**.
5. Insert the **MAX** and **MIN** functions in cells **B19** and **B20** respectively to determine the maximum and minimum rainfall. Make sure they both refer to cells **B3** through **B14**.
6. Select the five formulas in cells **B16** through **B20**. Use the fill handle to copy the formulas into the cells in column **C**.
7. Format the formulas in cells **B16** through **C20** to show one decimal place. Notice how the Total, Average, and Median are almost the same for the rainfall in the two cities. The difference is not apparent until you look at the other three statistics.
8. Save the workbook and leave it open for use in the next exercise.

	A	B	C	D
1		Annual Rainfall in Inches		
2		Buffalo	Seattle	Difference
3	Jan	3	6	Higher
4	Feb	2.4	4.2	Higher
5	Mar	3	3.6	Higher
6	Apr	3.1	2.4	Lower
7	May	2.9	1.6	Lower
8	Jun	2.7	1.4	Lower
9	Jul	3	0.7	Lower
10	Aug	4.2	1.3	Lower
11	Sep	3.4	2	Lower
12	Oct	2.9	3.4	Higher
13	Nov	3.6	5.6	Higher
14	Dec	3.4	6.3	Higher

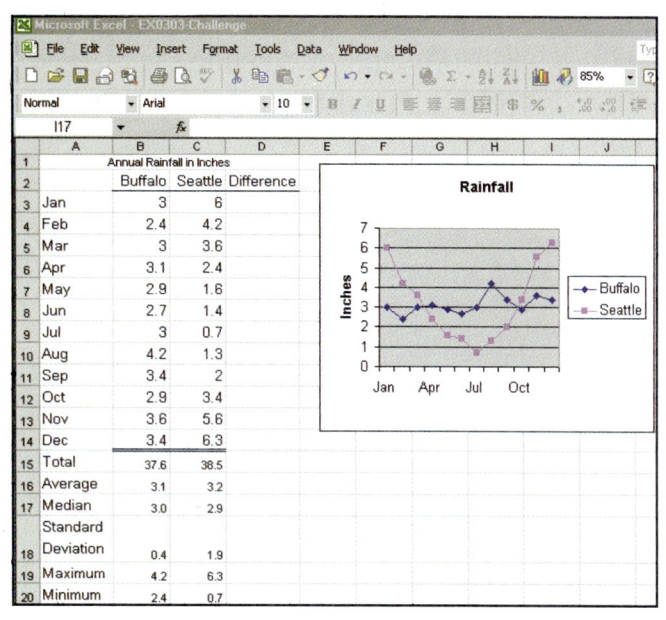

C5—Using the IF Logical Function

A difference between two sets of numbers may be apparent to the person who uses them but may not stand out to others. You can use a logical statement to test a given condition and then take action based on the result.

In this exercise, you look at the monthly rainfall in Buffalo and Seattle, compare them, and display the term **Higher** if the rainfall in Seattle is higher than Buffalo or **Lower** if it is lower.

Goal: Use Excel's logical IF function to display one of two words based on a comparison of rainfall.

1. In the **EX0303-Challenge** workbook, select the **Stats** sheet. Look at the rainfall for each month of the year—it is apparent that the rainfall in Seattle varies much more from month to month.

2. Select cell **D3** and insert the logical function, **IF**.

3. Type **C3>B3** in the **Logical_test** box.

4. Press Tab to move to the **Value_if_true** box and type **"Higher"** (include the quotation marks).

5. Press Tab to move to the **Value_if_false** box and type **"Lower"**. Click **OK**.

6. Use the fill handle to copy this formula into cells **D4** through **D14**. The resulting **IF** formulas indicate that the rainfall amounts in Seattle exceed those in Buffalo during the months of October through March, whereas Buffalo's numbers are higher from April through September.

7. Save the workbook and close it.

C6—Locating Data in a Table Using VLOOKUP

Challenge exercises C6 through C8 use different worksheets in the workbook **EX0304-Challenge**. Open **EX0304** from the **Student** folder on your CD-ROM disc and save it as **EX0304-Challenge** on your floppy disk.

If you are providing a quotation for a job, the price often depends on the cost of parts and labor. These costs vary depending on the item and the quantity purchased. It can be very time consuming to look up information in tables to include in your calculations. Excel has two functions that are designed to look up values in a table, column, or array. These are called **VLOOKUP** and **HLOOKUP**. VLOOKUP is used to look up values in a vertical column and HLOOKUP is used to look up values in a horizontal row. In this exercise, you will learn how to use the VLOOKUP function.

Goal: Use the VLOOKUP function to find and retrieve a value from a table for use in a formula.

To use the VLOOKUP function to find the correct value in a table and use it in a calculation, follow these steps:

1. Select the **Lookup** sheet, if necessary.

2. Use Help to find the description of the **VLOOKUP** function. Read the description and examine the example in cell **C4**. There are three arguments included in this formula. The first defines the value that is looked up in a table. The second argument defines the table or range of cells that should be examined. The third is the column that should be used to locate the matching value. Each column in

the defined table is identified with a number, 1, 2, 3, etc. (Note: The values in the first column of a table that is used with this function must be sorted in increasing order, as shown in column E of this example.)

3. Test the function in cell **C4** by changing values in cells **A4** and **B4**. Use one of the codes from column **1** of the **Quantity Charge** table for cell **A4** and either a **2** or **3** for cell **B4**. The number in cell **B4** indicates whether column **2** or **3** of the Quantity Charge table should be used to look up the value that matches the code in cell **A4**.

4. Find the **Multi-Color Charge** table. Insert the **VLOOKUP** function from the list of **Lookup & Reference** functions into cell **C18** and select the arguments so that it will find the correct charge for additional shirt colors and display it in cell **C18**.

5. Test the function by trying different numbers in cells **A18** and **B18**. Your sheet will differ from the example shown if you use different numbers when you test it.

6. Save the workbook and leave it open for use in the next exercise.

C7—Creating a Frequency Distribution

This exercise requires the Analysis ToolPak Add-in. Look under the **Tools** menu to determine if you have the **Data Analysis** option. If not, select **Tools**, **Add-Ins**, **Analysis ToolPak**. If you plan to do the Solver exercise, C8, select the Solver Add-in. You may need your Office 2002 CD-ROM disc, or ask your lab administrator to install these features.

If you are trying to determine how many of each kind of number you have in a group, you want to know the frequency distribution. For example, 25 people have answered a question that has five possible answers numbered 1 through 5, and you would like to know how many people chose each answer.

Excel provides two options for determining the frequency distribution. There is a Frequency function that can be found by using the **Insert**, **Function** menu option. The other is part of the Histogram tool in the Analysis ToolPak. The Histogram tool is much easier.

Goal: Learn how to use the Histogram tool to determine the number of people answering each option for a question.

1. In the **EX0304-Challenge** workbook, select the **Frequency** sheet.

2. Search for Help on the **Histogram** analysis tool.

3. Look at the example analysis that was done on the first question.

4. Use the Histogram analysis tool to produce a similar analysis of the second question. Use cells **B12** through **X12** as the input range, cells **T5** through **T9** as the bin range, and select cell **Y14** as the output cell that will be used as the upper-left corner of the output range.

5. Save the workbook and leave it open for use in the next exercise.

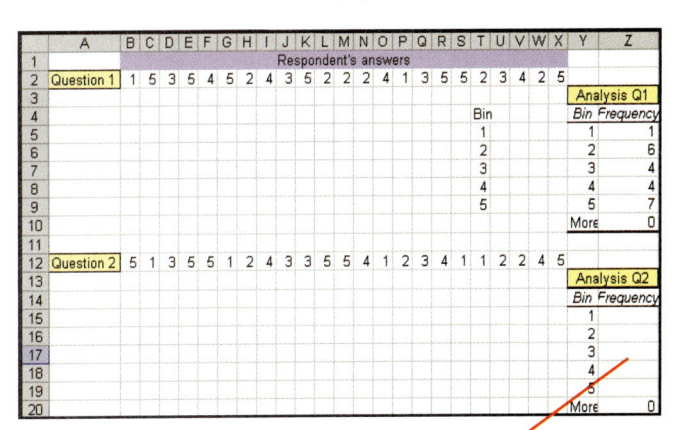

Results to be determined by the student

Challenge   EXC   77

C8—Using the Solver Add-in

This exercise requires the Solver Add-in. Look under the **Tools** menu to determine if you have the **Solver** option. If not, select **Tools**, **Add-Ins**, **Solver Add-in**. You may need your Office 2002 CD-ROM disc, or ask your lab administrator to install these features.

Solver is similar to Goal Seek, but it has more options. It can change more than one input cell, and you can specify constraints on several cells. You can have it determine the inputs to produce a match, a maximum, or a minimum value.

A classic physics problem is to determine how high a projectile will go if it is shot straight up at a given initial speed. The formula is $H = -16T^2 + ST$. This formula can be written in Excel as =−16*(*time cell reference*)^2+(*speed cell reference*)*(*time cell reference*). In the example sheet used for this exercise, the formula is =-16*B3^2+B4*B3. There are two ways to solve this problem. You could use differential calculus to find the derivative, set it equal to zero, solve for T, and then plug the value of T into the original formula. A second way would be to try increasing values of time in the formula until the value of the height stopped increasing and started decreasing. In order to solve for the time down to the nearest tenth of a second, you would have to do the formula many times.

The Solver works by trying different values in the formula, subject to the constraints you have imposed, until the target cell matches the value you have chosen or is a maximum or minimum if you have selected either of those options.

Goal: Use the Solver tool to find the maximum height to which a projectile will rise given an initial speed of 2,000 feet per second.

1. In the **EX0304-Challenge** workbook, select the **Solver** sheet
2. Search for Help on guidelines for using the Solver.
3. Use the Solver to determine the **Maximum** value for the formula in cell **B5** by changing the time values in cell **B3**.
4. Keep the Solver solution if it is between 50 and 100. The answer calculated by the program will be more accurate than the value displayed in the cell due to rounding of the display.
5. Save the workbook and leave it open for use in the next exercise.

	A	B
1	Find Maximum Height of a projectile	
2		
3	Time in seconds	62.5
4	Initial speed in feet/sec	2,000
5	Height	62,500

Time to maximum height rounded to one decimal place — Maximum height

C9—Using Date Functions to Determine Present Age

You can use Excel to calculate the difference between a fixed date and today's date. This may be useful for determining retirement benefits or simply recognizing birthdays in a retirement home.

Goal: Use the NOW() function to determine a person's present age.

1. In the **EX0304-Challenge** workbook, select the **Dates** sheet.
2. Enter a birth date such as **5/21/47** in cell **B3**.
3. Insert the **Date & Time** function, **NOW**, into cell **B4**.
4. Enter a formula into cell **B5** that will subtract the value in cell **B3** from the value in cell **B4**.
5. Select cell **B5** and click the **Comma Style** formatting button on the toolbar (to the right of the Percent Style formatting button). The number of days between the two dates is displayed in cell **B5**.
6. Select cell **B6** and enter a formula that will divide the contents of cell **B5** by **365.25**. Cell **B6** will display the difference in years. Format cell **B6** to display one decimal place.
7. Save the workbook and leave it open for use in the next exercise.

	A	B
1	Use Date Functions	
2		
3	Your Birth Date	5/21/47
4	Today's date	11/24/00 19:36
5	Days old	19546.82
6	Years old	53.5

C10—Using Named Cells in Formulas

Formulas that refer to cells by their column and row labels are short and compact but may be difficult to understand. It is possible to give cells names that reflect the meaning of their contents and then use those names in formulas.

Goal: Give names to the total cost and total retail values in cells D10 and F10 and then use these names in a formula to determine the gross profit.

1. In the **EX0304-Challenge** workbook, select the **Named Cells** sheet.

2. Select cell **D10**. Click in the **Name** box on the formula toolbar and type **Total_Cost**. Be sure to type the underscore character. Excel does not accept blanks in the cell names.

3. Select cell **F10**. Click in the **Name** box on the formula toolbar and type **Retail_Value**. Be sure to type the underscore character.

4. Select cell **E13** and type **=Retail_Value – Total_Cost**.

5. Save the workbook and close it.

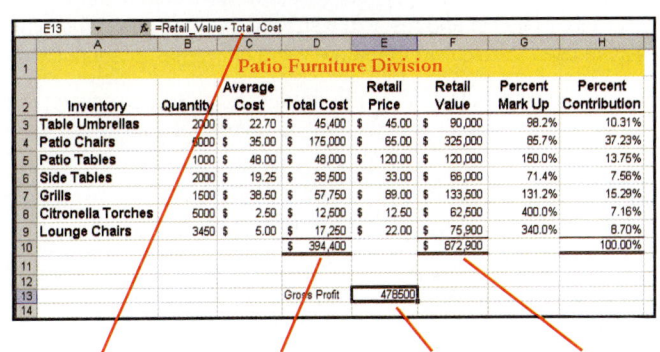

Result of formula using names | Cell named Total_Cost | Formula in cell E13 | Cell named Retail_Value

Challenge   EXC   79

ON YOUR OWN

If you want to have an income of your own when you retire, you need to save or invest money each year that will accumulate interest and result in a sizeable balance that you can draw from during your retirement. The FV function may be used to calculate the future value of a series of equal deposits in an interest earning account.

Set up a worksheet that calculates the future value of a series of deposits that you might make into a savings or investment account for your retirement. Criteria for grading will be:

1. Demonstration of the use of the FV financial function.

Some examples of features that students have learned to use in previous classes to enhance their personal retirement worksheet are:

- The rate of interest, the years to retirement, and monthly investment are in separate cells, and any formulas that use them refer to those cells so that these assumptions may be changed and all the dependant cells will be recalculated automatically
- The formula uses one month as a basis for calculation to show how much the student must save per month
- The monthly interest rate is calculated from the annual interest rate, and the number of months is calculated from the years to retirement
- All dollar amounts are formatted with zero decimal places
- A negative number is used for the investment amount to make the future value positive

2. Identify yourself. Place your name in a cell that is clearly visible.

3. To complete the project:
   - Save your file on your own disk. Name it **EX0305-Retire**.
   - Check with your instructor to determine if the project should be submitted in electronic or printed form. If necessary, print out a copy of the worksheet to hand in.

Lesson 4

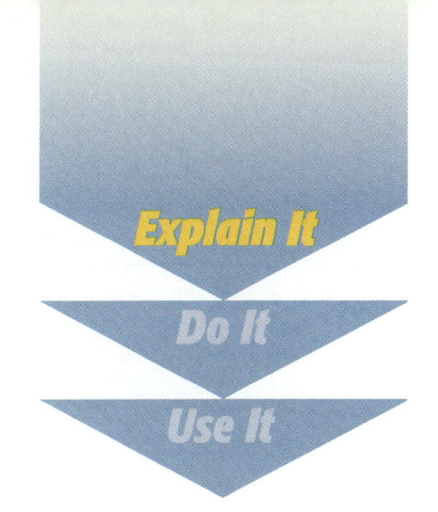

Understanding the Numbers Using a Chart

Task 1   Creating a Chart to Show a Trend
Task 2   Creating a Chart to Show Contributions to a Whole
Task 3   Creating a Chart to Make Comparisons
Task 4   Editing the Elements of a Chart and Adding a Callout
Task 5   Printing a Chart

INTRODUCTION

People process information in several different ways. Most of us recognize trends more readily if a line or a series of columns of differing heights represents them. We also recognize how one member of a group compares to the others if they are represented by slices of a pie chart.

This lesson is designed to provide you with the basic skills you need to create a variety of *charts* to represent your numerical data graphically. Excel's *Chart Wizard* guides you through the necessary steps. You will be working with store data from the Armstrong Pool, Spa, and Sauna Co.

VISUAL SUMMARY

By the time you have completed this entire lesson, you will have created a worksheet containing a data table and three charts that look like these:

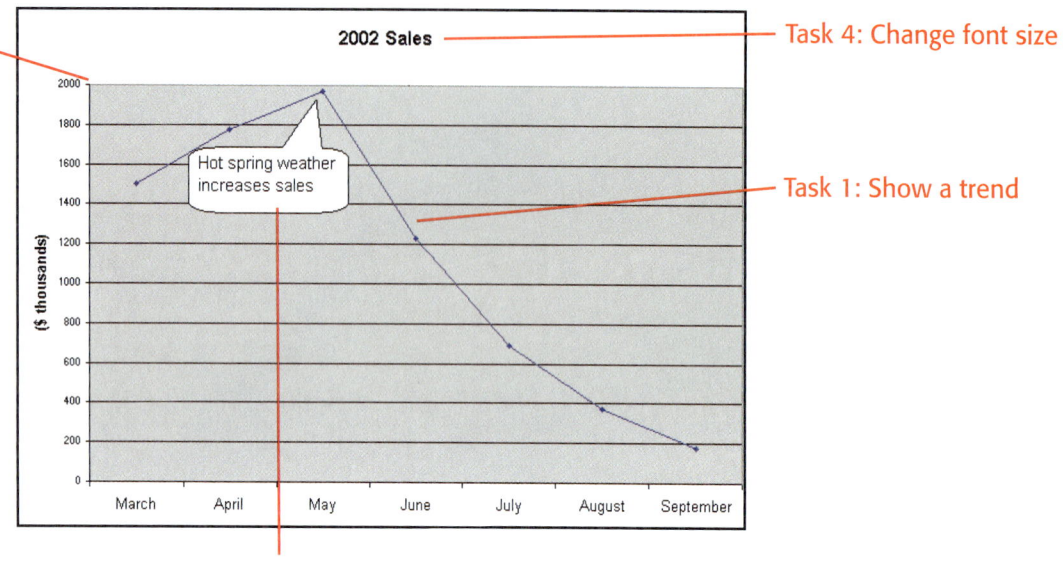

Task 4: Change the axis scale

Task 4: Change font size

Task 1: Show a trend

Task 4: Insert and modify a callout

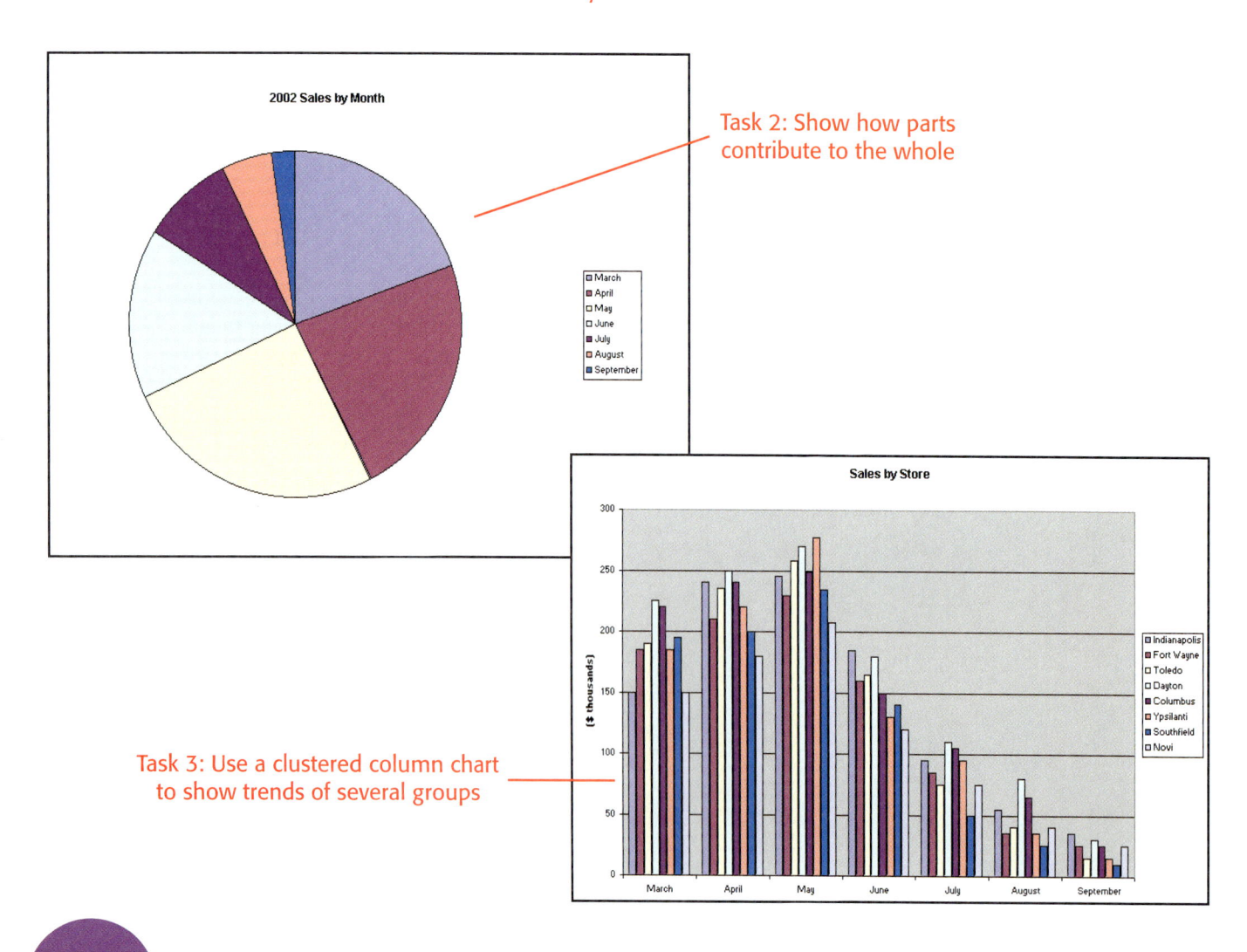

Task 2: Show how parts contribute to the whole

Task 3: Use a clustered column chart to show trends of several groups

82   EXC   Lesson 4   Understanding the Numbers Using a Chart

Task 1
CREATING A CHART TO SHOW A TREND

Why would I do this?
It is sometimes easier to analyze numbers when looking at a visual representation. A picture or *chart* helps, and some chart types are better than others for specific purposes. For instance, when you want to show a trend (change over time), a *line chart* is usually most effective.

In this task, you learn how to create a line chart to show the trend in sales for the Armstrong firm.

1 Open **EX0401** from the **Student** folder. Save it as **EX0401-Sales**.

The new title appears in the title bar.

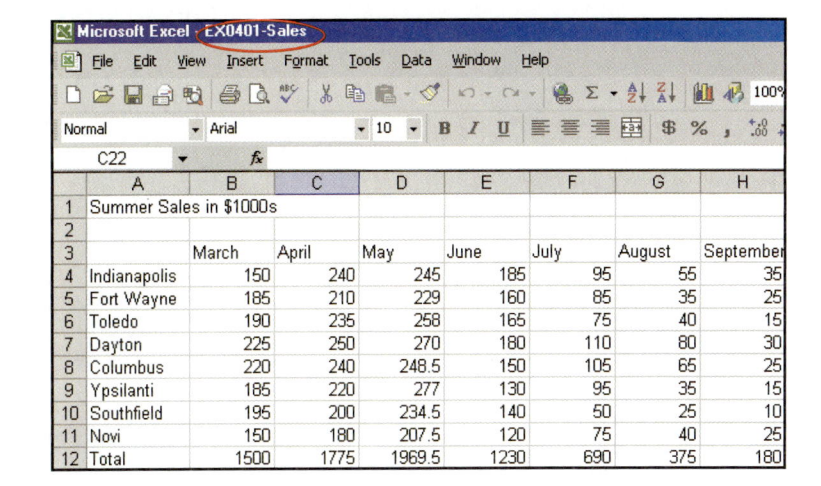

2 Move the pointer to cell **A3**. Click-and-drag to select cells **A3** through **H3**, and then release the mouse button.

Hold down Ctrl and select cells **A12** through **H12**.

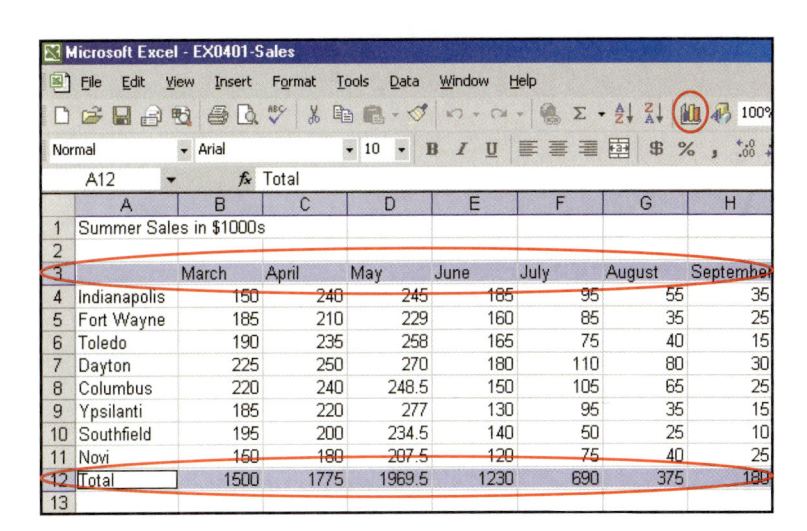

Task 1   Creating a Chart to Show a Trend   EXC   83

❸ Click the **Chart Wizard** button.

The first Chart Wizard dialog box is displayed.

Click **Line** in the **Chart type** area.

*Notice that the default **Chart sub-type** is a line with data markers. Each chart type has several variations that you can use to display the data.*

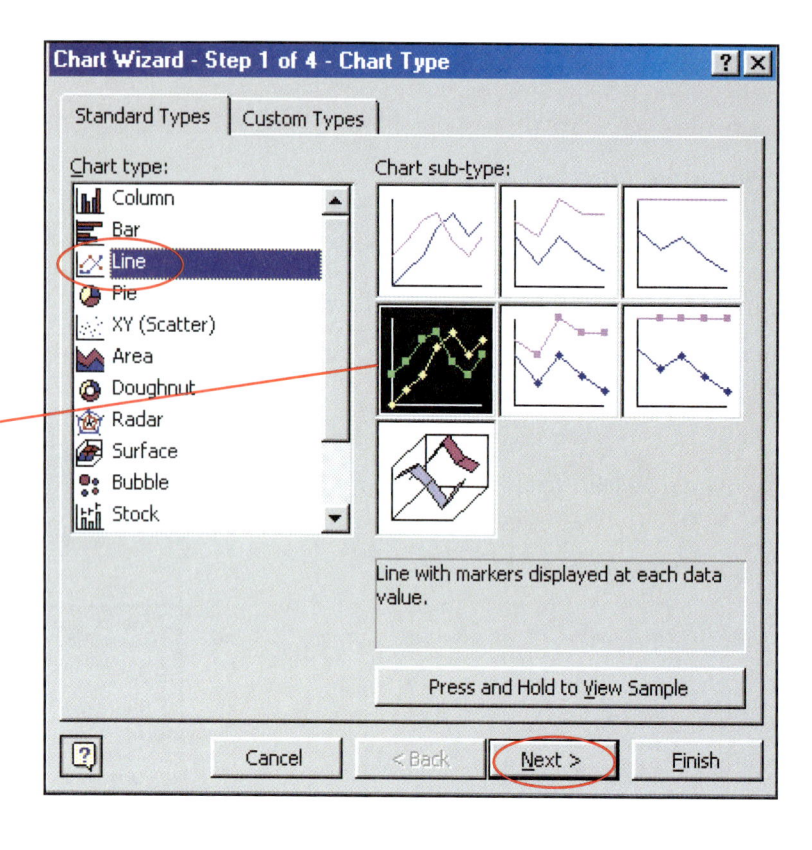

Default Chart sub-type

❹ Click **Next**.

*The second Chart Wizard dialog box is displayed. Make sure Rows is selected from the **Series in** area.*

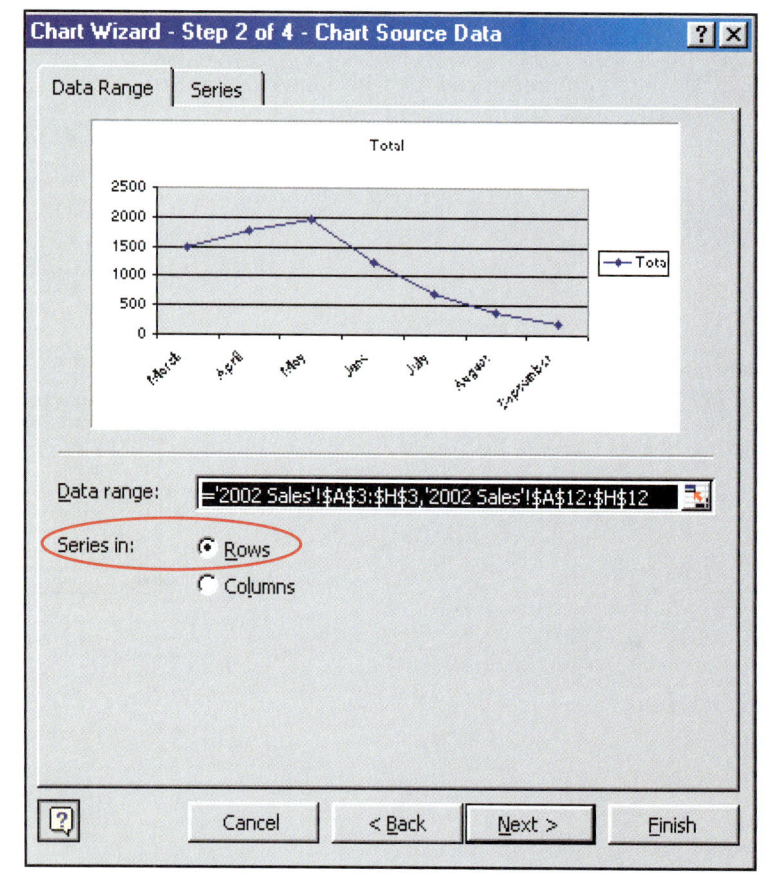

84   EXC   Lesson 4   Understanding the Numbers Using a Chart

5 Click **Next**.

The third Chart Wizard dialog box is displayed.

Click the **Titles** tab, if necessary. Replace the default title in the **Chart title** box with **2002 Sales**. Type **($ thousands)** in the **Value (Y) axis** box.

Legend

6 Click the **Legend** tab.

*A **legend** is a list that identifies a pattern or color used in an Excel chart.*

Click the **Show legend** box to turn the legend off.

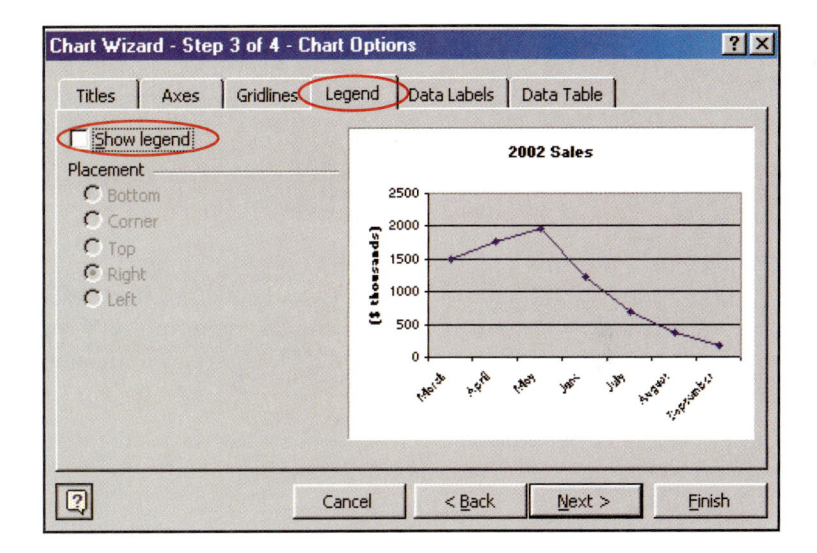

> **IN DEPTH**
> The first three Chart Wizard dialog boxes contain multiple tabs. These tabs let you control such things as the chart scale, whether to show vertical or horizontal gridlines, and how to label the data points.

7 Click **Next**.

The fourth Chart Wizard dialog box is displayed.

Click **As new sheet** to select it and type **2002 Sales Chart** in the adjacent box.

Task 1   Creating a Chart to Show a Trend   EXC   **85**

8 Click **Finish**.

The chart is shown full-size on its own sheet.

Click the **Save** button to save your work. If the Chart toolbar appears, close it.

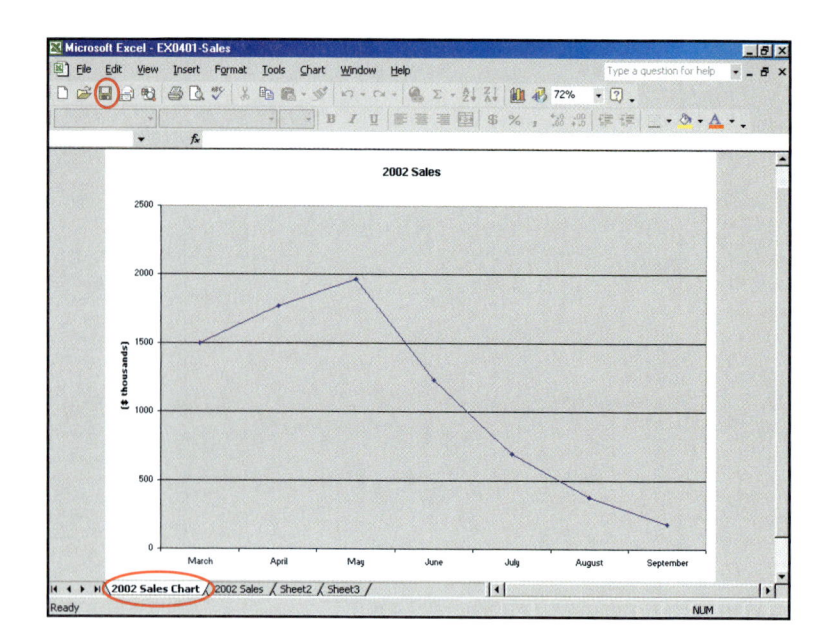

Task 2
CREATING A CHART TO SHOW CONTRIBUTIONS TO A WHOLE

Why would I do this?
In the previous task, you took a set of data and created a line chart to show a trend over time. You may find that it is often beneficial to graphically represent the contribution of various elements to the whole. The best way to illustrate parts of a whole is to use a *pie chart*.

In this task, you learn how to create a pie chart that shows the contribution each region made to the total sales amount for the year.

1 Click the **2002 Sales** sheet tab. If necessary, select cells **A3** through **H3**. Hold down Ctrl and select cells **A12** through **H12** if necessary.

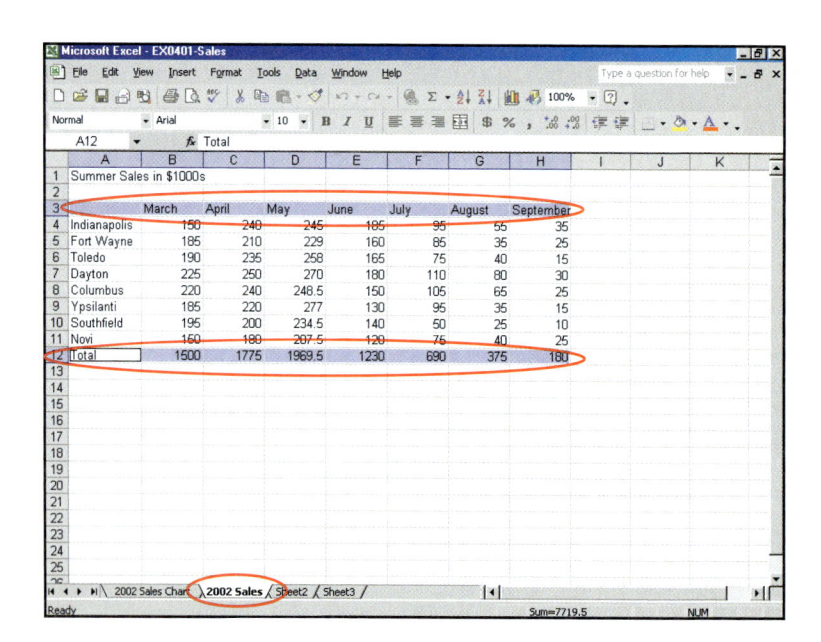

86 EXC Lesson 4 Understanding the Numbers Using a Chart

2 Click the **Chart Wizard** button.

The first Chart Wizard dialog box is displayed.

Click **Pie** in the **Chart type** area and select **Pie**, the default chart sub-type, in the **Chart sub-type** area.

Description of sub-type

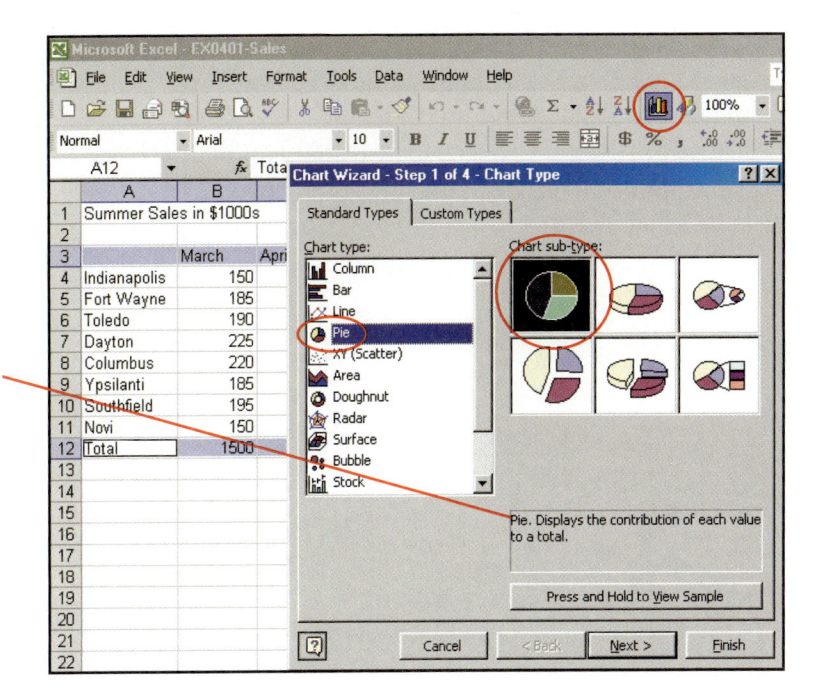

3 Click **Next**.

The second Chart Wizard dialog box is displayed.

Make sure **Rows** is selected from the **Series in** area.

The data you are charting is in rows.

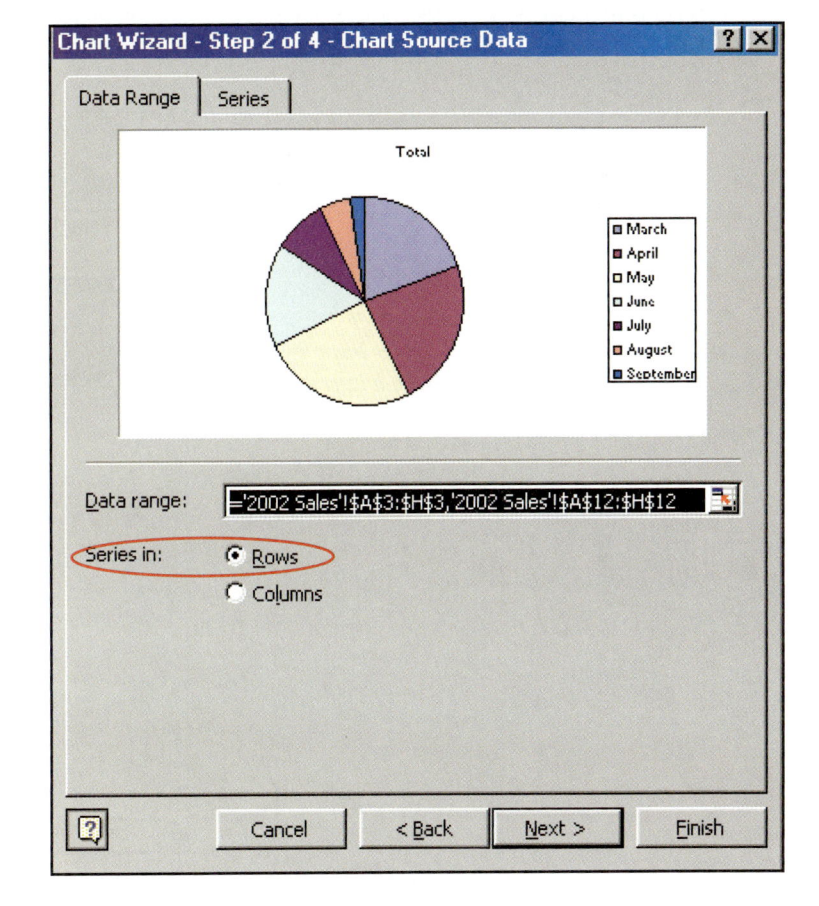

Task 2   Creating a Chart to Show Contributions to a Whole   EXC   **87**

4 Click **Next**.

The third Chart Wizard dialog box is displayed.

Click the **Titles** tab, if necessary. Replace the default text in the **Chart title** box with **2002 Sales by Month**.

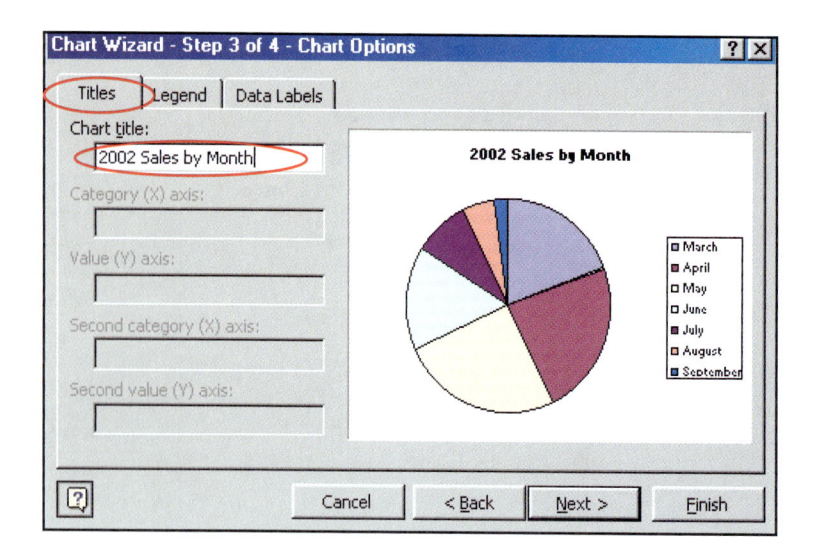

5 Click **Next**.

The fourth Chart Wizard dialog box is displayed.

Select **As new sheet** and type **2002 Sales by Month** in the adjacent box.

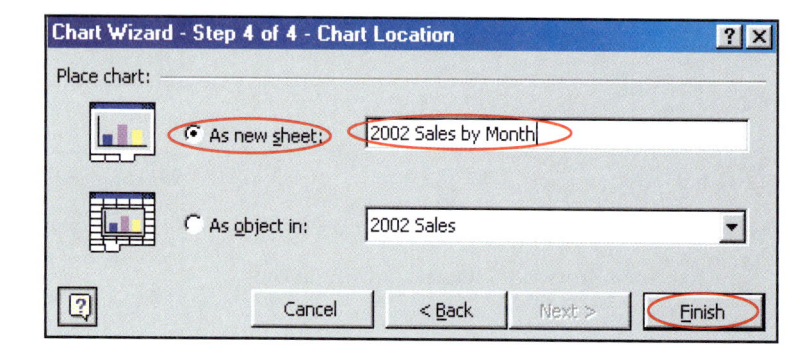

6 Click **Finish**.

The chart is placed on its own sheet. (You learn how to change the size of the title and legend in a later task.)

Save your work.

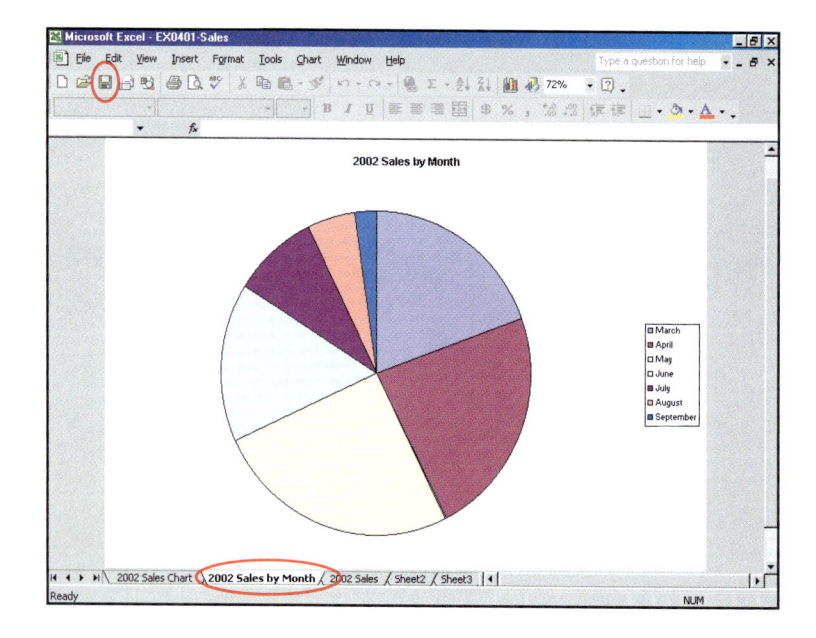

88   EXC   Lesson 4   Understanding the Numbers Using a Chart

Task 3
CREATING A CHART TO MAKE COMPARISONS

Why would I do this?
Perhaps the most common use for a chart is to make comparisons. For example, you might want to compare oil production by country over a series of years. To illustrate this type of comparison, a *column chart* (with vertical bars) or *bar chart* (with horizontal bars) is most often used.

In this task, you learn how to create a column chart that compares sales by city.

1 Click the **2002 Sales** sheet tab. Select cells **A3** through **H11**.

> **IN DEPTH**
> It is important that you do not include the total rows or columns when doing a comparison chart. If you included these figures, it would distort the chart, since the totals would be compared to regional and monthly sales amounts.

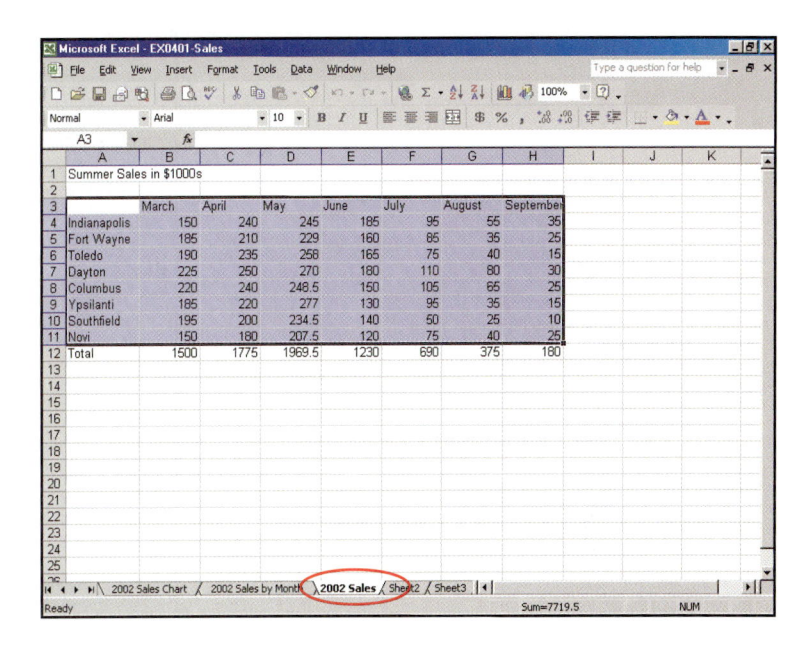

2 Click the **Chart Wizard** button.

The first Chart Wizard dialog box is displayed.

Click **Column** in the **Chart type** area and accept the **Clustered Column** option in the **Chart sub-type** area.

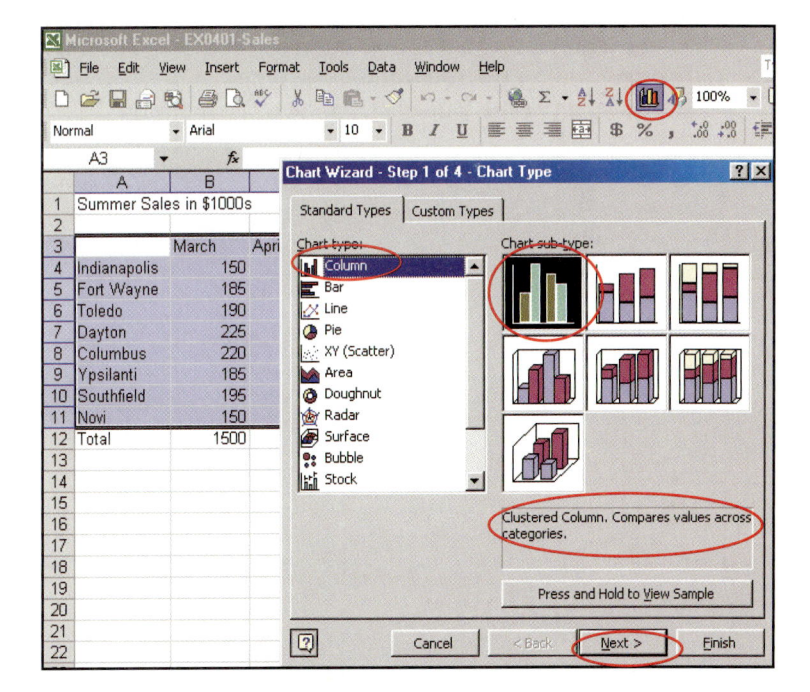

Task 3   Creating a Chart to Make Comparisons   EXC   89

3 Click **Next**.

The second Chart Wizard dialog box is displayed.

    Select **Rows** in the **Series in** area.

This keeps all of the sales figures from each month together.

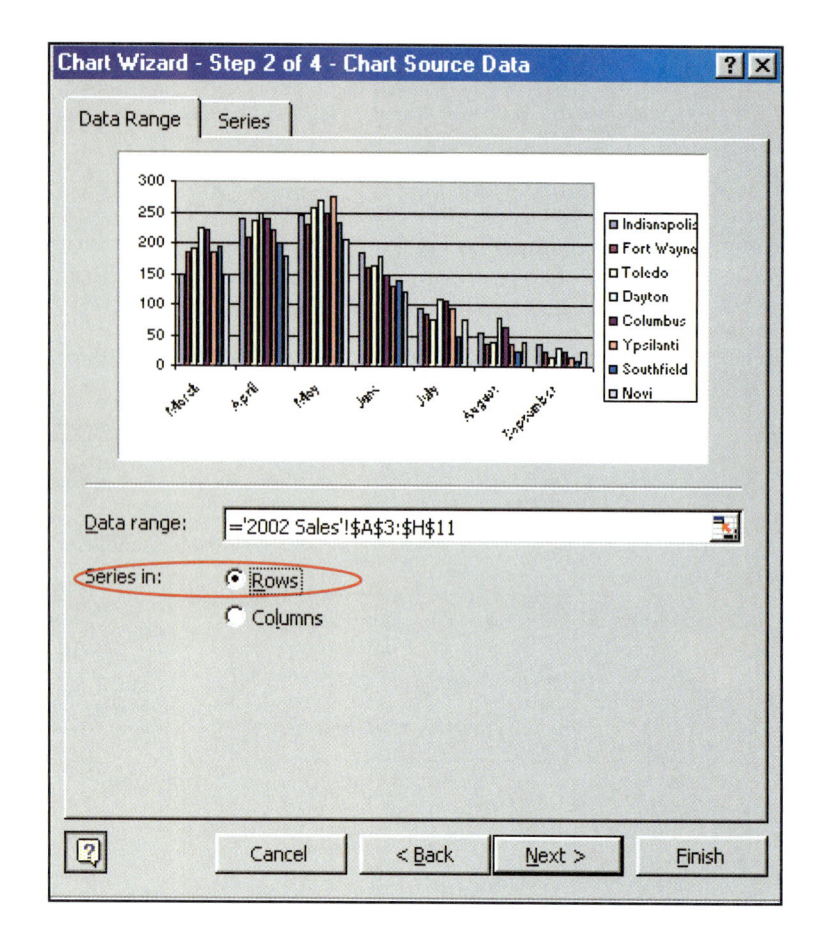

4 Click **Next**.

The third Chart Wizard dialog box is displayed.

    Click the **Titles** tab, if necessary, and type **Sales by Store** in the **Chart title** box. Type **($ thousands)** in the **Value (Y) axis** box.

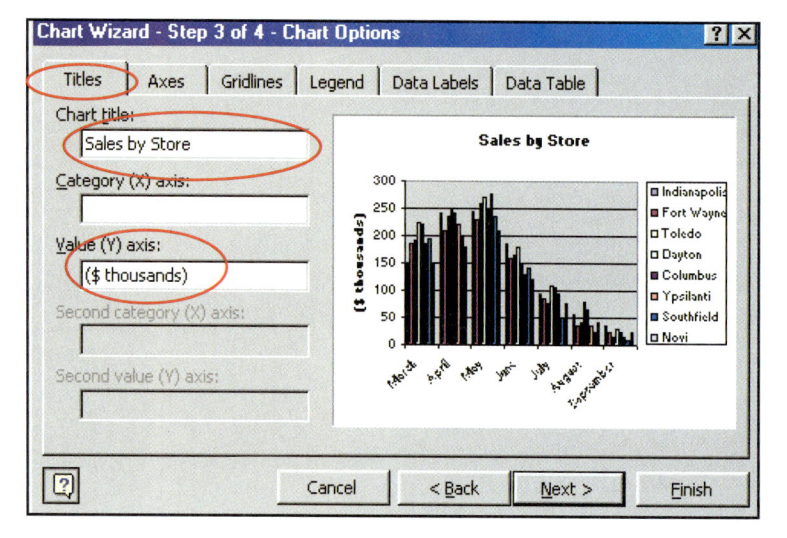

5 Click **Next**. Select **As new sheet** and type **2002 Sales by Store** in the adjacent box.

6 Click **Finish**.

The chart is on its own sheet.

Click the **Save** button to save your work.

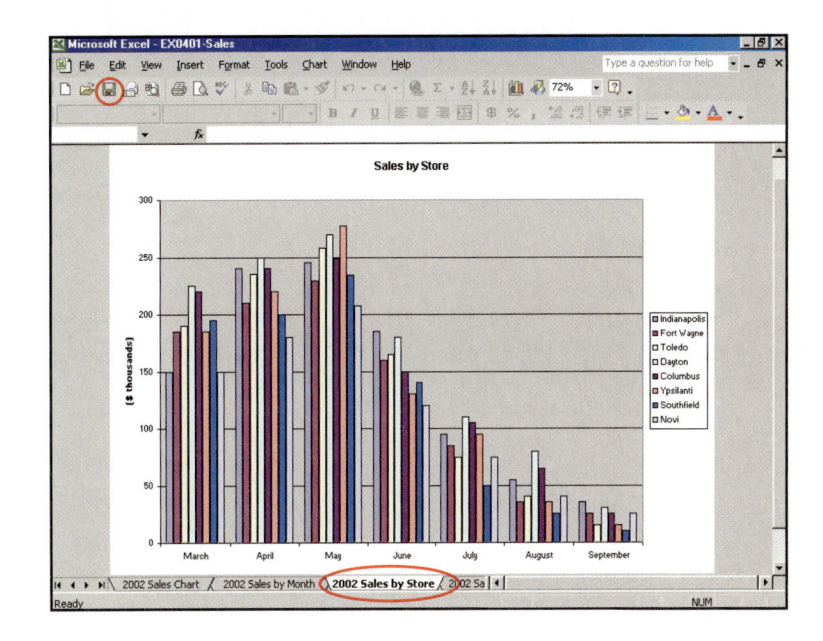

Task 4
EDITING THE ELEMENTS OF A CHART AND ADDING A CALLOUT

Why would I do this?
When you create a chart in Excel, the proportions of the various elements often need to be adjusted. For example, the text on the axes, titles, and legends on the charts may be too small. There are many options for customizing your charts in Excel, and they are easy to use.

In this task, you make changes to the 2002 Sales Chart to make it easier to read and to emphasize the variation from one month to the next.

Task 4 Editing the Elements of a Chart and Adding a Callout   EXC

1 Click the **2002 Sales Chart** sheet tab. Right-click on the title, **2002 Sales**.

A shortcut menu appears.

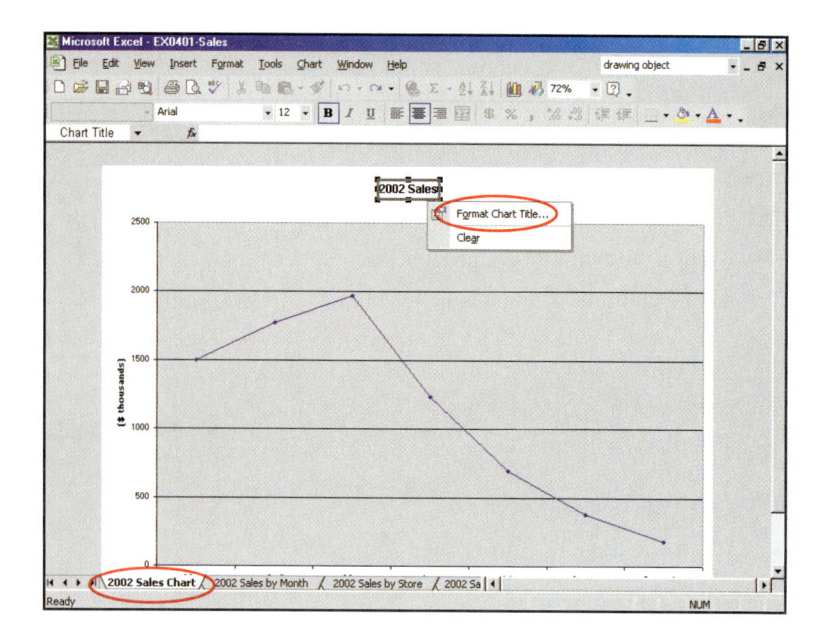

2 Select **Format Chart Title** from the shortcut menu and click the **Font** tab in the Format Chart Title dialog box. Scroll down the list of available font sizes and select **18**.

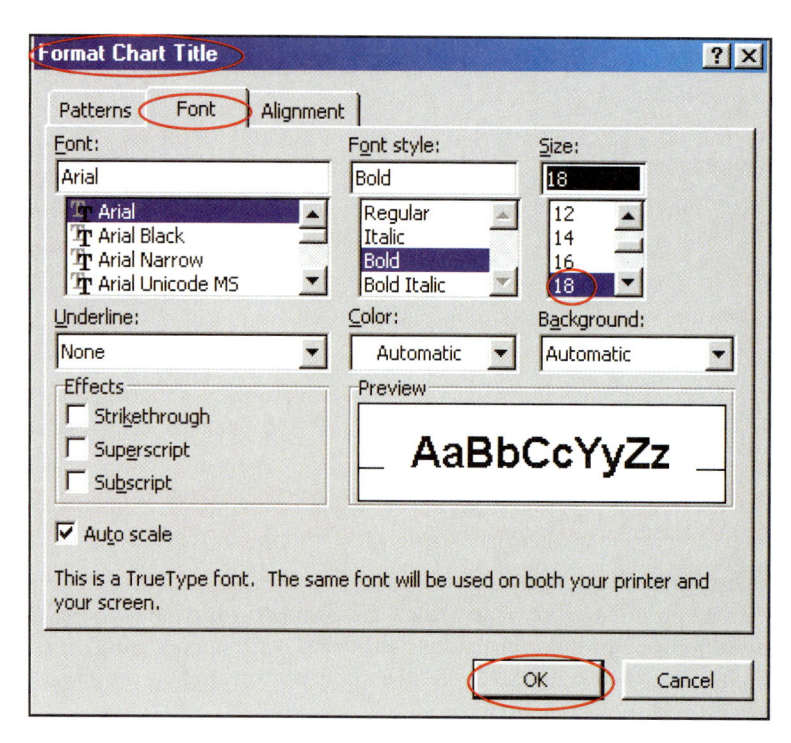

3 Click **OK**.

The title is now much easier to read.

4 Right-click on the **Value Axis Title ($ thousands)** and choose **Format Axis Title** from the shortcut menu. Change the size of the font to **14** points.

> **QUICK TIP**
> You can also open the Format dialog box quickly by double-clicking on any of the components of the chart. The dialog box that appears will contain all of the options available for the selected chart component.

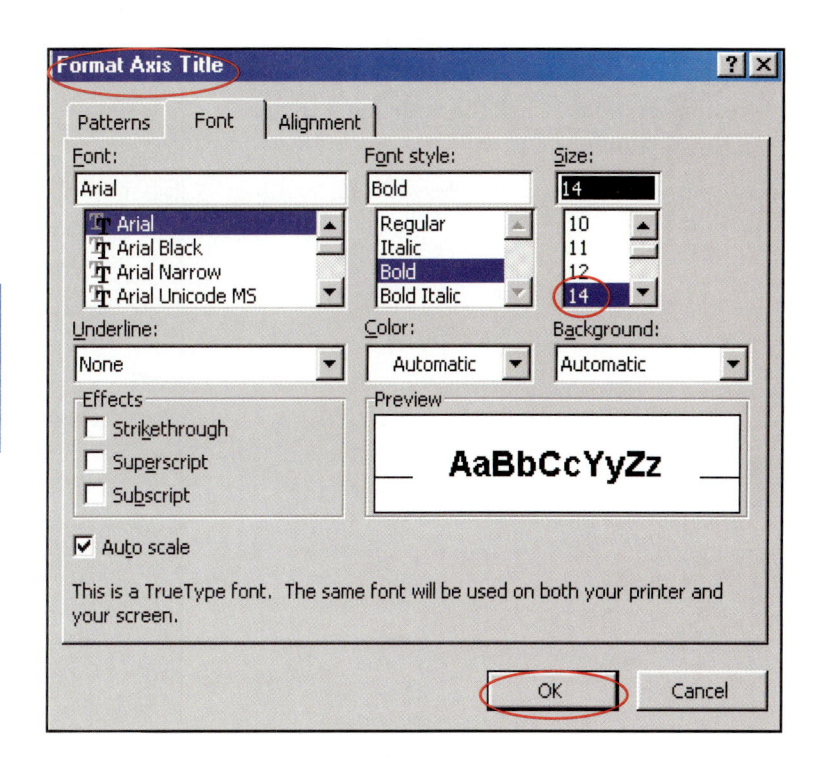

5 Click **OK**. Use the same procedure to change the size of the category axis labels to **14** points.

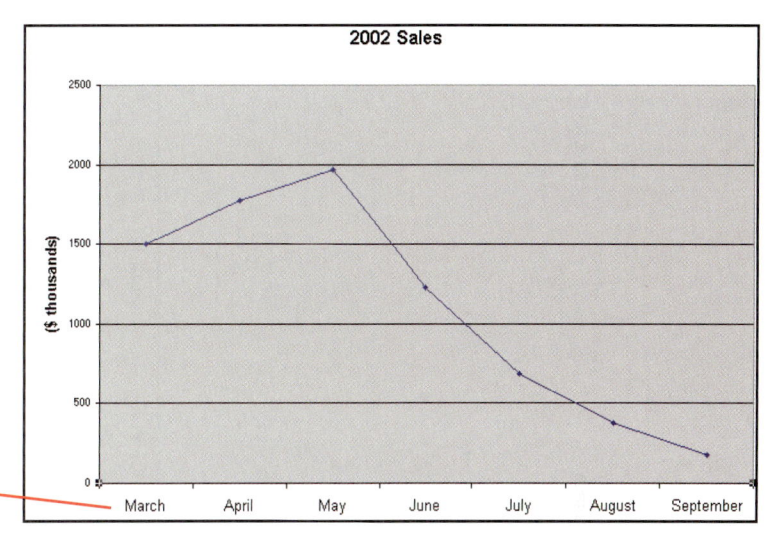

Category axis labels displayed using 14-point font

6 Move the pointer onto the numbers on the value axis.

The ScreenTip **Value Axis** *is displayed.*

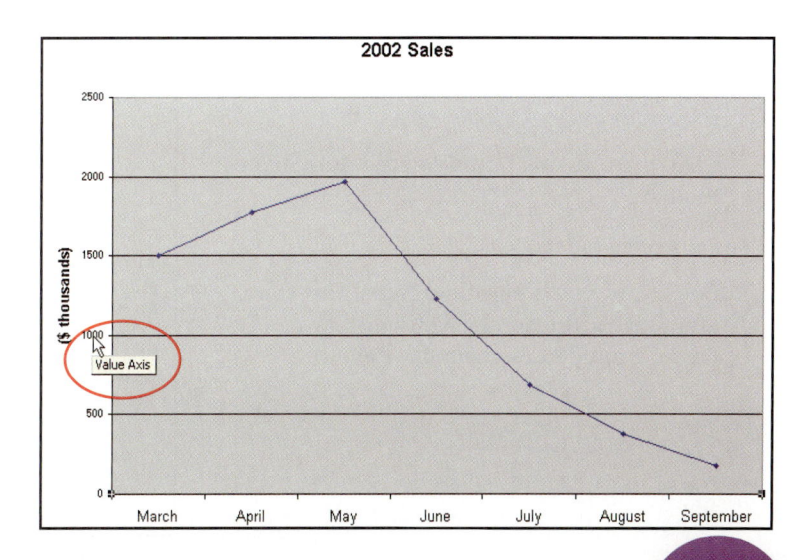

Task 4 Editing the Elements of a Chart and Adding a Callout   EXC   93

7 Right-click and select **Format Axis** from the shortcut menu. Click the **Scale** tab. Change the **Maximum** value to **2000**.

The highest point on the chart is below 2000.

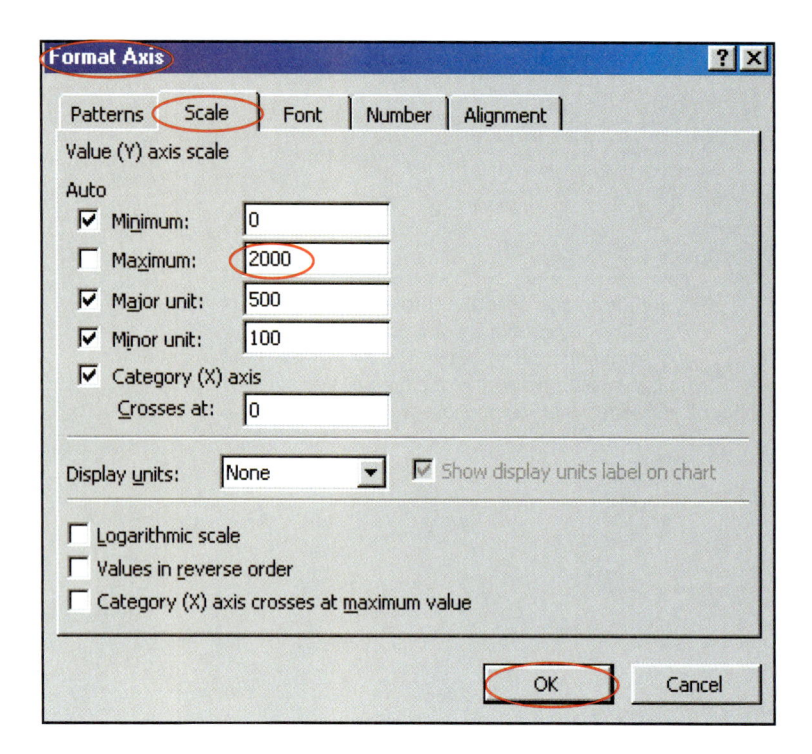

8 Click **OK**.

Notice the new scale emphasizes the difference in the values.

New scale ends at 2000

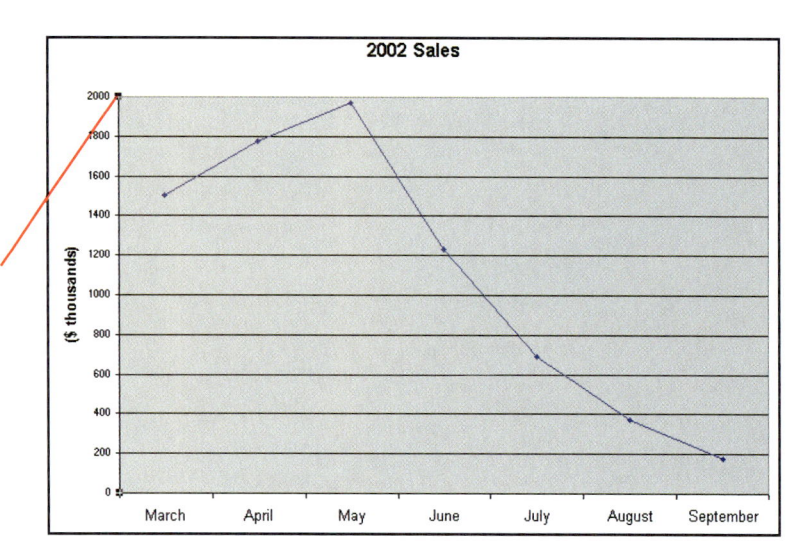

9 Choose **Insert**, **Picture**, **AutoShapes**.

The AutoShapes toolbar is displayed.

Click the **Callouts** button on the **AutoShapes** toolbar.

A menu of callout shapes is displayed.

Point at the second callout in the first row and wait for the ScreenTip to display its name, **Rounded Rectangular Callout**.

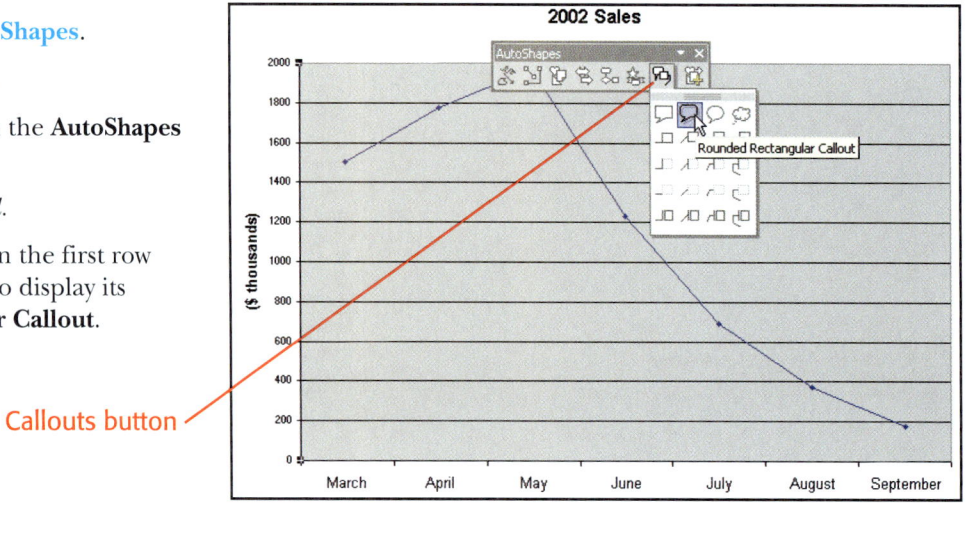

Callouts button

10 Click the **Rounded Rectangular Callout**.

The mouse pointer turns into cross hairs.

Click and drag a rectangular area that defines the size of the callout and release the mouse button.

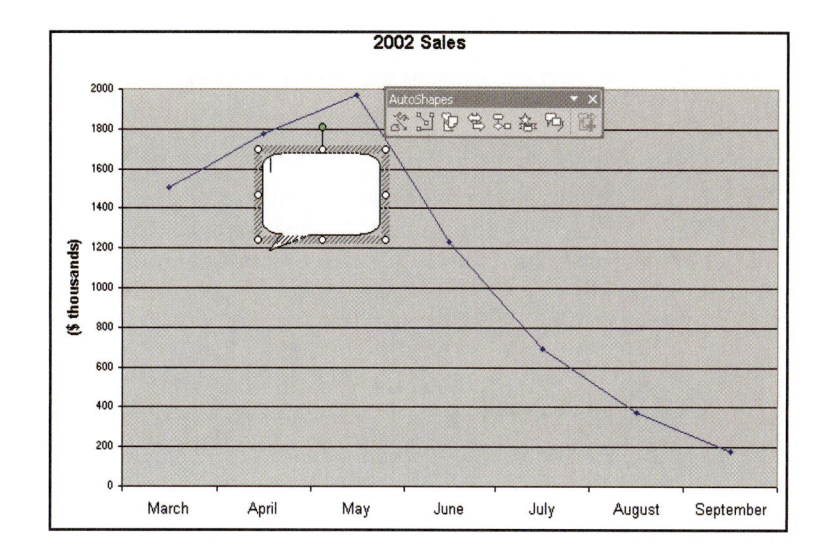

11 Change the font size to **16**. Type **Hot spring weather increases sales**.

The text wraps within the callout.

Click and drag the sizing handles so that the text fits on two lines.

Notice the tip of the callout is a yellow diamond.

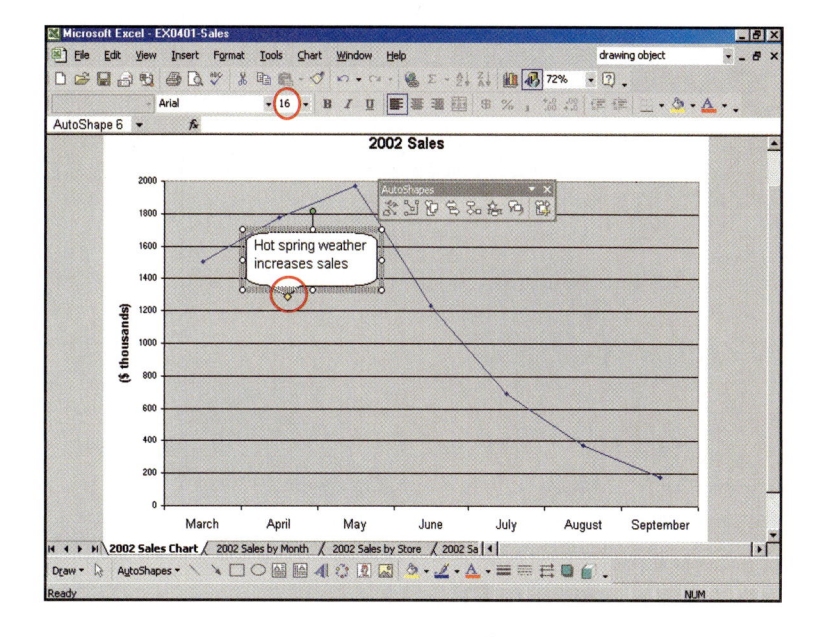

12 Click-and-drag the yellow diamond so the callout points at the peak of the chart. Press Esc to deselect the callout.

Close the **AutoShapes** toolbar. Save the changes you have made and leave the workbook open for use in the next task.

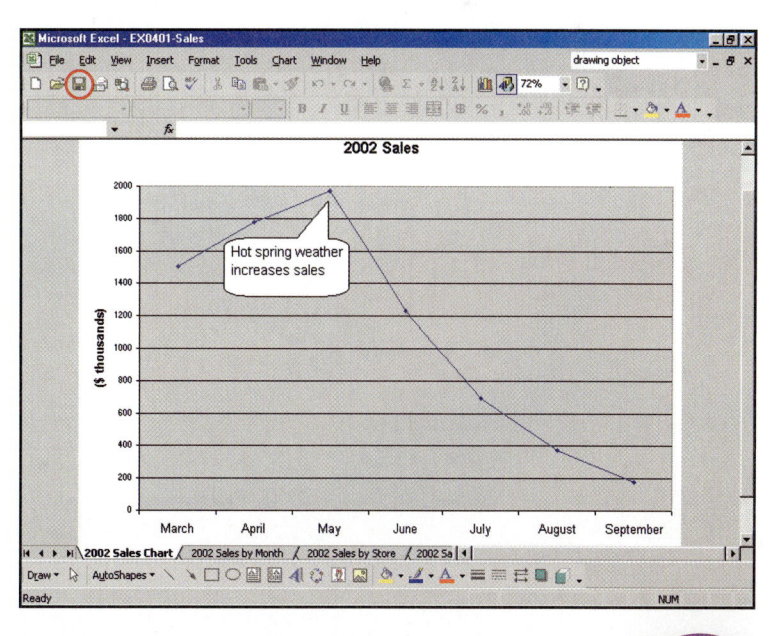

Task 4 Editing the Elements of a Chart and Adding a Callout   EXC   **95**

Task 5
PRINTING A CHART

Why would I do this?
Many spreadsheets are created for the sole purpose of generating one or more charts. These charts might be printed on paper to be included in a report or on overhead transparencies to be used as part of a presentation.

In this task, you learn how to print a chart.

1 Click the **2002 Sales by Store** sheet tab.

This sheet contains a column chart comparing sales by store.

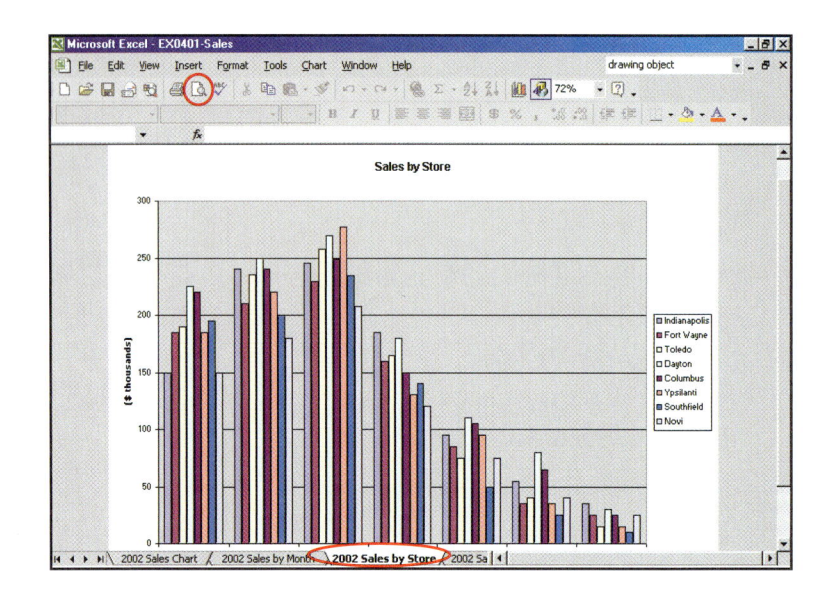

2 Click the **Print Preview** button.

The preview is displayed in grayscale in the figure. It may be in color if your default printer is a color printer.

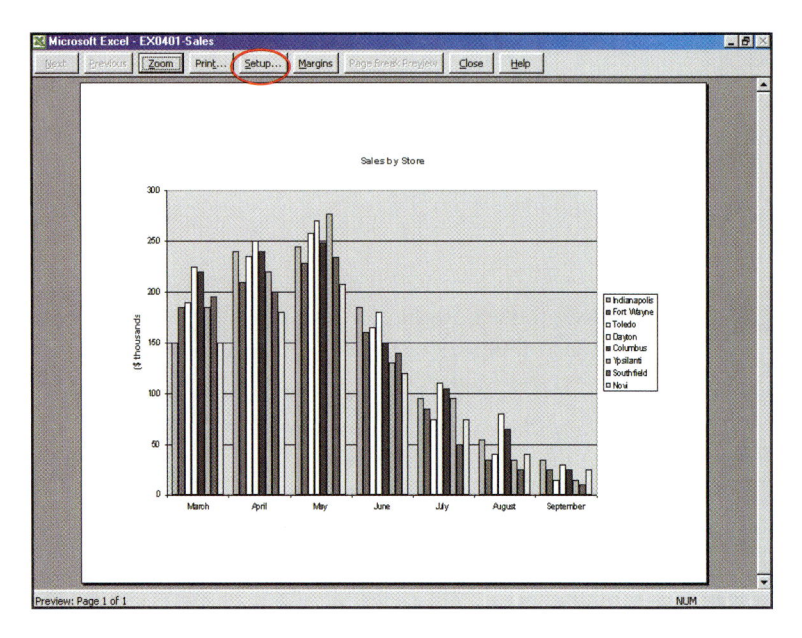

> **IN DEPTH**
> If your computer is connected to a color printer, the preview is displayed in color and the chart will print in color. Otherwise, the preview will not be shown in color.

96   EXC   Lesson 4   Understanding the Numbers Using a Chart

3 Click **Setup**. Click the **Header/Footer** tab. Click **Custom Header** and type your name in the **Left Section** of the header.

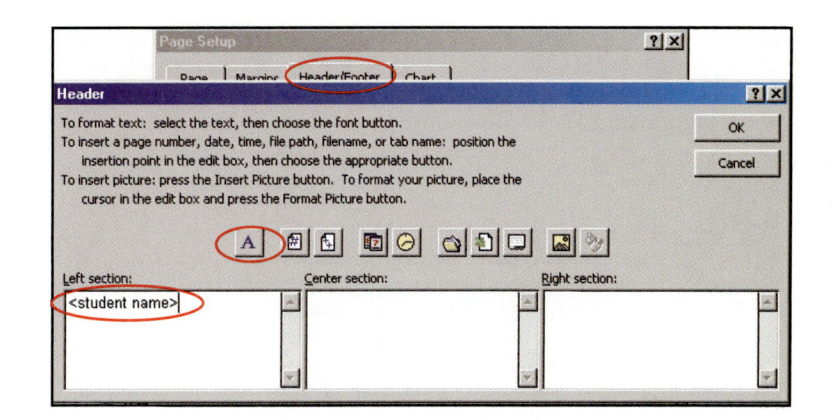

4 Select your name. Click the button with the large **A** on it and change the size of the font to **14** points and the **Font style** to **Bold Italic**.

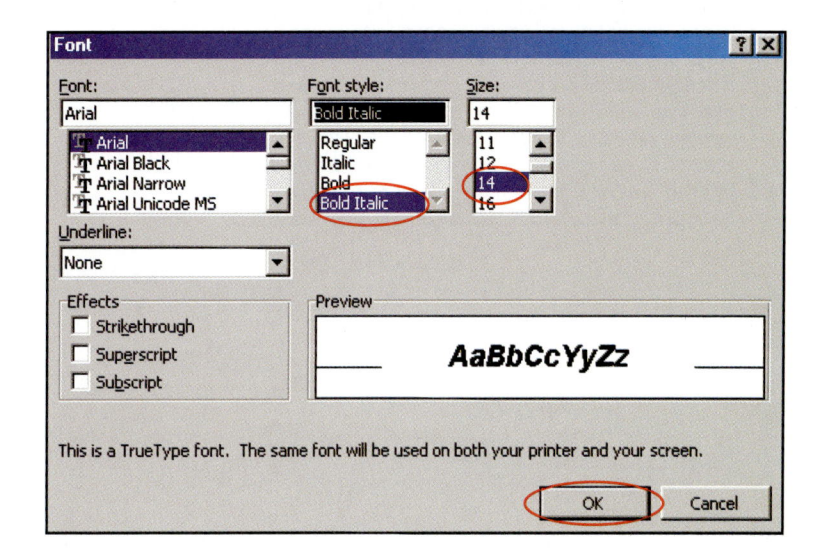

5 Click **OK** to return to the Header dialog box.

Click **OK** to return to the Page Setup dialog box.

Click **OK** to return to the Print Preview.

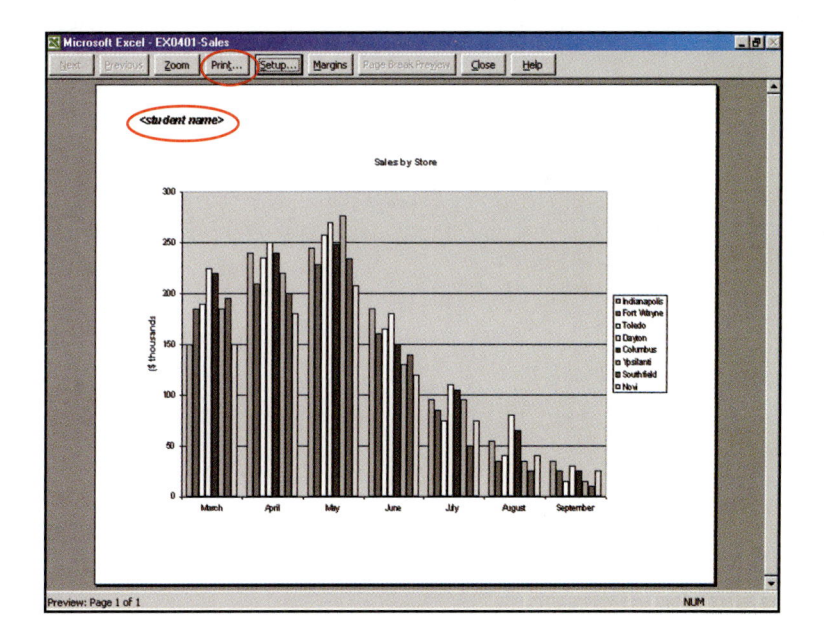

Task 5 Printing a Chart EXC

6 Click the **Print** button to print the chart. Click **OK** in the Print dialog box. Close the workbook and save the changes.

> **CAUTION**
>
> If you plan to create transparencies from your charts, keep several issues in mind. If you plan to print the transparency directly from your printer, you must use a transparency that is designed for your type of printer. Colors on transparencies seldom look as dark or saturated as those onscreen or on paper. If your office has transparencies that work with your copier, you would be wise to print the charts on regular paper and then use the copier to transfer them to transparencies. Transparency material is expensive, and you usually have to buy an entire box. Preview your work and print samples on paper to avoid costly reprints. Also, be aware that transparencies sometimes jam when you try to feed several through the printer or copier.

The exercises that follow are designed for you to review and use what you have learned in this lesson. You also have the opportunity to practice your skills and then expand on them by applying them to new situations.

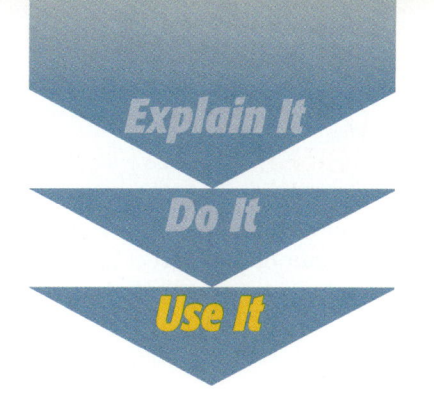

Explain It

Do It

Use It

COMPREHENSION

Comprehension exercises are designed to check your memory and understanding of the basic concepts in this lesson. You distinguish between true and false statements, identify new screen elements, and match terms with related statements. If you are uncertain of the correct answer, refer to the task number following each item (for example, T4 refers to Task 4), and review that task until you are confident you can provide a correct response.

TRUE-FALSE

Circle either T or F.

T F 1. The Chart Wizard walks you through the creation of a chart. **(T1)**

T F 2. Pie charts are used to show trends. **(T2)**

T F 3. If the printer you use is a color printer, the print preview will be in color. **(T5)**

T F 4. When selecting data to chart, always include the row and column totals. **(T3)**

T F 5. When you right-click on a chart title, it automatically sizes the font to produce a title that spans three-fourths of the printed page. **(T4)**

T F 6. Column charts and bar charts are both used to illustrate data that shows comparisons. **(T3)**

MATCHING QUESTIONS

A. Column chart   D. **Print Preview** button
B. Category (X) axis   E. Line chart
C. Value (Y) axis   F. Pie chart

Match the following statements to the word or phrase that is the best match from the list. Write the letter of the matching word or phrase in the space provided next to the number.

1. ____ A chart type used to make comparisons **(T3)**

2. ____ Displays chart as it will look when printed **(T5)**

3. ____ A chart type used to show trends over time **(T1)**

4. ____ The chart axis at the bottom of the chart **(T4)**

5. ____ The chart axis at the left side of the chart **(T4)**

6. ____ A chart type used to show contributions to a whole **(T2)**

Comprehension   EXC

IDENTIFYING PARTS OF THE EXCEL SCREEN

Refer to the figure and identify the numbered parts of the screen. Write the letter of the correct label in the space next to the number.

1. _____
2. _____
3. _____
4. _____
5. _____
6. _____
7. _____
8. _____
9. _____
10. _____

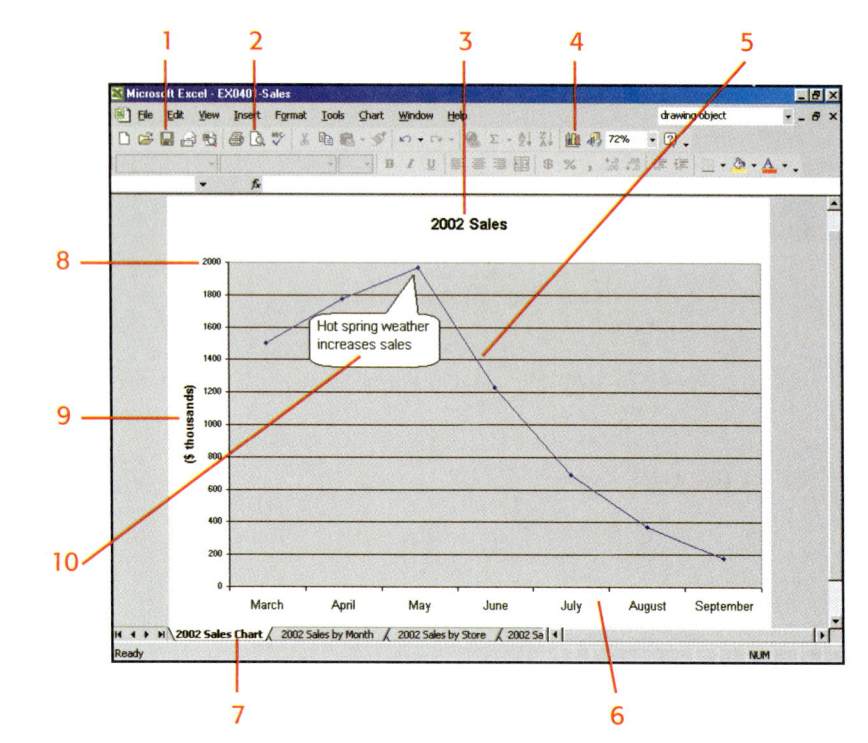

A. **Save** button (T1)

B. Category axis (T4)

C. **Print Preview** button (T6)

D. Callout (T4)

E. Value axis title (T4)

F. **Chart Wizard** button (T1)

G. Sheet tab (T2)

H. Chart title (T1)

I. Maximum scale value (T4)

J. Line connecting data points (T1)

REINFORCEMENT

Reinforcement exercises are designed to reinforce the skills you have learned by applying them to new situations. Detailed instructions are provided along with a figure, where appropriate, to illustrate the result. The reinforcement exercises that follow should be completed sequentially. Leave the file open at the end of each exercise for use in the next exercise until you are specifically directed to close it.

Open **EX0402** and save it as **EX0402-Reinforcement** on your floppy disk for use in the following exercises.

In these exercises, you examine a table of statistics showing the fatalities and injuries due to tornadoes in Michigan over a forty-year period. Charts are very useful when displaying trends, comparisons, or contributions to the whole.

R1—Creating and Printing a Pie Chart

A pie chart may be used to show how each decade has contributed to the total number of casualties. See the following steps for more detail.

1. Select cells **A2** through **A6**. Hold down Ctrl and select cells **E2** through **E6** on the **Casualties** sheet.

2. Click the **Chart Wizard** button. In the first dialog box, choose the **Pie** chart type, and then choose the **Pie with a 3-D visual effect** chart sub-type (the middle choice on the top row).

3. In the second dialog box, choose **Columns**, if necessary.

4. In the third dialog box, change the title to **Michigan Tornado Casualties by Decade**.

5. In the fourth dialog box, choose to save the chart as a new sheet named **Pie Chart**.

6. Change the size of the font in the title and the legend to **18** points.

7. Choose **File**, **Page Setup** and add your name to the custom header on the left side using **Bold Italic**, **12**-point font. Preview and print the chart if your instructor requires it. Save your work.

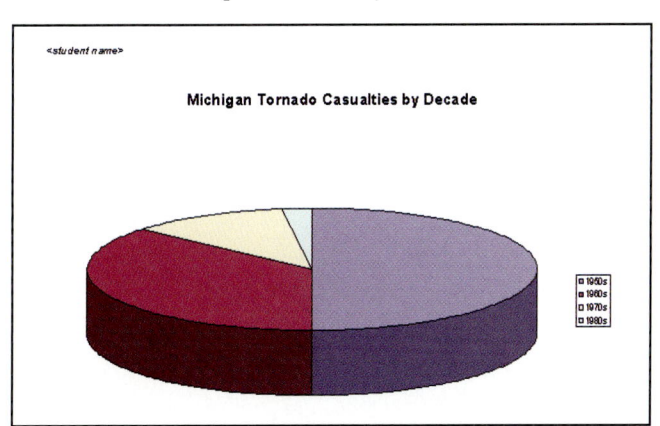

R2—Creating and Printing a Column Chart

Column charts are useful for showing comparisons. In this exercise, you compare the number of tornadoes in each decade. See the following steps for more detail.

1. Select the **Casualties** sheet. Select cells **A2** through **B6**.

2. Click the **Chart Wizard** button. Choose the **Column** chart type, and then choose the **Clustered column with a 3-D visual effect** chart sub-type (the first choice in the second row).

3. Proceed to step 3 of the Chart Wizard and change the title to **Michigan Tornadoes by Decade**.

4. In the fourth dialog box, place the chart on a new sheet named **Column Chart**.

5. Change the size of the title font to **18** points. Select and delete the legend. Change the size of the X and Y axis labels to **12** points.

6. Choose **File**, **Page Setup** and add your name to a custom footer in the lower left. Print the chart if your instructor requires it. Save your work.

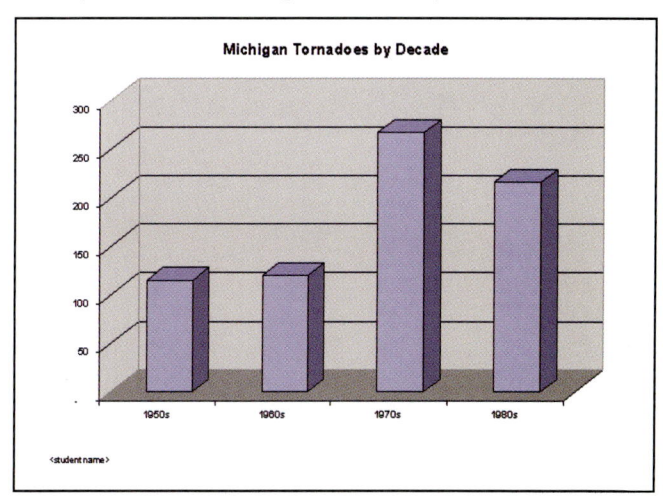

R3—Showing a Trend with a Line Chart

Create a chart to show the trend in total casualties. See the steps below for more detail.

1. Select the **Casualties** sheet. Select cells **A2** through **A6** and cells **E2** through **E6**.

2. Click the **Chart Wizard** button and select the **Line** chart type and **3-D Line** as the sub-type.

3. Proceed with the Chart Wizard and change the chart title to **Tornado Casualties in Michigan**.

4. Save as a new sheet with the name **Line Chart**.

5. Delete the legend. Change the size of the font in the title to **18** points.

6. Add your name to the custom header in the upper left. Preview and print the chart if your instructor requires it. Save the workbook and close it.

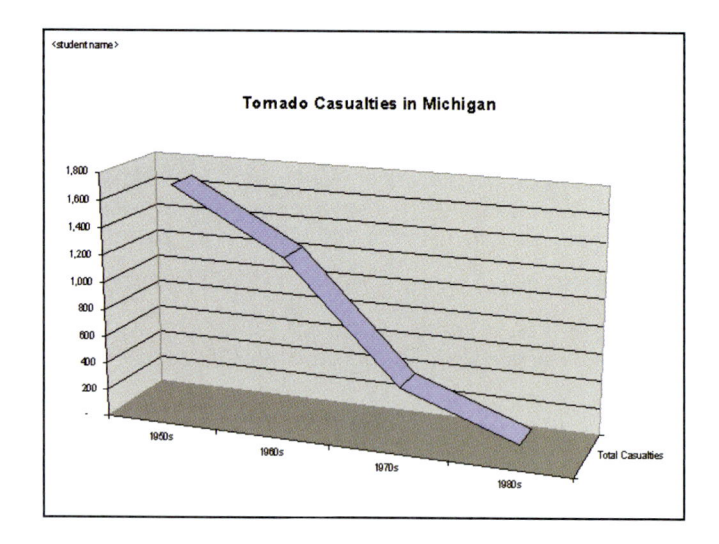

CHALLENGE

Challenge exercises are designed to test your ability to apply your skills to new situations with less-detailed instructions. These exercises also challenge you to expand your repertoire of skills by using commands that are similar to those you have already learned. The desired outcome is clearly defined, but you have more freedom to choose the steps needed to achieve the required result.

Challenge exercises C1 through C4 use the workbook **EX0403-Challenge**. The exercises are related but may be done individually. Open **EX0403** from the **Student** folder and save it as **EX0403-Challenge**.

In these Challenge exercises, you work with data concerning the consumption of energy compared to gross national product (GNP) for sixteen countries around the world. You will use Excel's charting capability to determine if the amount of energy that a person uses is proportional to the amount of goods they produce. In other words, if a person in an affluent country consumes ten times as much energy as a person in a poor country, do they produce ten times as much? If the amount of goods produced is directly proportional to the energy consumed, a line chart of the data should be a fairly straight line.

In these exercises, you examine this data to see if such a relationship exists, using some of the advanced Excel charting tools.

C1—Placing a Chart on the Same Sheet as the Data

If a chart is small, it may be placed on the same sheet as the rest of the data. In this example, you chart the energy used per person by country, and then save it on the same sheet as the data. This makes it easier to compare the chart with the data.

Goal: Create a column chart that displays the country and the energy used per capita and place it on Sheet1 with the data. Adjust the font size of the category labels so they all display.

Use the following guidelines:

1. Select **Sheet1**. Select the data (and headings) in the **Country** and **Energy** columns.

2. Create a column chart and save it as an object in **Sheet1**. Accept all defaults, including the chart title.

3. Delete the legend.

4. Deselect the chart and change the **Zoom** to **50%** so you can see more of the page. Click-and-drag the chart to a place below the data and drag one of its handles to stretch the chart so that it spans columns **A** through **H**.

5. Change the font of the Category (X) axis labels to **8** point. Change the **Zoom** back to **100%**. All the country names should display. If they do not, widen the chart further.

6. Change **Page Setup** to **Landscape** orientation. Work with the **Print Preview** option to make sure the chart will fit on one page and all the country names will print (see the figure).

7. Add your name to the custom header. Print the page with the chart.

8. Save the workbook. Leave the workbook open for use in the next exercise.

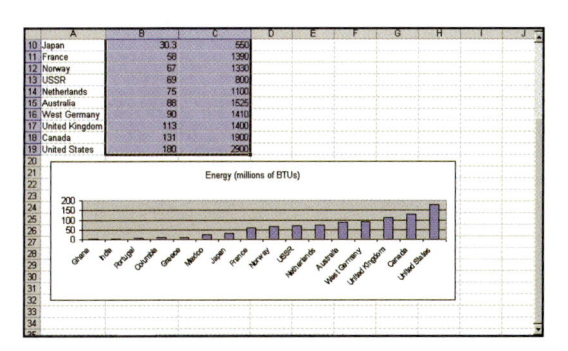

C2—Charting Related Data Using the X-Y Chart

If you are charting two columns of numbers where the second column is dependent on (or related to) the first column, you should use an X-Y chart, sometimes called a scatter chart. The data points are scattered on the chart to indicate each intersection of the X and Y coordinates, and the intervals on the category (X) axis are forced to be equal.

When plotting real-life data, you seldom get an exact relationship. You look to see if the points represent a general trend, such as a straight line or a curve. In our example, the energy used per person is displayed on the category (X) axis and the GNP per person is displayed on the value (Y) axis.

Goal: Represent the per capita Gross National Product as it relates to the amount of energy used per person.

Use the following guidelines:

1. Select **Sheet1**. Select the **Energy** and **GNP** columns (cells **B3** through **C19**). Use the Chart Wizard and create an X-Y scatter chart.

2. Enter **GNP per Energy Used** as the chart title, **Millions of BTUs** for the X axis title, and **Dollars** for the Y axis title.

3. Delete the legend.

4. Save the chart on its own sheet named **My X-Y chart**.

5. Add your name to the custom header and print the chart if your instructor requires it.

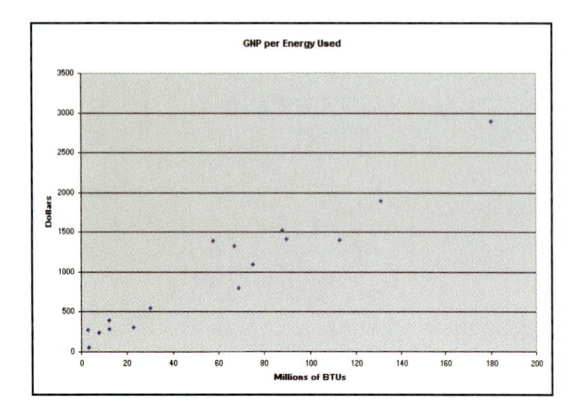

C3—Adding Data Labels to an X-Y Chart

Excel makes it easier to determine the exact values of a point on a data chart by displaying the data value next to the data point.

You can add data labels to a chart using the shortcut menu that displays when you right-click on a data point on the chart.

Goal: Use the shortcut menu to display the Y-axis value next to each data point on an X-Y chart.

1. Select the **XY Chart** sheet. It is similar to the chart that you may have created if you did the previous Challenge exercise. Right-click on one of the chart's data points.

2. Choose **Format Data Series** from the shortcut menu. Choose **Data Labels** and select labels for both the **X Value** and the **Y Value**.

3. Add your name to the custom header and print the chart. Leave the workbook open.

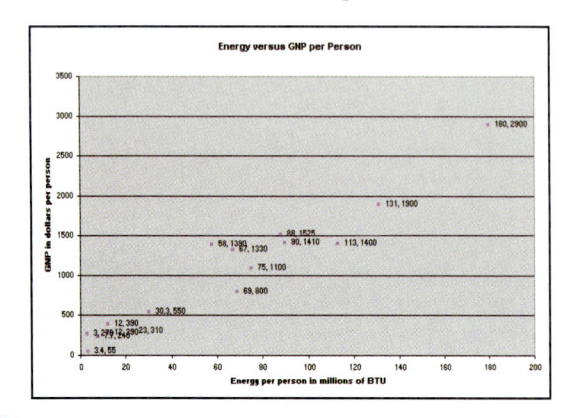

C4—Adding a Trend Line to an X-Y Chart

If there is a linear relationship between the values displayed on the category (X) axis and those on the Y-axis of an X-Y chart, the data points will be close to a straight line. Excel can calculate the straight line that is the best fit to the data points and add it to the chart.

The method of determining the formula for the best fitting straight line is called a linear regression analysis. The degree of fit is represented by the R^2 value. A perfect fit would have an R^2 value equal to 1. If the R^2 value is close to 1, you may use the equation of the straight line to estimate new values of GNP if you know the energy used per person.

Goal: Add the trend line to the XY chart that is the best fit to the data. Use the R^2 value to evaluate the relationship between the X values and the Y values. Display an equation of the relationship.

1. Select the **XY chart** sheet. Right-click on one of the data points and choose **Add Trendline**.

2. Choose the **Linear** trend line. Click the **Options** tab and choose to display the R-squared value and the equation on the chart.

3. Locate the R-squared value and the equation. Drag them to the upper-left portion of the chart. Change the font to **14** points.

4. Add your name to the custom header and print the chart. Save and close the workbook.

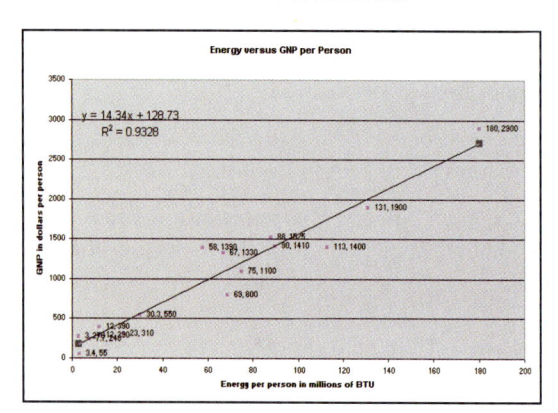

C5—Charting Problem Data

The Chart Wizard makes assumptions that are often helpful when setting up charts. If a table of data has an unexpected value in it, the wizard can produce unusable results unless you know how to change some of the settings.

The data in this exercise represents the number of passengers that rode on commercial airlines from 1981 to 1998. The data for one of the years is missing, and the text, **Not Available**, occupies that cell. The wizard does not handle this well.

Goal: Manually adjust the settings used in the Chart Wizard to display a chart where one of the pieces of data is missing.

1. Open **EX0404** from the **Student** folder and save it as **EX0404-Challenge**.

2. Select cells **A3** through **B21**. Click the **Chart Wizard** button. Choose the **Column** chart type and the **Clustered Column** sub-type, if necessary, and then go to the next step.

The sample chart in this step indicates that there is a problem. **Columns** is selected, as it should be; the problem is that the wizard guessed incorrectly when it assigned the cells to their respective roles in the chart.

3. Click the **Series** tab. The years should be used as Category (X) labels, but they are shown in the **Series** box as data to be charted. Select the series that starts with **Year** and click **Remove**.

4. Click the **Collapse Dialog Box** button next to the **Category (X) axis labels** box. Select cells **A4** through **A21**. Click the **Expand Dialog Box** button. This helps but there is still a problem. The label and legend are wrong and there should be eighteen years of data displayed, but there are only eleven.

5. Click the **Collapse Dialog Box** button next to the **Name** box. Select cell **B3**. Click the **Expand Dialog Box** button. This fixes the title and legend.

6. Click the **Collapse Dialog Box** button next to the **Values** box. Select cells **B4** through **B21**. Click the **Expand Dialog Box** button. All of the years display properly with a gap for 1987, when there was no data (see figure).

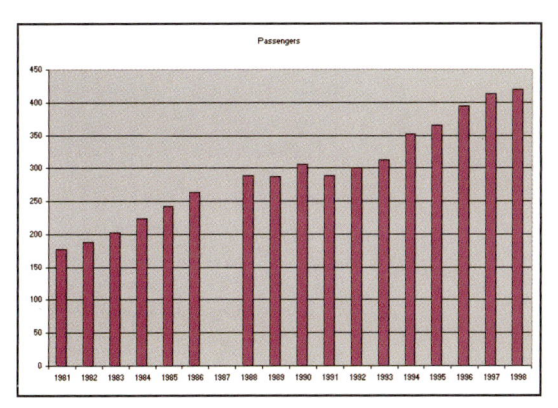

7. Go to step 3 of the wizard. Click the **Legend** tab and deselect **Show legend**.

8. Go to step 4 of the wizard. Choose **As new sheet** and enter **Passengers** as the sheet name.

9. Add your name to a custom header. Save the workbook and close it.

C6—Exploding, Rotating, and Annotating a Chart

Sometimes you want to make a point dramatically. An attractive chart that isolates and identifies the key elements is very helpful.

Excel has several advanced charting options to help create more dramatic charts. In this exercise, you learn to use a pie chart that separates the individual slices. You will rotate the chart to bring the element of most interest to the front, and then add a callout to explain its significance.

Goal: Make an exploded pie chart of the sources of electric energy and identify the amount of new capacity we would need from sources that do not emit carbon dioxide if we are to reduce our carbon dioxide output to 1990 levels from electricity generation.

1. Open **EX0405** from the Student folder and save it as **EX0405-Challenge**.

2. Select cells **A1** to **E2**. Click the **Chart Wizard** button. Click the **Custom Types** tab, scroll down, and choose the **Pie Explosion**.

3. Change the chart title to **Electric Energy in the United States**.

4. Place the chart on a new sheet named **Electricity**.

5. Choose **Chart**, **3-D View**. Choose a rotation of **180** to bring the **New** slice to the front.

6. Choose **Insert**, **Picture**, **AutoShapes** from the menu bar. Click the **Callouts** button and choose the **Rounded Rectangular Callout**. Drag the outline of the callout below and to the right of the **New** slice.

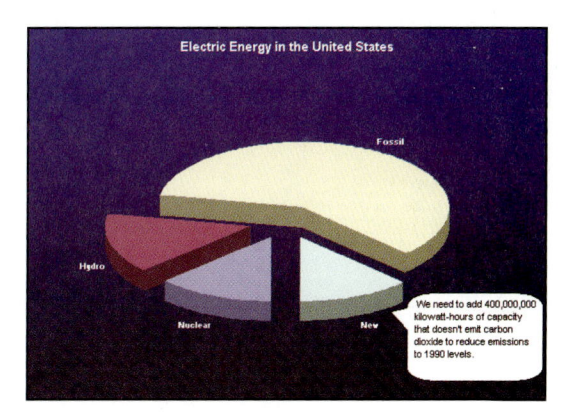

7. Change the font size to **12** and type **We need to add 400,000,000 kilowatt-hours of capacity that doesn't emit carbon dioxide.**

8. Adjust the size of the callout if necessary and move the yellow diamond to point at the **New** slice.

9. Change the font color of the title to **white** and its font size to **16**. Close the **AutoShapes** toolbar.

10. Add your name to the custom header. Save your work and print the chart. Close the workbook.

Challenge   EXC

ON YOUR OWN

When you are trying to determine where the household money is going or when you are discussing this topic with other members of the household, it is useful to be able to display the situation with a chart.

Set up a worksheet that shows how much of the household's income is spent by category. Create a pie chart that displays how each expenditure compares to the other. The following criteria will be used for grading:

1. Demonstration of the use of the charting skills taught in this lesson.
2. Demonstration of a pie chart to display the household expenses.

Some examples of features that students have learned to use in previous classes to enhance their personal household expenses chart are listed below:

- Use of a legend or labels to identify slices of the pie chart
- Labels of adequate size for easy reading
- Use of data labels to place dollar amounts or percentages next to each slice
- 3-D effects when appropriate
- Identification of amounts as weekly, monthly, or yearly
- Saved as its own sheet
- Name in the header or footer

3. Identify yourself. Place your name in the footer so that it is visible in **Print Preview**.

4. To complete the project:
   - Save your file on your own disk. Name it **EX0405-Expenses**.
   - Check with your instructor to determine if the project should be submitted in electronic or printed form. If necessary, print out a copy of the worksheet to hand in.

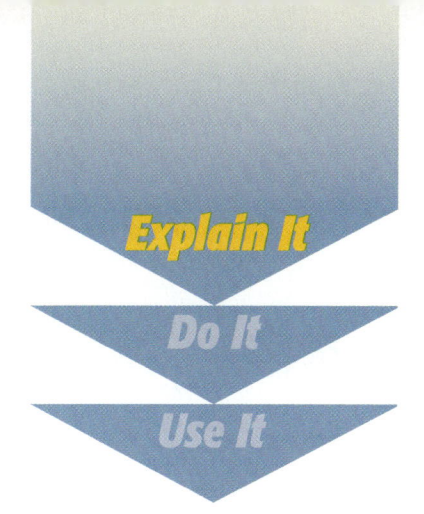

Lesson 5

Integrating Excel with Word and the Internet

Task 1   Deleting, Inserting, Renaming, and Moving Sheets
Task 2   Designing a Summary Sheet
Task 3   Linking the Results of Several Sheets to a Summary Sheet
Task 4   Pasting a Worksheet into a Word Document
Task 5   Saving a Worksheet as a Web Page
Task 6   Previewing the Web Page

INTRODUCTION

Excel has several powerful tools that you can use to connect a worksheet with other worksheets or to connect a worksheet to other documents on your computer. You can create summary sheets to compare the totals of several different sheets and paste the results into a Word document to illustrate the message in that document.

You can share the worksheet with a wider audience by saving it as a Web page that can be loaded on a Web server.

In this lesson, you learn how to link the totals from individual product sheets to a summary sheet. You also learn how to paste this worksheet into a letter and save it as a Web page.

Jack Armstrong, president of Armstrong Pool, Spa, and Sauna Company, decided to share the sales results from the previous year with his employees. He plans to send out a letter that shows a summary of quarterly sales figures and to provide these figures on an interactive web page.

VISUAL SUMMARY

By the time you have completed this lesson, you will have created a year-end summary worksheet and pasted it into a document. You will also have a web page that could be uploaded to a server and shared on the Internet. The worksheet, Word document, and web page will look like this:

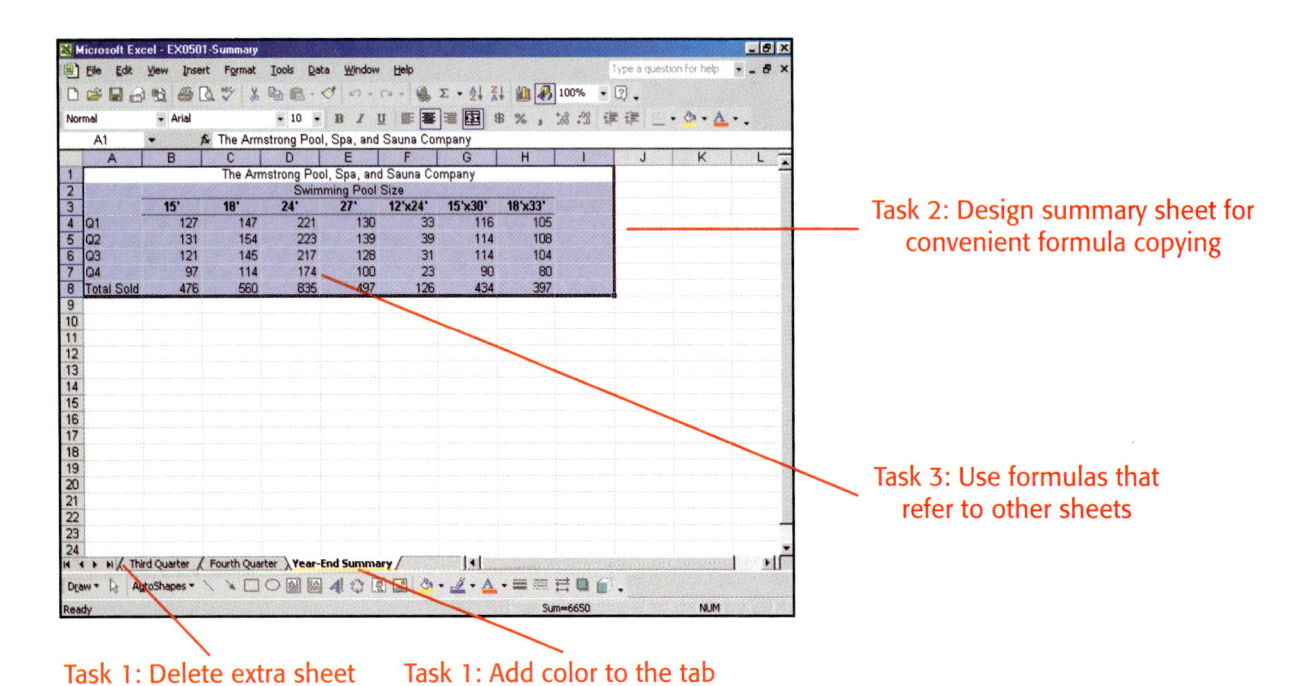

Task 1: Delete extra sheet

Task 1: Add color to the tab

Task 2: Design summary sheet for convenient formula copying

Task 3: Use formulas that refer to other sheets

Task 4: Paste worksheet into a Word document

Task 5: Save worksheet as a Web page

Task 6: Preview the worksheet in a browser

Task 6: Export web page worksheet to Excel

EXC Lesson 5 Integrating Excel with Word and the Internet

Task 1
DELETING, INSERTING, RENAMING, AND MOVING SHEETS

Why would I do this?
It may make sense to divide your data into several separate sheets when you are working with it. This makes the data easier to manage and to chart. However, you often need to bring the results of these sheets together in one place so that they can be compared and summarized. When you are ready to summarize your work, you may need to add a worksheet and place it into your workbook in a particular location.

In this task, you delete a sheet, add a new sheet to use as a year-end summary sheet, give it a name, and move the sheet to a new position in the sequence of worksheets.

1 Open **EX0501** from the **Student** folder. Save it as **EX0501-Summary** on your disk.

The new title appears in the title bar.

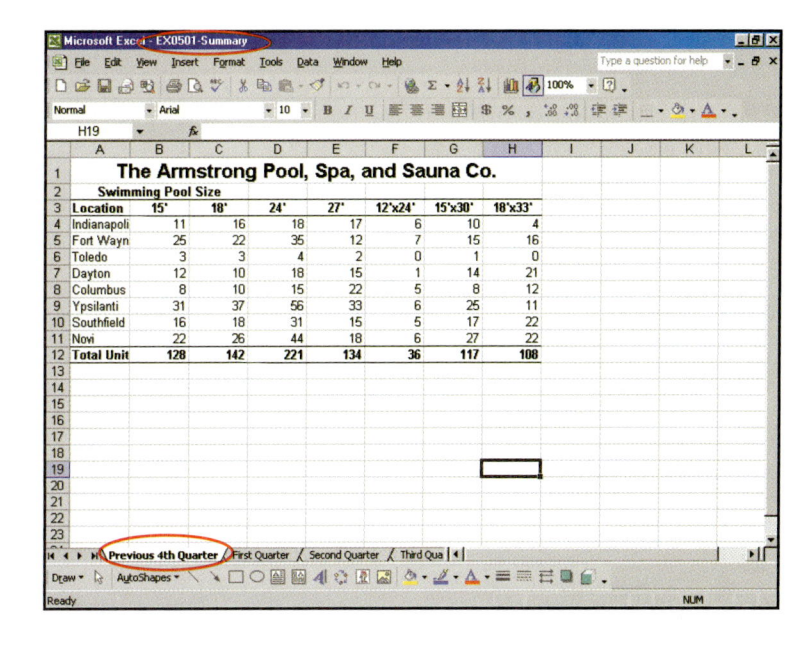

2 Right-click on the **Previous 4th Quarter** sheet tab and choose **Delete** from the shortcut menu. Click the **Delete** button to confirm the deletion.

The sheet is deleted from the workbook.

Choose **Insert**, **Worksheet**.

A blank worksheet is added. It is called Sheet1.

Double-click the **Sheet1** tab to select it and type **Year-End Summary**. Press ⏎Enter.

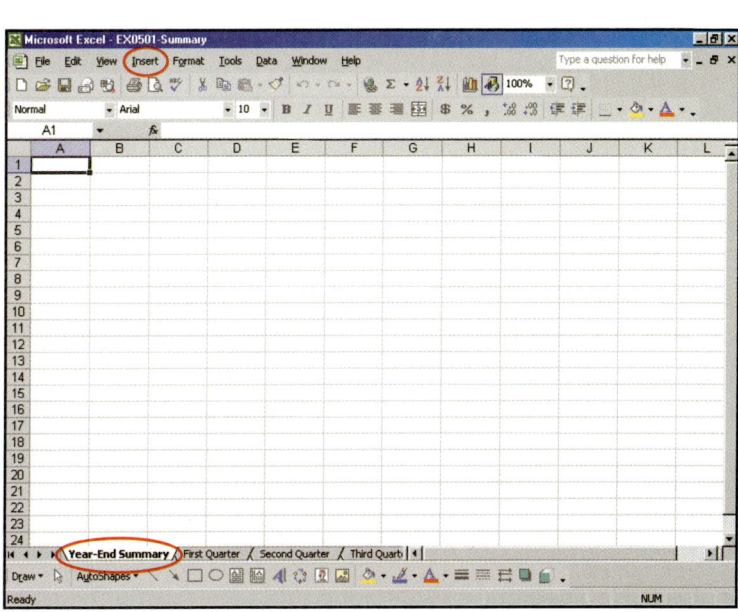

3 Move the pointer onto the new tab. Click-and-drag the tab to the right to make this sheet the last one.

Notice that there is a small arrow indicating where the sheet will be placed.

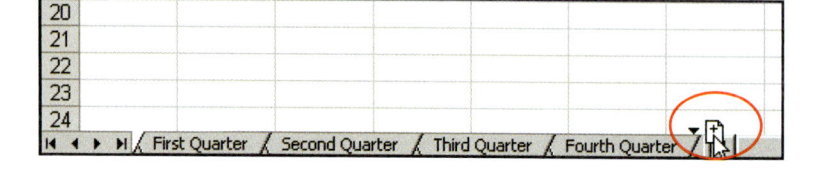

4 Release the mouse button.

The sheet is placed last.

5 Right-click on the **Year-End Summary** tab and choose **Tab Color** from the shortcut menu

The Format Tab Color dialog box is displayed.

Click the **Yellow** color box in the bottom row.

6 Click **OK**.

A thin yellow line is displayed beneath the text.

Click the **Fourth Quarter** tab.

The Year-End Summary tab displays a yellow background color.

Task 2
DESIGNING A SUMMARY SHEET

Why would I do this?
The summary sheet consolidates the data from several other sheets. Because this is summary information that may be communicated to others, you want to organize it so that it is easy to chart. To create charts the data must be arranged into adjacent cells in rows or columns. Therefore it is important that the design of the worksheet allows for easy comparison charting.

In this task, you set up labels for a sheet that summarizes the sales from each of the quarters represented by the other four sheets.

1 Click the **Year-End Summary** tab. Select cell **A1** and type **The Armstrong Pool, Spa, and Sauna Company**. Press **Enter**.

Select cells **A1** through **I1**. Click the **Merge and Center** button.

2 Select cell **B2**. Type **Swimming Pool Size**. Press **Enter**.

Select cells **B2** through **H2**. Click the **Merge and Center** button.

3 Click the **Fourth Quarter** sheet tab and select cells **B3** through **H3**.

Click the **Copy** button.

Cells B3 through H3 have a marquee around them to show that they have been copied.

4 Click the **Year-End Summary** sheet tab and select cell **B3**.

Click the **Paste** button.

The column headings from the Fourth Quarter sheet are pasted into these cells.

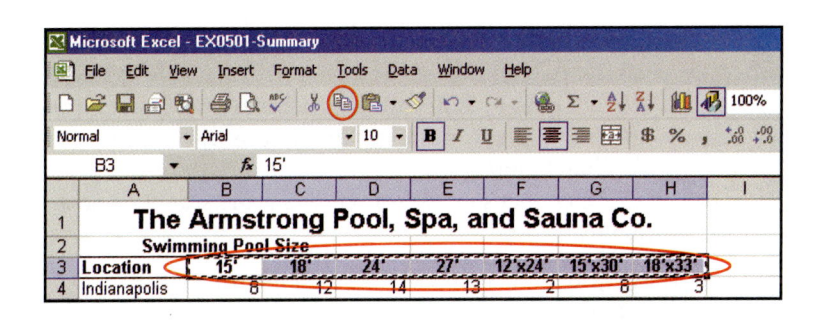

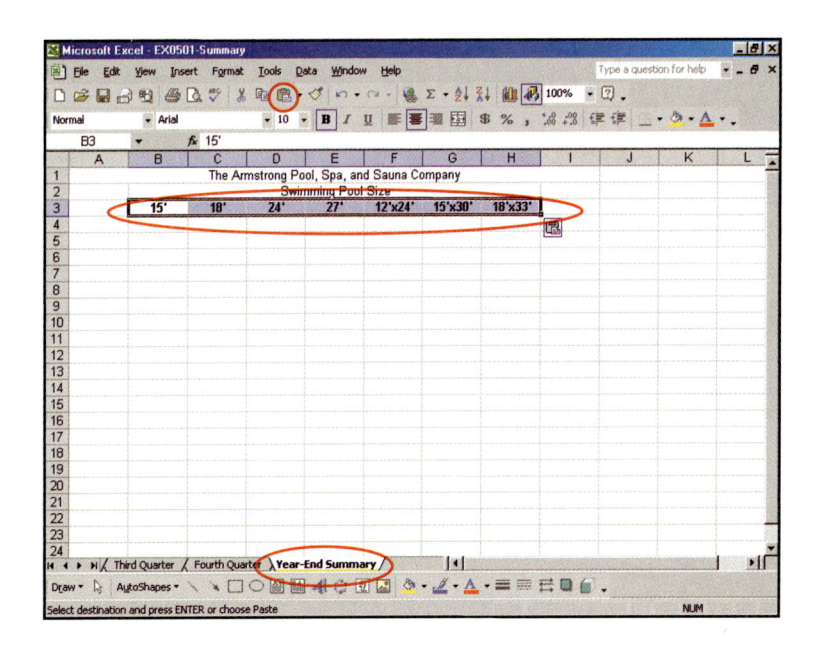

5 Select cell **A4**, type **Q1**, and press **Enter**.

> **IN DEPTH**
> When labeling columns or rows that will be charted at a later time, use brief labels that will not take up too much space on the chart, such as the Q1 label.

Task 2 Designing a Summary Sheet   EXC   111

6 Select cell **A4**. Drag the fill handle down from cell **A4** to **A7** and release the mouse button.

The cells fill with a series from Q1 through Q4.

Use the fill handle

Task 3
LINKING THE RESULTS OF SEVERAL SHEETS TO A SUMMARY SHEET

Why would I do this?
When you copy and paste information from one sheet to another, no link is established between the data in the two worksheets. To be able to change data in one sheet and have that change reflected in a summary worksheet, you need to create a connection between the worksheets. You do this by entering a formula in the summary sheet that contains a reference to a particular cell in the source worksheet. If you make changes in the source sheet, the summary sheet will reflect the change automatically.

For example, if you copy the data from the First through Fourth Quarter sheets and paste it into your Year-End Summary sheet, the values do not change in the Year-End Summary whenever you update the data in the quarterly report sheets. However, if you place a formula in a cell in the Year-End Summary sheet, you can make it refer to specific cells in the quarterly worksheet and it will update itself automatically.

In this task, you place formulas in the summary sheet that refer to the totals by category in each of the quarterly sales sheets.

1 Make sure that the **Year-End Summary** sheet is selected and select cell **B4**.

Type **=** to indicate that the following entry is a formula.

> **IN DEPTH**
> After the = sign, you could type the complete formula in cell B4 if you knew the cell references you wanted to select. In this case, as you will see, it is easier to use your mouse to locate the cell references because the cells to which you refer are on another sheet.

2 Click the leftmost **Tab Scrolling** button to find the **First Quarter** sheet tab.

Click the **First Quarter** tab.

Notice that the name of the sheet is written in the Formula bar between single quotation marks, followed by an exclamation mark.

Tab scrolling buttons

3 Click cell **B12**.

Notice that the formula in the Formula bar now refers to this sheet and cell.

> **QUICK TIP**
> You could have typed the formula shown in B12 into cell B4 in step 2 if you knew the cell reference was B12 and how to state the formula.

4 Click the **Enter** button on the Formula bar.

The screen automatically returns to the Year-End Summary sheet, and the value from cell B12 on the First Quarter sheet is displayed in cell B4 where you placed the formula.

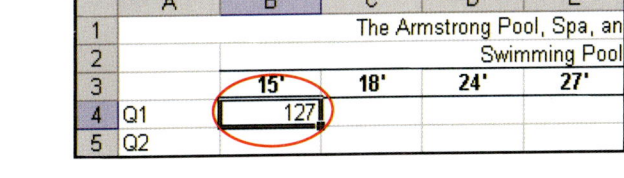

5 Drag the fill handle from cell **B4** to **H4** and release the mouse button.

The cells from C4 through H4 are filled with relative formulas that refer to cells C12 through H12 on the First Quarter sheet.

Task 3 Linking the Results of Several Sheets to a Summary Sheet   EXC   113

6 Select cell **B5** and type **=**. (Do not type the period shown at the end of the previous sentence, just the equals sign.) Switch to the **Second Quarter** sheet, select cell **B12**, and click the **Enter** button.

Drag the fill handle from cell **B5** to **H5** and release the mouse button.

The values from the second quarter are filled in.

7 Repeat this process in rows **6** and **7** to display the values from the **Third Quarter** and **Fourth Quarter** sheets.

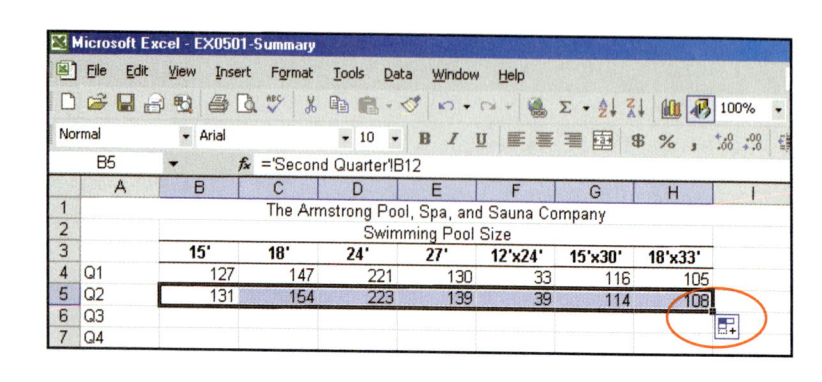

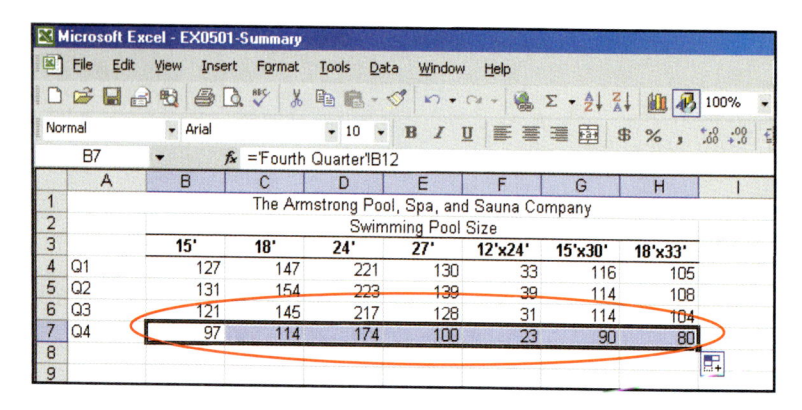

8 Select cell **A8**. Type **Total Sold** and press Tab.

Select cells **B4** through **H8**.

The selected area includes the columns to be totaled and the empty cells at the bottom of each column.

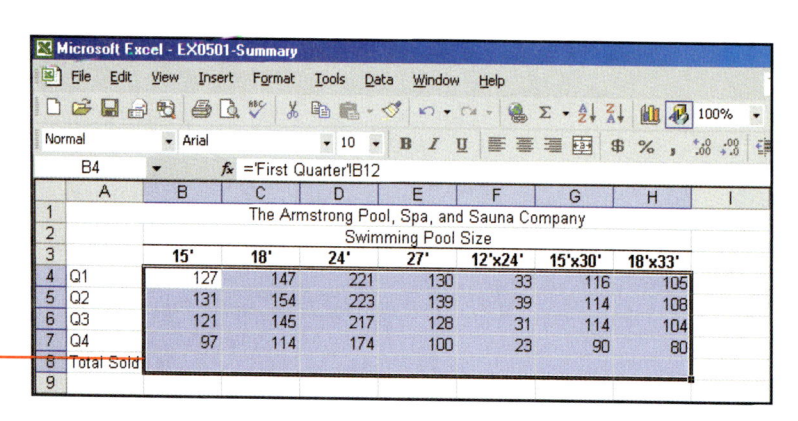

Include the empty cells in row 8

9 Click the **AutoSum** button.

Each column is totaled.

Click the **Save** button.

You may leave the workbook open for use in the next task.

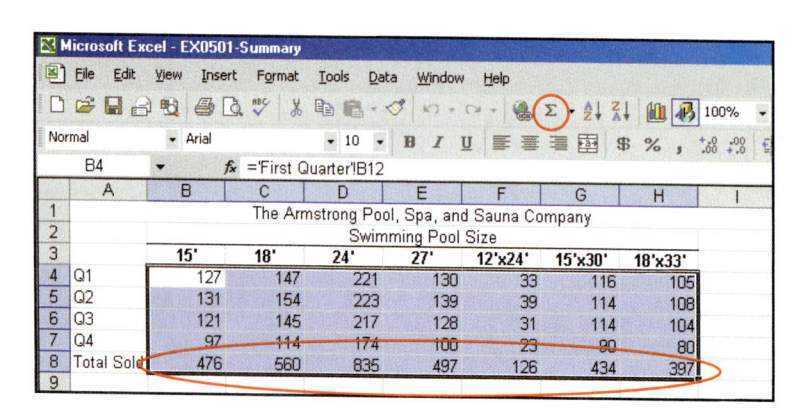

114   EXC   Lesson 5   Integrating Excel with Word and the Internet

Task 4
PASTING A WORKSHEET INTO A WORD DOCUMENT

Why would I do this?
A worksheet can be used to calculate summary information, but it usually needs further explanation. If you paste the worksheet into a Word document, you can use the document to explain the accompanying numbers.

In this task, you paste the Year-End Summary worksheet into a memo document.

1 Launch Word and open the document **EX0502** from the **Student** folder. Save the file on your disk as **EX0502-Memo**.

The letter has a space for the table.

Choose **View**, **Print Layout**, if necessary, to select this view of the document.

> **IN DEPTH**
> It is usually a good idea to view a document in the Print Layout view to see how inserted objects will really look when the document is printed.

2 Use the taskbar to switch to the **EX0501-Summary** workbook in Excel.

Select the **Year-End Summary** worksheet if necessary.

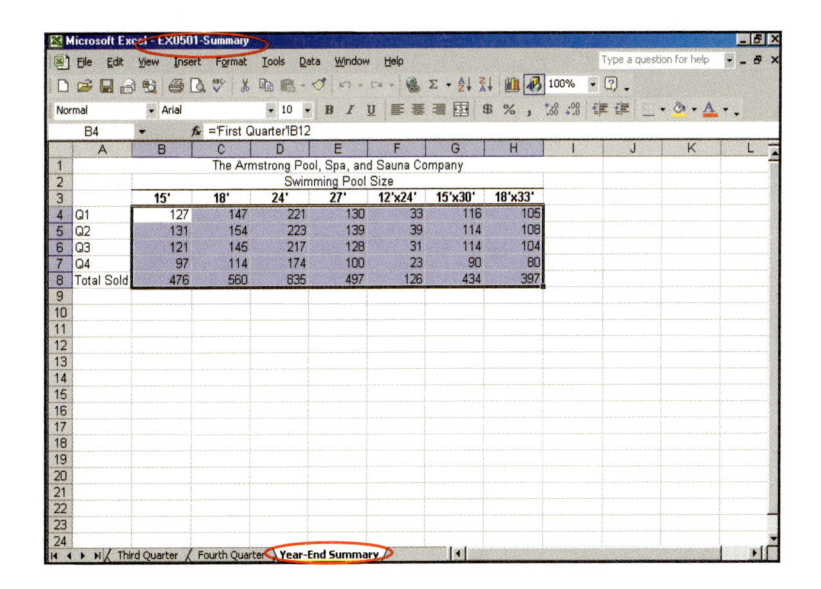

3 Select cells **A1** through **I8**.

Click the **Copy** button.

> **CAUTION**
> The range of cells in the previous step ends at cell I8. Be careful not to confuse the letter I with the number 1.

Cells to be copied

Task 4 Pasting a Worksheet into a Word Document   EXC   **115**

4 Use the taskbar to switch to the **EX0502-Memo** document.

Click on one of the blank lines between the body text paragraphs.

The worksheet will be inserted at the insertion point.

> **QUICK TIP**
>
> You can switch between applications and open worksheets and documents quickly by holding Alt and pressing Tab to display icons for each open document or application. The application used most recently prior to the current one is selected. If you release the Alt key, the selection will jump to it. If you press Tab, the selection moves to the next icon and will select this item if you release the Alt key.

5 Click the **Paste** button on the toolbar.

The selected cells of the worksheet are pasted into the document as a Word table.

> **IN DEPTH**
>
> If you change the values in the worksheet, the values in the new table in Word will not automatically update. If you would like to connect the worksheet and the document so that the table in the Word document updates when changes are made to the worksheet, choose Edit, Paste Special. A dialog box is displayed in which you can choose to Paste link the worksheet.

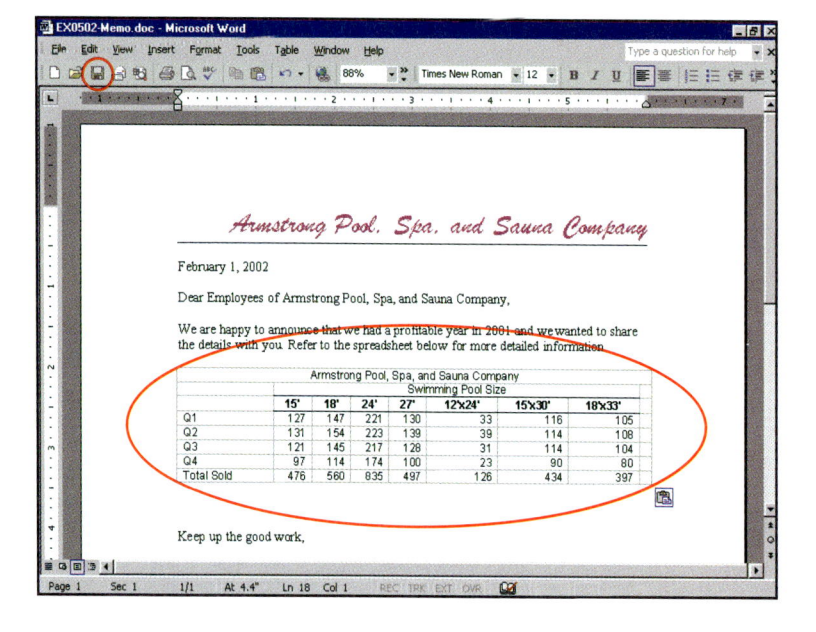

EXC   Lesson 5   Integrating Excel with Word and the Internet

6 Click the **Save** button, then close Word.

Switch back to the **EX0501-Summary** workbook if necessary.

Click the **Save** button to save the workbook.

Task 5
SAVING A WORKSHEET AS A WEB PAGE

Why would I do this?
Excel 2002 uses a Web language called Extensible Markup Language, or *XML*, that was introduced with Office 2000. It allows you to interact with a worksheet using a browser. You can save your worksheet as an interactive Web page that can be used by anyone on the Web who has permission to view your site.

In this task, you learn how save the Year-End Summary worksheet as an XML Web page.

1 Confirm that cells **A1** through **I8** are still selected.

The empty cells in column I will be used in the next task.

Include the empty cells

2 Choose **File**, **Save as Web Page**.

The Save As dialog box opens.

Select the **Excel Exercises** folder in the **Save in** box, if necessary.

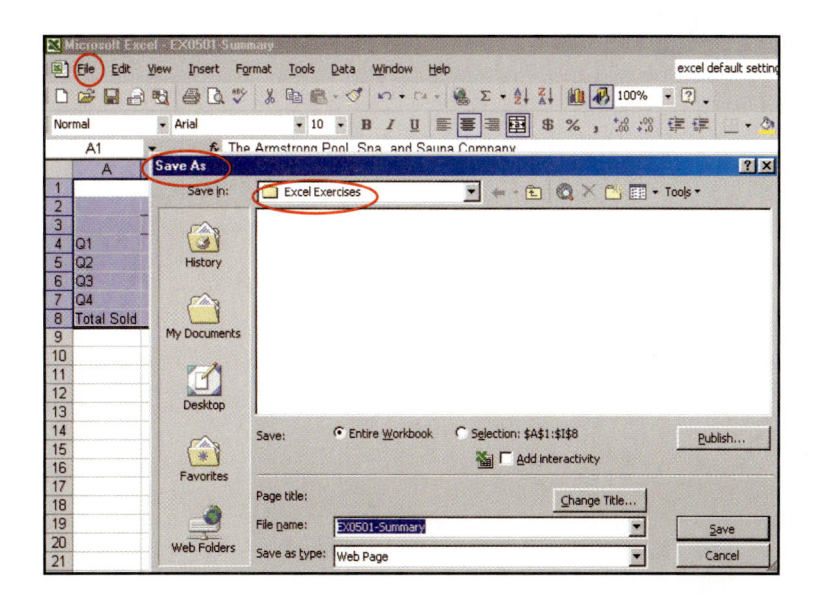

Task 5 Saving a Worksheet as a Web Page EXC 117

3 Enter the name **EX0501-Web Page** in the **File name** box.

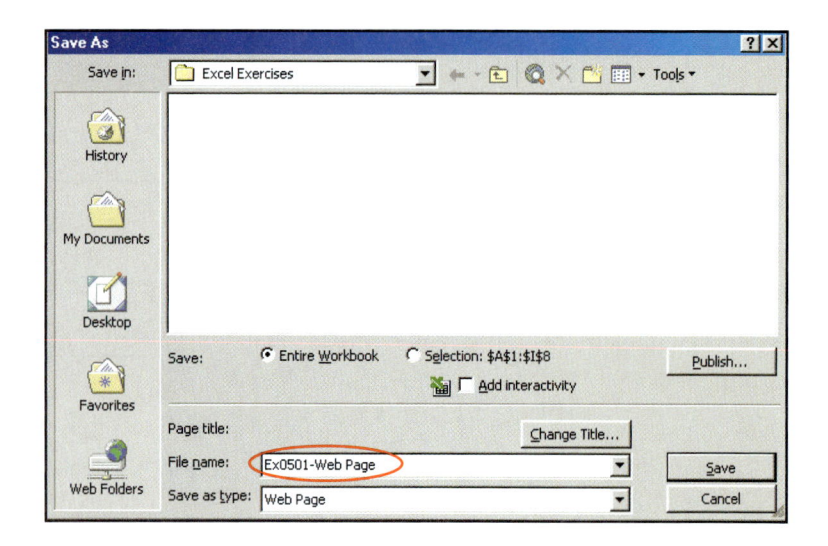

4 Click the **Selection: $A$1:$I$8** option and the **Add interactivity** check box.

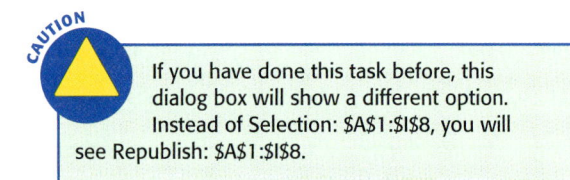

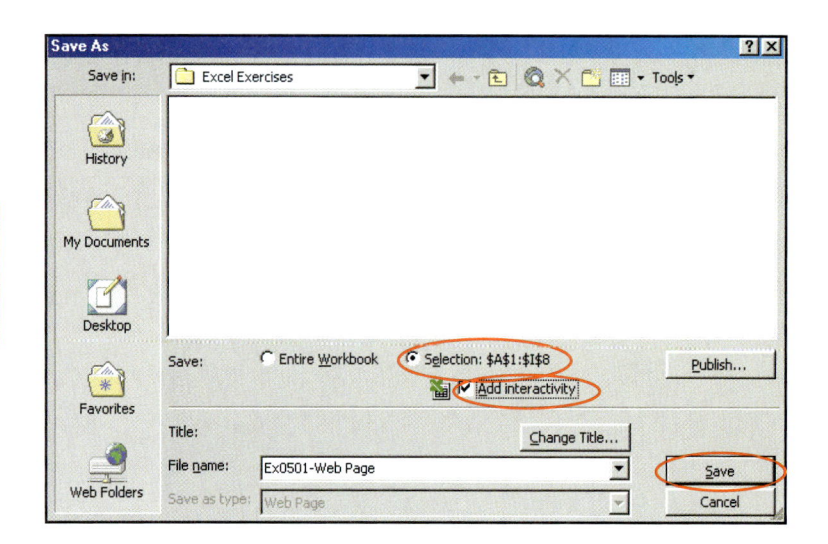

> ⚠ **CAUTION**
> If you have done this task before, this dialog box will show a different option. Instead of Selection: $A$1:$I$8, you will see Republish: $A$1:$I$8.

5 Click **Save**.

A warning box tells you that the formulas that refer to the other worksheets will not work on the Web page. This means that the Web page will not be linked to the quarterly sales worksheets.

  Click **OK**.

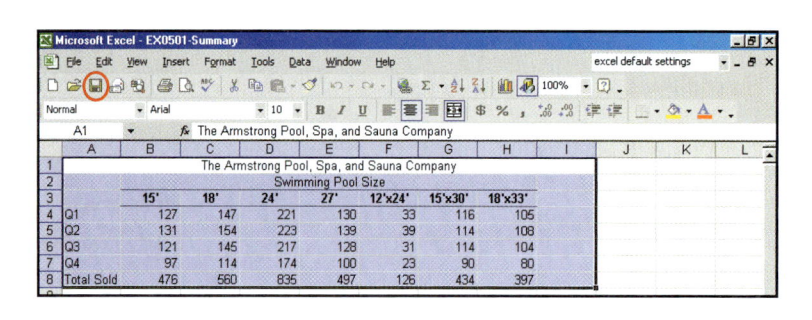

6 Click the **Save** button on the toolbar to save your changes, then close Excel.

118   EXC   Lesson 5   Integrating Excel with Word and the Internet

Task 6
PREVIEWING THE WEB PAGE

Why would I do this?
Recent versions of Web browsers, such as Microsoft's Internet Explorer 5.0 or later versions, can read files that have XML features. Older browsers display a static page. Using the XML feature, you can interact with a worksheet on the Web in new ways.

In this task, you launch Internet Explorer 5.0 or 5.5 and browse the **EX0501-Web Page** file on your disk as if it were posted to a Web server.

1 Launch Microsoft Internet Explorer or another browser that supports XML.

The browser opens and displays the default home page. Yours will differ from the figure.

> Choose **File**, **Open**. Click the **Browse** button. Locate the folder in which you saved the web page in the previous task and select it.

The Open dialog box displays options for opening existing web pages. You can browse your disks to locate the web pages. Notice the file name uses .htm to identify it as a web page.

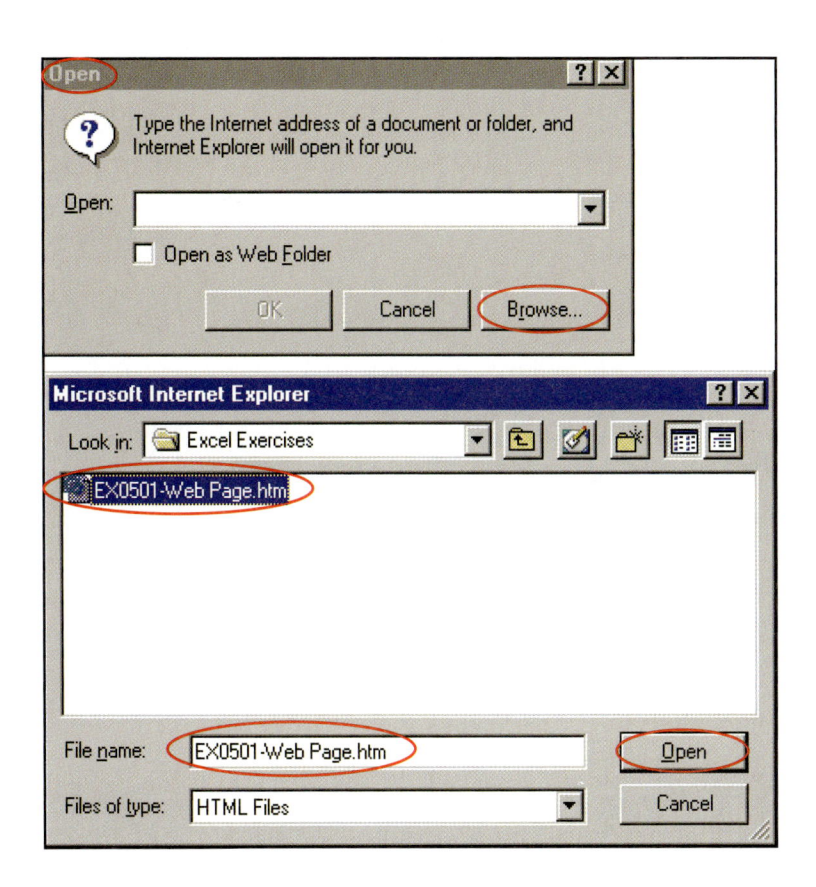

> **CAUTION:** If you are not connected to the Internet, the browser displays an error message. You do not need to be connected to the Internet to practice using this feature.

2 Click **Open**.

The Open dialog box displays the location of the web page.

> Click **OK**.

The worksheet displays in the browser as an interactive web page.

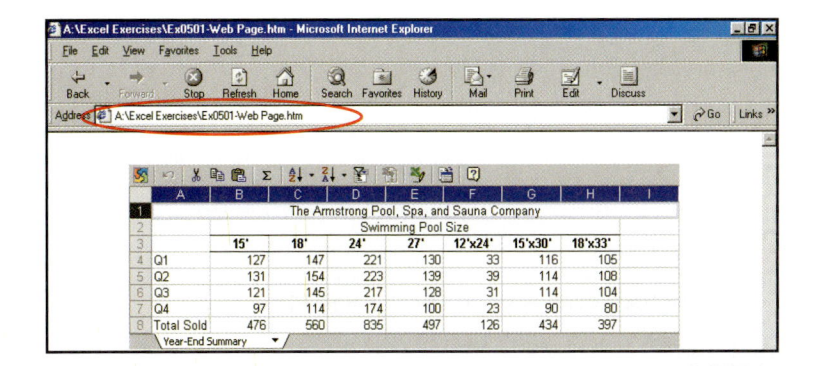

Task 6   Previewing the Web Page   EXC   119

❸ Select cell **I4**.

Notice that this worksheet summarized the total number of pools sold by size of pool at the bottom of each column but did not summarize the total number of pools sold each quarter at the end of each row. Notice that some of the worksheet tools from Excel are available on a toolbar at the top of the page.

Double-click the **AutoSum** button.

The Q1 row total is displayed.

First quarter total

❹ Select cell **I2** and enter your last name.

❺ Click the **Export to Excel** button.

*The Excel program launches and the worksheet displays in **Read Only** mode.*

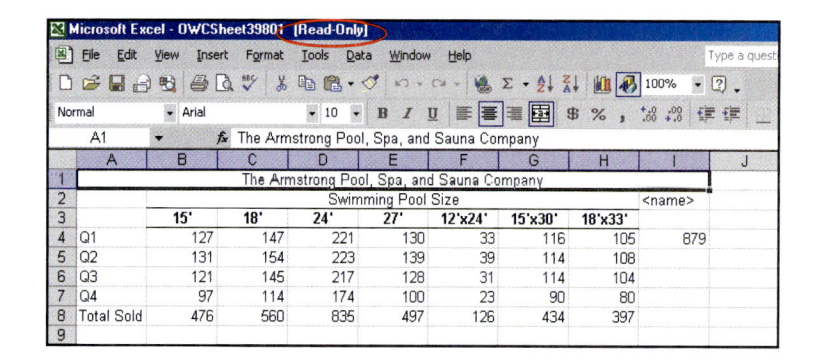

❻ Choose **File**, **Save As**. Type the name **EX0501-Web Sheet**, in the **File name** box. Set the **Save as type** box to **Microsoft Excel Workbook**. Change the folder displayed in the **Save in** box to the disk and folder where you keep your files.

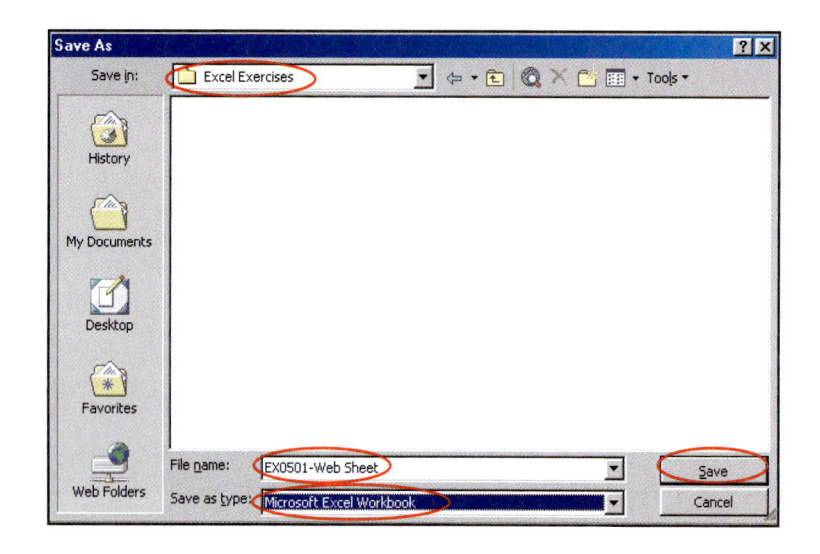

❼ Click **Save**.

Close the workbook and Excel. Close the browser.

EXC   Lesson 5   Integrating Excel with Word and the Internet

The exercises that follow are designed for you to review and use what you have learned in this lesson. You also have the opportunity to practice your skills and then expand on them by applying them to new situations.

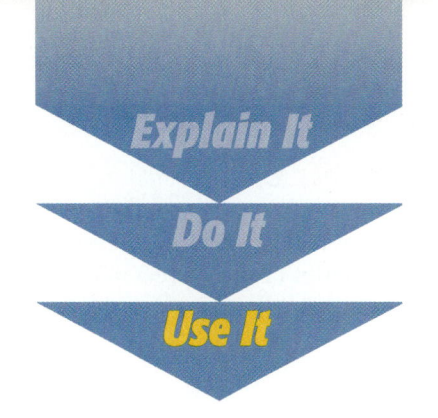

COMPREHENSION

Comprehension exercises are designed to check your memory and understanding of the basic concepts in this lesson. You distinguish between true and false statements, identify new screen elements, and match terms with related statements. If you are uncertain of the correct answer, refer to the task number following each item (for example, T4 refers to Task 4), and review that task until you are confident you can provide a correct response.

TRUE-FALSE

Circle either T or F.

T   F   1. To move a worksheet in Excel, you click-and-drag the sheet tab to a new position. **(T1)**

T   F   2. If you want cells in one worksheet to reflect changes that are made in another worksheet, you start with an equal sign in the destination cell. **(T3)**

T   F   3. In a formula, a reference to another worksheet is indicated by an exclamation point at the beginning and the end of the worksheet name. **(T3)**

T   F   4. If a cell contains a formula that refers to a cell in another sheet, you cannot use the Fill function with that cell. **(T3)**

T   F   5. To save the sheet as an interactive page suitable for publishing on the Internet, choose **File**, **Save as HTML**. **(T5)**

T   F   6. The Extensible Markup Language that makes interactive worksheets possible is known by the acronym, EML. **(T5)**

MATCHING QUESTIONS

A. table
B. insertion point
C. ='Sheet1!A2'
D. XML
E. Export to Excel
F. Tab scrolling buttons

Match the following statements to the word or phrase that is the best match from the list. Write the letter of the matching word or phrase in the space provided next to the number.

1. ____ Used to move a sheet tab into view so it can be selected **(T1)**

2. ____ A range of cells turns into this when pasted into a document using the **Paste** button **(T4)**

3. ____ A button on an interactive Web page that sends a worksheet to Excel **(T6)**

4. ____ A formula showing a reference to a cell on another worksheet **(T3)**

5. ____ A language used to make worksheets interactive on the Internet **(T5)**

6. ____ Place where the cells will go if pasted into a document **(T4)**

IDENTIFYING PARTS OF THE EXCEL SCREEN

Refer to the figure and identify the numbered parts of the screen. Write the letter of the correct label in the space next to the number.

1. _____
2. _____
3. _____
4. _____
5. _____
6. _____
7. _____

A. Reference to a cell in the Second Quarter sheet (T3)

B. Name of a sheet as it is used in a formula (T3)

C. **Print Preview** button (T4)

D. Name of currently displayed sheet (T2)

E. **AutoSum** button (T4)

F. Tab scroll buttons (T1)

G. Color added to sheet tab (T1)

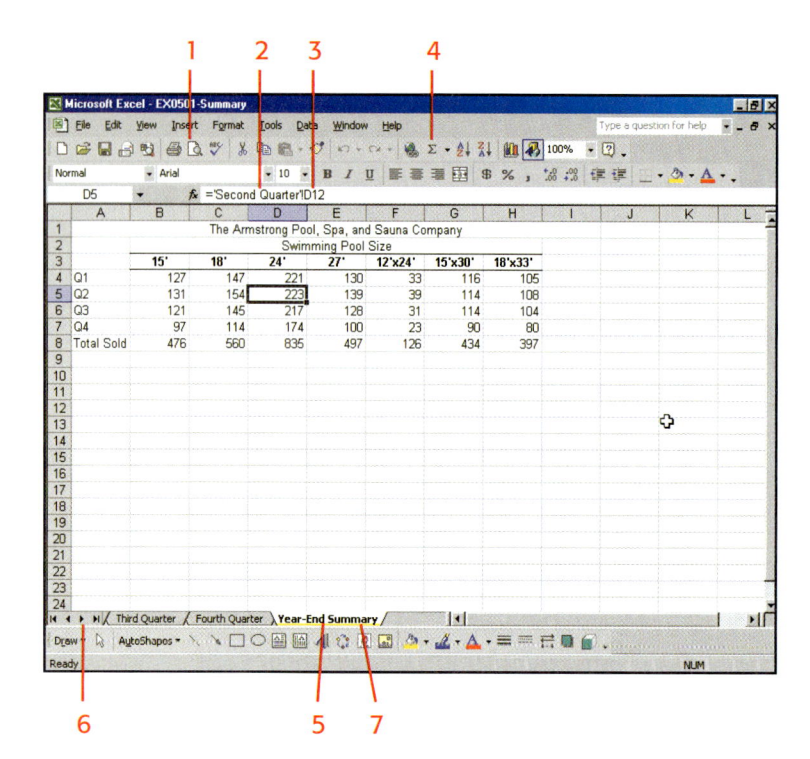

REINFORCEMENT

Reinforcement exercises are designed to reinforce the skills you have learned by applying them to new situations. Detailed instructions are provided along with a figure, where appropriate, to illustrate the result. The reinforcement exercises that follow should be completed sequentially. Leave the file open at the end of each exercise for use in the next exercise until you are specifically directed to close it.

Open **EX0503** and save it as **EX0503-Reinforcement** on your floppy disk for use in the following exercises. Replace source file with new file that uses year 2001 instead of 2000.

R1—Summarizing Income and Expenses by Quarter

Many companies provide quarterly reports to stockholders. The data provided in the first sheet displays the income and expenses by month. You summarize this data on Sheet2 into three-month periods or quarters.

1. Select **Sheet2**. Select cell **B4**, where the sum of the incomes for the months of January, February, and March should be displayed.
2. Click the **AutoSum** button once to place the SUM function in cell **B4**.
3. Click the **2001** sheet tab and drag across cells **B9** though **D9** to identify the total income for the first three months of the year.
4. Press ⏎Enter or click the **Enter** button on the formula bar. The total income for those three months, **66699**, displays in cell **B4** of **Sheet2**.
5. Repeat this process to represent the total income for April, May, and June in cell **C4**. The number **74549** displays in cell **C4**. (Do not use the fill handle for this exercise.)
6. Repeat this process to find the remaining two quarterly summations of income and the four quarterly expenses.
7. Select cell **F4** and use the **AutoSum** function to add the four quarters of income. (The total should be **321668**.) Repeat this process for the total expenses in cell **F5**. (The total expenses should be **312352**.)
8. Rename **Sheet2** as **Quarterly Report**.
9. Right-click on the Quarterly Report tab and change the tab color to light blue. Save the workbook and leave it open for use in the next exercise.

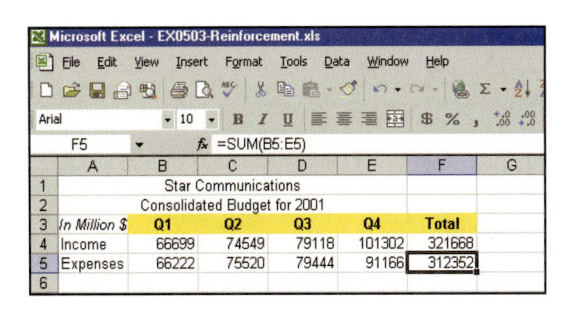

R2—Pasting the Quarterly Report into a Word Document

The Quarterly Report worksheet may be copied and pasted into a Word document for convenient reporting.

1. Select the **Quarterly Report** sheet, if necessary. Select cells **A1** through **F5**.
2. Click the **Copy** button.
3. Start Word and open a blank document, if necessary.
4. Click the **Paste** button on the toolbar. The worksheet cells are pasted into the document as a table.
5. Save the document on your disk as **EX0503-Report**.
6. Close the document and close Word.

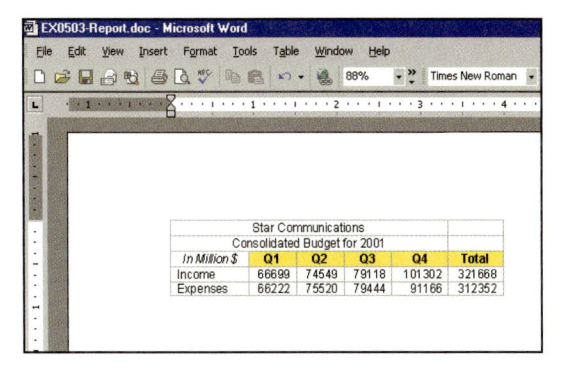

R3–Saving a Summary Sheet as an Interactive Web Page

You can share this data with others by saving it as a Web page that can be placed on a Web server or in a folder that is available to others on a local area network.

1. Select the **Quarterly Report** sheet, if necessary. Select cells **A1** through **F6**. (Be sure to include row **6**.)

2. Save the selected area as a Web page on your disk. Choose the **Add interactivity** option and name it **EX0503-Web Page**.

3. Start your browser and enter the file's location in the browser's **Address** box or browse for its location using **File**, **Open**, and the **Browse** button.

4. In cell **B6**, type **=B4-B5** and press Enter to determine the difference between income and expenses for the first quarter.

5. Select cell **B6**, if necessary, and click the **Copy** button. Select cells **C6** through **F6** and click the **Paste** button.

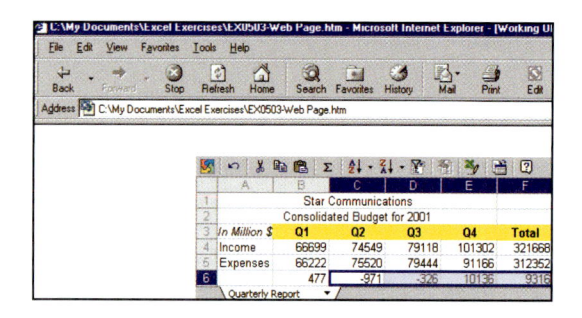

6. Click the **Export to Excel** button. Save the file as an Excel workbook named **EX0503-Web Sheet**.

7. Close the workbook.

CHALLENGE

Challenge exercises are designed to test your ability to apply your skills to new situations with less detailed instruction. These exercises also challenge you to expand your repertoire of skills by using commands that are similar to those you have already learned. The desired outcome is clearly defined, but you have more freedom to choose the steps needed to achieve the required result.

The following Challenge exercises use the file **EX0504**, which is similar to the file you edited in the lesson. They also use a Word document file, **EX0502**, that is opened in Word. Challenge exercises C1 to C3 use the same files, but they may be done independently.

Start Microsoft Word. Open **EX0502** from the **Student** folder and save it on your disk as **EX0502-Challenge**.

Start Excel, if necessary. Open **EX0504** from the **Student** folder and save it on your floppy disk as **EX0504-Challenge**.

C1—Pasting a Worksheet into a Document as a Workbook

It is possible to paste a worksheet into a Word document in several ways depending on the application. A worksheet can be copied and pasted in such a way that it is converted into a Word table. It is also possible to paste it as an actual worksheet that you can activate and edit. If you paste the worksheet into a Word document as a working worksheet, you also can choose to maintain a link between the document and the parent worksheet so that changes in one are reflected in the other.

Goal: Paste the Armstrong Pool, Spa, and Sauna Co. worksheet into a letter to the employees, then activate the worksheet and look at various sheets within the workbook.

Use the following guidelines:

1. Select cells **A1** through **I8** on the **Year-End Summary** sheet and copy it.
2. Switch to the **EX0502-Challenge** document in Word and place the insertion point in one of the blank lines between the paragraphs.
3. Choose **Edit**, **Paste Special**. Paste the object as a **Microsoft Excel Worksheet Object** (do not link it).
4. Delete extra blank lines in the document as needed. Double-click on the table to activate the worksheet.
5. Save the document. Close the Word document and close Word. Close the workbook.

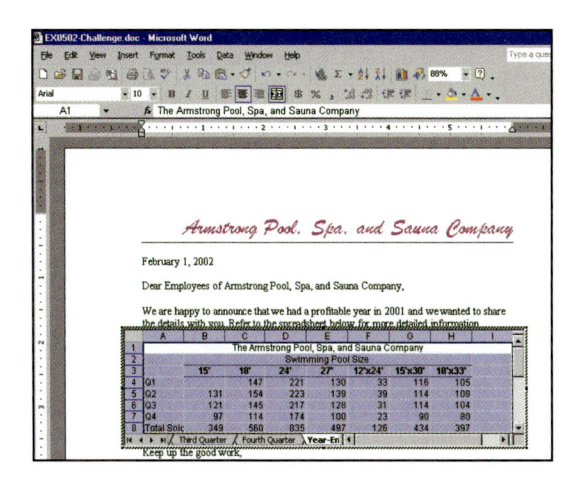

C2—Saving a Workbook as a Web Page

If a workbook has several sheets, you can save the entire workbook as a Web page.

Goal: Save the workbook as a series of Web pages that can be selected using navigation buttons.

Use the following guidelines:

1. Open **EX0504-Challenge**, if necessary. See the instructions preceding the first Challenge exercise if you do not have this file.
2. Choose **File**, **Save as Web page** from the menu. Choose **Entire Workbook**. Change the name of the file to **EX0504-Web Pages** in the **File name** box. Save it to your disk.

3. Launch your Web browser (Internet Explorer 5.0 or later, or another browser capable of reading XML). Choose **File**, **Open**, **Browse** to locate the file on your disk and open it. (If your file is on the floppy disk, the address is probably A:\Excel Exercises\EX0504-Web Pages.htm).

4. Open the Web page. The workbook has sheet tabs as shown in the figure.

5. Navigate the different sheets of the workbook using the sheet tabs at the bottom of the page.

6. Close the browser. Close the workbook.

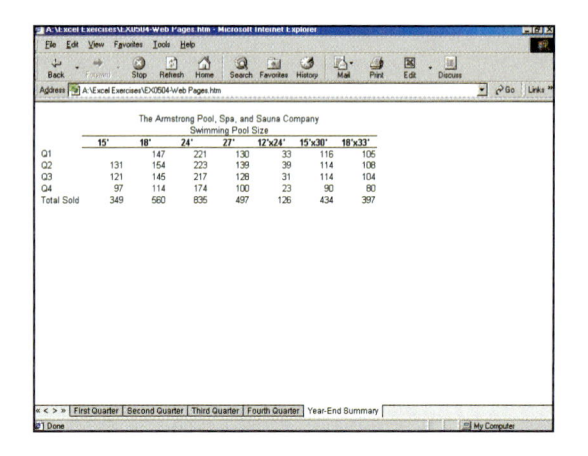

C3—Inserting a Hyperlink to a Document

If you are using a Word document with a worksheet, it is useful to jump directly to the document, even if it isn't open. A convenient way to do this is to insert a *hyperlink*. A hyperlink is a connection between a word or label in one location to a file in another location. When you click on a hyperlink, it connects you directly to information in another file.

Goal: Place a hyperlink in a worksheet that links to a Word document.

1. Open **EX0504-Challenge**, select the **Year-End Summary** sheet if necessary, and select cell **A10**. Type **Go to Document** and enter it. Select the cell again if necessary.

2. Click the **Insert Hyperlink** button.

3. Click the down arrow next to the **Look in** box. Locate the Word document **EX0502-Memo**, select it, and click **OK**. The text will change color to indicate that it is a hyperlink.

4. Click the new hyperlink. The document opens in Word. Notice the Web navigation toolbar above the document.

5. Click the **Back** button to return to the worksheet.

6. Save the changes you have made and close the workbook.

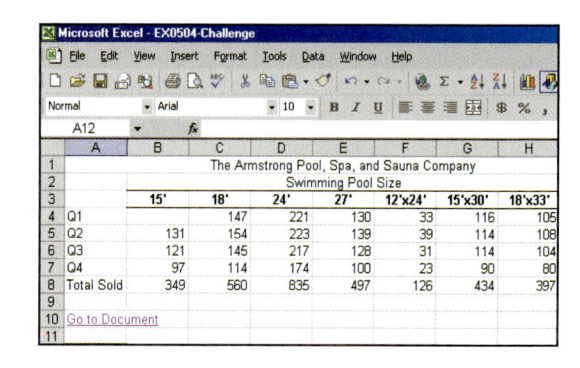

C4—Using Named Cells and Adding Comments

If a cell or range of cells is often copied, used in formulas, or returned to frequently, it is useful to give it a name of its own. The name of the cell may be used when selecting, copying, or writing formulas.

You may also add comments that provide additional information to a worksheet. Cells with small red triangles in the corners indicate the presence of a comment. The comment appears when the pointer is placed on the cell.

Goal: Assign names to cells and ranges of cells and then use those names in place of the cell address. Add a comment to the summary sheet to explain the new section.

1. Open **EX0504-Challenge** and select the **First Quarter** sheet. Select cell **I12** and double-click the **AutoSum** button to add up the total number of pools sold of all sizes.

2. Click on the name of the cell **I12** in the **Name** box at the left end of the formula bar to select it and type **Q1_Total**. Press ↵Enter. (Names of cells cannot have spaces in them. The underscore character may be used to simulate a space between words.)

3. Repeat this process for the other three quarters, naming the cells **Q2_Total**, **Q3_Total**, and **Q4_Total** respectively.

4. Go to the **Year-End Summary** sheet and select cell **A1**. Click the cell name in the **Name** box and type **Title**. Press ↵Enter.

5. Click the new name, **Title**, in the **Name** box to select it and click the **Copy** button.

6. Select cell **A13** and click the **Paste** button. The title is pasted into cells A13 through I13.

7. Select cells **A4** through **A8**. Click the name of the cell in the **Name** box and type **Row_Labels**. Press ↵Enter.

8. Click the new name, **Row_Labels**, in the **Name** box and click the **Copy** button. Select cell **A14** and click the **Paste** button.

9. Select cell **B14**. Enter **=Q1_Total**. The value of the named cell from the First Quarter sheet is displayed. Select cell **B15** and enter **=Q2_Total**. Repeat this process for cells **B16** and **B17** to enter formulas that refer to the totals in the third and fourth quarters respectively.

10. Select cell **B18**. Enter **=Q1_Total + Q2_Total + Q3_Total + Q4_Total**. Cell names can be used in formulas.

11. Choose **Edit**, **Go To** from the menu. Choose **Q1_Total** from the list in the Go to dialog box and click **OK.** You can use this method to go directly to a named cell in a worksheet.

12. Return to the **Year-End Summary** sheet. Select cell **B18** and choose **Insert**, **Comment** from the menu. Select the default user name and type your name followed by **This cell uses named cells in a formula**. Click in an unused cell to finish. Move the mouse pointer onto cell **B18** to view your comment.

13. Save the workbook and close it.

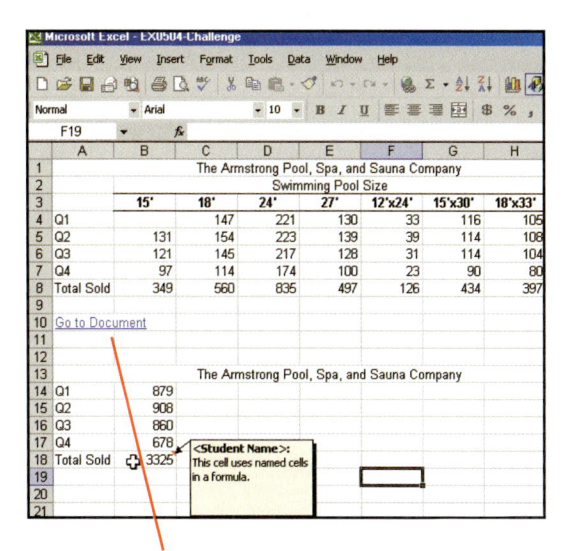

Not present if you did not do exercise C3

C5—Pasting a Table from Word into a Worksheet

You may find a table of data in a Word document and desire to analyze it in more detail using Excel. You may copy a table and paste it directly into Excel.

Goal: Copy a table of fatality statistics from a Word document into a blank worksheet.

1. Launch Word and open **EX0505** from the **Student** folder.

2. Scroll to the second page of the document and click anywhere in the table. Choose **Table**, **Select**, **Table** from the menu.

3. Click the **Copy** button. Close the document and close Word.

4. Switch to Excel. Click the **New** button at the left end of the **Standard** toolbar or select it from the **Toolbar Options** list if it is not displayed on your combined toolbar.

5. Click the **Paste** button. The table is inserted but is not formatted properly. Widen column **A** to display **North Carolina** on a single line.

6. Choose **Format**, **AutoFormat** from the menu. Choose **Classic 2** and click **OK**.

7. Save the file on your disk as **EX0505-Word Table**. Close the workbook.

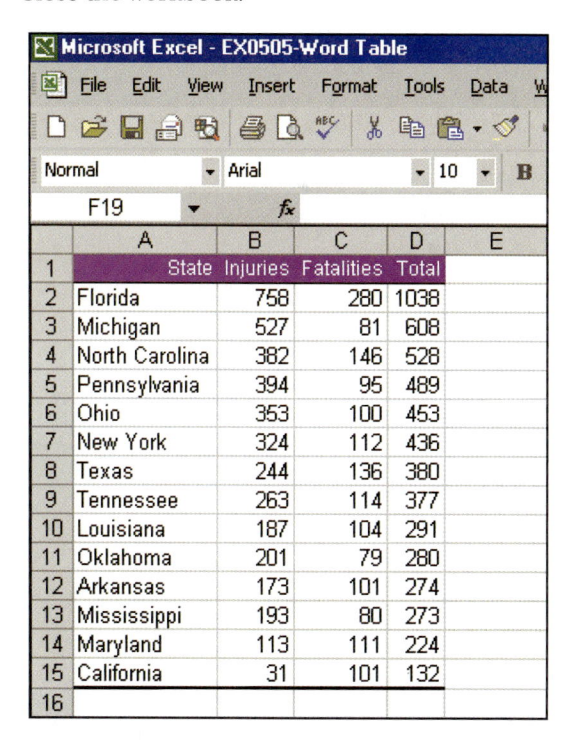

Challenge   EXC   **127**

ON YOUR OWN

Create a set of worksheets to help itemize your deductions for tax purposes. Create a set of individual worksheets that are used to list and summarize your tax-deductible expenses. Create a summary sheet that displays the total from each of the other sheets next to a label. Write a brief letter in Word to an accountant and paste the summary table into the letter.

Criteria for grading will be:

1. Demonstration of the use of formulas that refer to cells on other worksheets.
2. Demonstration of the ability to paste a worksheet into a Word document.

Some examples of features that students have learned to use in previous classes to enhance their personal tax worksheets are as follows:

- Set up a worksheet for one expense with attractive formatting and copy that sheet for use with the other types of expenses
- Round all dollar amounts displayed to the nearest dollar
- Refer to an itemized tax return to see what categories a person would use to itemize expenses
- Rename each sheet tab to identify the type of deduction
- Include at least three of the four most common categories: Medical, Taxes, Gifts, Job Expenses, and Miscellaneous
- Set up a summary sheet that would be easy to chart with the labels and totals for each expense in a simple row-and-column format.

1. Identify yourself and the year. Place your name in a cell that is clearly visible on the summary worksheet and use your name in the letter at the bottom.
2. To complete the project:
    - Save the workbook and the letter on your own disk. Name the workbook **EX0506-Tax** and the letter **EX0507-Tax**.
    - Check with your instructor to determine if the project should be submitted in electronic or printed form. If necessary, print out a copy of the workbook and the letter to hand in.
    - If your school or company has a server that supports web discussions, place the workbook on the discussion server. Post comments from two different computers that simulate a discussion between yourself and your accountant. Use Tools, Online Collaboration, Web Discussions to post comments.

Glossary

Absolute reference   a cell reference that will not change when copied or filled into other cells.

Application   one of the components of the Microsoft Office XP suite, such as Word, Excel, or Access. An application is often referred to as a program in this book.

Arguments   numbers or words used by a function to perform its operation.

Bar chart   a chart that compares values across categories. The data columns are horizontal.

Calculations   mathematical operations involving data in the worksheet cells.

Cell   a bounded area forming part of a whole that is identified by a column letter and a row number.

Chart   a graphic representation of a series of numbers; sometimes referred to as a graph.

Chart subtype   a variation on a basic chart type that allows for different emphasis and views of a chart.

Chart Wizard   a mini-program that walks you through the steps involved in creating a chart.

Clipboard   see Office Clipboard.

Column chart   a chart that compares values across categories. The data columns are vertical.

Column heading   the letter at the top of each column of an Excel worksheet that identifies the column.

Fill handle   a small box at the lower-right corner of a selected cell that can be used to fill in a series of cells.

Font   a typeface style that determines the appearance of text.

Formatting toolbar   a toolbar that contains buttons used to format fonts and alignment. It may share the same row with the standard toolbar.

Formula bar   the toolbar that displays the contents of the selected cell. If the cell has a formula in it, the formula bar displays the formula rather than the calculated result of executing the formula.

Formula   a representation of the cell locations and the mathematical or logical operations that are performed on the contents of those cells.

Horizontal scrollbar   the bar at the bottom of a window that enables you to move left and right to view information too wide for the screen.

Hyperlink   a special protocol that is used to connect to another file on your computer or network, to a Web site on the Internet, or between Web pages.

Insertion point   a flashing vertical line that indicates the position where text will be entered. It is sometimes called a cursor.

Legend   a list that identifies a pattern or color used in a chart.

Line chart   a chart that includes a line running through each data point. It is usually used to show trends.

Marquee   a box of moving, blinking lines that resembles the flashing lights around the marquee of a theater.

Office Assistant   a Microsoft Office help program that enables you to ask questions by typing in sentences or phrases. When you ask a question of the Office Assistant, a series of possible related topics are displayed. You can choose the most appropriate topic for more information.

Pie chart   displays the contribution of each value to the whole.

Point size   the height of the letters plus the spacing between rows is measured in points. There are 72 points per inch.

Program   one of the components of the Microsoft Office XP suite, such as Word, Excel, or Access. A program is often referred to as an application in this book.

Registered programs   Windows records information about the programs that are installed on a computer, including the three letter file extensions that the program uses to identify files that it uses or creates.

Relative reference   a cell reference that will change when the formula is copied, moved, or filled into other cells.

Row heading   the number at the left of the row that is used to identify cells in that row.

Sheet   a synonym for worksheet, identified by tabs at the bottom of the window.

Standard toolbar   a toolbar that contains commonly used buttons such as Save, Print, Cut, Copy, and Paste. It may share the same row with the Formatting toolbar.

Start button   the button on the left side of the taskbar that is used to run programs, change system settings, get help, or shut down the computer.

Task pane   a pane that opens on the right side of the window, which is used to display commonly used tools.

Vertical scrollbar   the bar at the right side of a window that enables you to move up and down to view information too long for the screen.

Workbook   a collection of worksheets saved under one filename.

Worksheet   a set of cells that are identified by row and column headings.

XML   an abbreviation for Extensible Markup Language which is a standard for describing data in Web pages. The older Web page design language, HTML, defines how elements of a Web page are displayed, while XML defines what those elements contain.

Index

A

absolute cell references, 55, 58-59
Add Trendline option (charts), 104
addition
    basic formulas, 51-52
    referencing multiple cells, 53
addresses
    of cells, 6
age, current, calculating, 78
Align Left button (Formatting toolbar), 35
Align Right button (Formatting toolbar), 35
aligning
    text in cells, 34
        angular displays, 44
        horizontal alignment, 35
        orientation options, 35
        text wrapping, 34
Alignment tab (Format Cells dialog box), 34
    Horizontal listbox, 35
    Orientation window, 35
        angular displays, 44
    Wrap text option, 34
All Borders option (Borders button), 37
Analysis ToolPak Add-In, adding to Excel, 77
angular text alignment, 44
annotating pie charts, 105
Annual Percentage Rates (APR), including in formulas, 63
Answer Wizard tab (Help system), 20
APR (Annual Percentage Rates), including in formulas, 63
arguments
    in functions, 66
    wizard dialog box for, 68
        PMT function example, 66-67, 69
arithmetic calculations
    basic formulas for, 52-53
    combining operations, 55-59
    referencing multiple cells, 53-54
arrows
    on keyboards, CE11
    navigating spreadsheets using, 4-5
    navigating worksheets using, 6
asterisk (*) symbol, in formulas, 52
Auto Fill option (fill handles), 56
    absolute cell references with, 58-59
    combining relative with absolute cell formulas, 60-62
    relative cell references with, 56-57
AutoFilter option (Data, Filter menu), 46
Autohide feature, CE4
AutoShapes toolbar (Insert, Pictures menu), Callouts button, 94
AutoSum button, 12-13
    itemizing expenses, 21
    summarizing expenses, 21
    tracking operating costs, 22
averages, calculating (AVERAGE function), 75

B

backslash (\) symbol, 53
bar charts, 89
bolding
    cell contents, 36
    column and row headings, 6
borders, adding to cells, 37-38
Borders button (Formatting toolbar)
    All Borders option, 37
    Thick Border option, 37
    Top and Double Bottom Border option, 38
browsers, Web, previewing worksheets in, 119-120
buttons
    AutoShapes toolbar
        Callouts, 94-95
    Formatting toolbar
        alignment buttons, 35
        Borders, 37
        Comma Style, 29
        Currency Style, 29
        Decrease Decimal, 29
        Fill Color, 38
        Font Color, 38-39
        Increase Decimal, 30
        Merge and Center, 33, 111
    in dialog boxes, 14
    Menu bar
        Close, 16
    Office taskbar
        Start, CE3
    on worksheets
        Select All, 27
    Redo, 11
    Standard toolbar
        AutoSum, 12-13
        Chart Wizard, 84
        Copy, 111
        Insert Hyperlink, 126
        Paste, 111
        Print Preview, 96
        Print, 16
        Redo, 11
        Save, 13
        Undo, 11
    Title bar
        Close, 16

C

calculations, 51
    AutoSum, 12-13
        itemizing expenses, 21
        summarizing expenses, 21
        tracking operating costs, 22
    basic operations, 51-53
        referencing multiple cells, 53-54
    built-in formulas, loan repayment example, 63-69
    combining operations, 55-59
        relative with absolute formulas, 60-62
    complex, Solver tool for, 78
    date functions, 78
    frequency distributions, 77
    Goal Seek tool
        desired loan amount, 74
        interest rate calculations, 74
    logical functions, 76
    lookup functions, 76-77
    named cells in, 79
    percentage increases/decreases, 75
    statistical functions, 75
    sums, 12-13, 21-22
callouts, adding to charts, 94
Callouts button (AutoShapes toolbar), 94
categories of formulas, viewing, 65
category axis (charts), formatting labels for, 93
cell addresses, 6
cell ranges
    indicating in formulas, 60
cell references
    absolute, 58-59
    case sensitivity, 55
    colons (:) in, 60
    relative, 56-57
        combining with absolute 60-62
cells, 3
    AutoSum calculations, 12-13, 21-22
    entering text and numbers, 7-9
    errors in, correcting, 9
    formatting, 29
        alignment options, 34-35, 44
        borders, 37-38
        column width, 32-33
        Comma Style, 29
        Currency Style, 29
        dates, 30-31, 45
        Decrease Decimal, 29
        fill colors/shading, 38
        font color options, 38-39
        font options, 36
        Increase Decimal, 30
        organizing data visually, 44
    formulas in
        absolute formulas, 58-59
        basic addition and subtraction, 51-52
        basic multiplication and division, 52-53
        combining relative with absolute formulas, 60-62
        copying formulas into, 55-57
        referencing multiple cells, 53-54
        relative formulas, 57
    groups
        contiguous cells, 28-29
        noncontiguous cells, 28
    individual, selecting, 5-6
    locking, 45
    marquees around, 12
    merging, 33, 111
        splitting merged cells, 46
    moving, 46
    named cells, creating and using, 79, 126-127
    in preexisting templates, modifying, 22
    referencing, 5
    selecting, 27
Center button (Formatting toolbar), 35
centering cells, 111
Chart Wizard, 81
    accessing, 84
    column charts
        adding 3-D effects, 101
        clustered columns, 89-91
        handling missing data, 104-105
    line charts
        formatting options, 85
        naming and saving charts, 85-86
        selecting data source, 84
        titles and labels, 85
        titles and legends, 85
    pie charts, 86
        adding titles, 88
        creating, 87
        exploding and rotating, 105
        naming and saving, 88
    selecting chart type, 84
charts, 81
    bar charts, 89
    column charts, 89
        adding titles, 90
        creating, 89-90, 101
        handling problem data, 104-105
        naming and saving, 91
    creating transparencies from, 98
    formatting and editing, 91
    line charts
        creating, 83-84
        formatting options, 85
        naming and saving, 85-86
        titles and legends, 85
    pie charts, 86
        adding callouts, 94-95
        adding titles, 88

  creating, 87
  editing, 92-93
  exploding, rotating and annotating, 105
  formatting and editing, 92
  formatting value axis, 93
  formatting, 94
  naming and saving, 88
 placing on worksheets, 103
 printing, 96
  adding headers, 97
  font options, 97
 when to use, 83
 X-Y charts
  adding data label, 104
  adding trend lines, 104
  creating chart, 103-104

Clear Formats option (Edit menu), 31
Close button (Menu bar), 5, 16
closing
 Excel application, 5, 16
 worksheets, 16
Collapse Dialog Box option, 67
colon (:), in cell references, 60
colors
 adding to cells, 38
 for fonts, 38-39
 screen versus transparencies, 98
column charts, 89
 clustered columns
  adding titles, 90
  creating, 89-90
  handling problem data, 104-105
  naming and saving, 91
 placing on datasheets, 103
 printing, 96
  adding header, 97
  setting font options, 97
 3-D effects in, 101
columns, 3
 filtering contents of, 46
 merging cells and centering text, 33
 selecting
  whole columns, 27-28
  cells in, 28-29
 widths, enlarging, 32-33
Comma Style button (Formatting toolbar), 29
commas, formatting large numbers with, 29-30
Contents tab (Help system), 20
 Document Fundamentals, 21
contiguous cells, selecting, 28-29
copying
 copying worksheets into Word documents, 115-116
 formula fill handles for, 55-59
 moving merged data, 111
Create New Folder button (Save As dialog box), 15
Currency Style button (Formatting toolbar), 29

cursors. *See* **pointers**
Customize dialog box (Toolbars submenu), CE14-15
customizing
 toolbars, CE13-15
cut-and-paste method. *See* **copying**

D

dashes, in cells, 7
data. *See also* **calculations**
 charting
  bar charts, 89
  column charts, 89-91, 101
  handling problem data, 104-105
  line charts, 83-86
  pie charts, 86-88, 92-94, 105
  X-Y charts, 103-104
 entering, 8-9
 finding in tables
  HLOOKUP function for, 76
  VLOOKUP function for, 76
 frequency distributions, 77
 managing
  dividing into sheets, 109-110
  summary sheets, 110-114
 merged, moving, 111-112
 organizing visually, cell formatting for, 44
 showing trends in, 83
Data Analysis option, adding to Excel, 77
data calculations. *See* **calculations**
data labels (X-Y charts), 104
Data menu
 Filter submenu, AutoFilter option, 46
data points, in charts, labeling, 85
datasheets
 creating multiple, 109-110
 linking to summary sheets, 112-114
 placing charts on, 103
dates
 calculating present age, 78
 Date & Time function, 78
 formatting, 30-31
  two-digit dates, 45
Decrease Decimal button (Formatting toolbar), 29
defaults
 cell references, fill formulas, 57
 line chart sub-type, 84
 most recently used functions, 65
 toolbars, CE13
 worksheets, number of, 3
disks, saving Excel files on, 13-15
division calculations
 basic formulas, 52-53
 referencing multiple cells, 54
Document Fundamentals (Help system, Contents tab), 21

documents, Office
    formatting font size, CE15-16
    from multiple applications
        opening simultaneously, CE9-10
        switching between, CE10-11
    opening existing documents, CE6-7, CE8
    renaming and saving, CE7-8
dollar sign ($) symbol, with formulas, 58-59
double-clicking mouse, problems with, 11

E

Edit menu
    Clear Formats option, 31
    Paste Special option, 125
editing
    cell contents, data
        correcting typing errors, 9
    charts, 91
        pie chart example, 92-94
    formulas, 55
    preventing using locking, 45
    Redo button, 11
    Undo button, 11
empty cells, 7
equal sign (=), in formulas, 51
errors, error handling
    in formulas, redoing, 54
    typing errors, 9-12
Excel application
    starting, CE9-10
    closing, 16
exiting applications. *See* **closing applications**
Expense Statement template (Spreadsheet Solutions), 22
expenses
    itemizing, example of, 21
    operating, example of, 22
    summarizing, example of, 21
exploding pie charts, 105
Export to Excel button (Internet Explorer), 120

F

File menu
    Print dialog box, CE17
    Save As dialog box, CE7-8, CE13-14
        Create New Folder button, 15
    Save As Web Page option, 118-119
filename extensions
    default names, CE4, CE13
    registered programs, 13
files, saving, CE8, 13-15
fill colors, adding to cells, 38

fill handles
    Auto Fill features, 56-59
    copying formulas using, 55
filtering column contents, 46
financial formulas, built-in
    PMT function, 66-69
    viewing, 65
floppy disks
    creating new folders on, 15
    saving files to, CE8, 14-15
folders, creating new, 15
Font Color button (Formatting toolbar), 38-39
Font listbox (Format Cells, Font tab), 36
font size, customizing, 15-16
Font tab (Format Cells menu), 36
fonts
    color options, 38-39
    formatting in charts, 97
    in callouts, 95
    in cells, formatting options, 36
    in charts, formatting options, 92-93
Format Axis dialog box (chart shortcut menu), 94
Format Axis Title dialog box (chart shortcut menu), 93
Format Cells dialog box (Format menu), 30-31
    Alignment tab, 34
    Font tab, 36
    Protection tab, 45
Format Chart Title dialog box (chart shortcut menu), 92-93
Format menu
    Format Cells dialog box, 30-31
        Alignment tab, 34
        Font tab, 36
        Protection tab, 45
formatting
    borders, 37-38
    cell contents
        font color options, 38-39
        font options, 36
        organizing data visually, 44
    cells
        moving, 46
        splitting merged cells, 46
    charts, 91
        adding callouts, 94-95
        pie chart example, 92-94
    columns
        enlarging, 32-33
        headers, 33
    dates, 30-31
        two-digit dates, 45
    fill colors/shading, 38
    large numbers
        Comma Style, 29
        Currency Style, 29

Decrease Decimal, 29
Increase Decimal, 30
text, alignment options, 34-35, 44
text in callouts, 95
Formatting toolbar
   alignment buttons, 35
   Borders button), 37
   Comma Style button, 29
   Currency Style button, 29
   customizing location, 3
   display options, 13, 15
   Decrease Decimal button, 29
   Fill Color button, 38
   Font Color button, 38-39
   Font Size button, CE15-16
   Increase Decimal button, 30
   Merge and Center button, 33, 111
Formula bar
   editing formulas in, 55
formulas, 51. *See also* **functions**
   activating, 12
   asterisk (*) symbol in, 52
   AutoSum
      activating, 13
      itemizing expenses, 21
      summarizing expenses, 21
      tracking operating expenses, 22
   basic operations, 51-53
      referencing multiple cells, 53-54
   built-in formulas, 65
      PMT function, 66-69
      viewing formula categories, 65
   colons (:) in, 60
   combining operations in, 55-56
      absolute cell references, 58-59
      relative cell references, 56-57
      relative with absolute formulas, 60-62
   creating using Goal Seek dialog box, 74
   date functions, calculating present age, 78
   editing, 55
   equal sign (=) in, 51
   frequency distributions, 77
   handling errors in, 54
   identifying cell ranges for, 12
   loan repayment functions, 63-64
   logical functions, IF, 76
   lookup functions
      HLOOKUP, 76
      VLOOKUP, 76-77
   marquees in, 12
   named cells in, 79, 126-127
   percentage increases/decreases, calculating, 75
   printing, 59
   slash (/) symbol in, 53
   Solver tool, 78

   statistical functions
      AVERAGE, 75
      MIN/MAX, 75
      STDEVP, 75
   sums, 12
   viewing keyboard shortcuts for, 59
frequency distributions, calculating, 77
functions
   arguments in, 66
   built-in formulas
      accessing, 65
      PMT function, 66-69
   date, calculating present age, 78
   logical, 76
   lookup
      HLOOKUP, 76
      VLOOKUP, 76-77
   statistical functions
      AVERAGE, 75
      MIN/MAX, 75
      STDEVP, 75
   statistical functions, 75

G

Goal Seek dialog box (Tools menu)
   calculating desired loan amount, 74
   calculating interest rates, 74
gridlines, enabling in charts, 85

H

Header/Footer tab (Print Preview, Setup button)
   Custom Header option, 97
headers
   adding to charts, 97
headings
   column headings, 6
      merging in multiple columns, 33
      selecting columns using, 27-28
help system
   Answer Wizard tab, CE20
   Contents tab, CE20
      Document Fundamentals, CE21
   Index tab, CE20
   Office Assistant, CE18-21
Histogram tool (Data Analysis tools), 77
HLOOKUP function, 35
Horizontal listbox (Format Cells, Alignment tab), 35
hot keys, on menus, CE11
hyperlinks
   inserting in worksheets, 126
hyphenating wrapped text, 34

I

IF logical function, applying in formulas, 76
Increase Decimal button (Formatting toolbar), 30
Index tab (Help system), CE20
Insert Function dialog box, 65
    formula categories, 65
Insert Hyperlink button/dialog box (Standard toolbar)
    linking to Word documents, 126
Insert menu
    Function dialog box, 65
    Pictures submenu, AutoShapes toolbar, 94
insertion points, CE8
    moving in cells, 10
    positioning for within-cell edits, 11-12
integrating Office applications, CE1-2
    opening multiple applications, CE9-10
    switching between applications, CE10-11
interest rates
    Goal Seek tool for, 74
    calculating, 63-64
italicizing cell contents, 36
itemizing expenses, example of, 21

K

keyboard
    arrows on, using in cell selection, 29
    keyboard shortcuts
        menu hot keys, CE11
        viewing formulas, 59
    navigating worksheets using, 6-7, 9
        customizing cursor movement, 8

L

labels
    in charts
        data point labels, 85
        X-Y charts, 104
large numbers, formatting, 29
    Comma Style, 29
    Currency Style, 29
    Decrease Decimal, 29
    Increase Decimal, 30
legends, adding to charts, 85
Legends tab (Chart Wizard), 85
line charts, 83-84
    creating titles and legends, 85-86
    formatting options, 85
    when to use, 83
linear regression, applying to X-Y charts, 104
linking
    data sheets to summary sheets, 112-114
    worksheets, document hyperlinks, 126
loan amounts, calculating using Goal Seek tool, 74
loan payments, formulas for, 63-64
    built-in formulas, 65
    Loan Payment tab, 63-64
    PMT function, 66-69
locking options, 45
logical functions (IF function), 76
Logical_test box, 76
lookup functions
    HLOOKUP, 76
    VLOOKUP, 76-77

M

marquees, 12
MAX function, 75
maximizing windows, 5
medians, calculating, 75
Menu bar, Close button, 16
menus, CE11
    accessing from shortcut menu, 30
    Data menu
        AutoFilter option, 46
    Edit menu
        Clear Formats option, 31
        Paste Special option, 125
    File menu
        Save As dialog box, 13-15
        Save As Web page, 118-119
    Format menu
        Alignment tab, 36
        Format Cells dialog box, 30-31, 34, 45
    Help menu, 18
    Insert menu
        Function dialog box, 65
        Pictures, AutoShapes option, 94
    keyboard shortcuts, CE11
    Tools menu, CE11-12
        Data Analysis option, 77
        Goal Seek dialog box, 74
        Solver tool, 78
    View menu
        Toolbars submenu, CE13-15
Merge and Center button (Formatting toolbar), 33, 111
merging cells, 33, 111
    splitting merged cells, 46
Microsoft Excel Worksheet Object, 125
MIN function, 75
missing data, handling in charts, 104-105
monthly interest rate, calculating, 63-64
mouse device
    double-clicking problems, troubleshooting, 11
    enlarging column widths, 32-33
    pointers, *18*

selecting cell groups
   contiguous cells, 28-29
   noncontiguous cells, 28
selecting columns, 28
selecting/deselecting toolbars, CE16
selecting individual cells, 5-6

Move selection after Enter option (Tools, Options menu), 8

moving
   cells, 46
   merged data, 111-112

multiple applications
   opening simultaneously, CE9-10
   switching between, CE10-11

multiple data sheets
   advantages of using, 109
   creating, 109-110

multiplication
   basic formulas, 52-53
   referencing multiple cells, 54

N

Name box, 6

named cells
   creating and using, 126-127
   using in formulas, 79

navigating
   between worksheets, 3
   drop-down menus, CE11
   within worksheets
      customizing cursor movement, 8
      horizontal scrollbar, 4-5
      keyboard arrows, 6
      tab keys, 7, 9
      vertical scrollbar, 4

New from Templates section (Task Pane), 22

noncontiguous cells, selecting, 28

numerical data, numbers
   entering into cells, 7-9
   formatting
      Comma Style, 29
      Currency Style, 29
      Decrease Decimal, 29
      font options, 36
      Increase Decimal, 30
   rounding of, in displays, 29-30
   updating and changing, 9

O

Office Assistant
   show/hide options, CE18, CE21
   using, CE19-20

Office suite, advantages of using, 1-2
Office taskbar, Start button, CE3
Open dialog box (Standard toolbar), CE6-7, CE9
opening applications, CE3, CE6-7
opening files, from Windows Explorer, CE8
operating expenses, tracing, example of, 22
Options, Edit tab (Tools menu), 8
Orientation window (Format Cells, Alignment tab), 35
   angular displays, 44

P

Paste button (Standard toolbar)
   moving merged data, 111

Paste Special option (Edit menu), 125

pasting
   Word tables into worksheets, 127
   workbooks into Word documents, 125

payment (PMT) function, 66-69
percentage increases/decreases, calculating, 75
physics problems, solving using Solver tool, 78

pie charts
   callouts, adding, 94-95
   category axis, 93
   creating, 87
   editing, 92-93
   exploding, rotating and annotating, 105
   formatting and editing, 92
   naming and saving, 88
   scale modifications, 94
   titles, adding, 88
   when to use, 86

PMT (payment) function, 66, 68
   argument wizard, 66-67, 69
   viewing calculated payment, 69

pointers, CE8

previewing
   worksheets, in Word documents, 115

Print button/dialog box, CE16-17
Print Layout view (View menu), 115

Print Preview feature
   adding headers, 97
   previewing charts, 96
   setting font options, 97

printing
   charts, 96
      adding headers, 97
      font options, 97
   worksheets
      printing formulas with, 59

Programs submenu (Office), CE1
   locating Office applications, CE3

Protection tab (Format Cells dialog box), Wrap text option, 45

R

ranges, cell
    calculating, function for, 75
    using in formulas, 12, 21-22
Redo button (Standard toolbar), 11
referencing cells, nomenclature for, 5
registered programs, filename extensions, 13
regression lines, adding to charts, 104
relative cell references, 55-57
renaming files, CE7-8
right-mouse button, accessing shortcut menus, 30
rotating pie charts, 105
rounding data
    in displays, 29-30
rows, 3
rulers, enabling, CE4

S

Save As dialog box (File menu), 7-8, 13-14
    Create New Folder button, 15
Save As Web Page option (File menu), 118-119
Save button (Standard toolbar), 13
saving
    charts, 86
        column charts, 91
        placing on datasheets, 103
        as separate sheet, 85
    files, 7-8
    workbooks and worksheets, 13-15
scale, in charts, modifying, 85, 94
scrollbars
    horizontal, 4-5
    using in cell selection, 28
    vertical, 4
security issues
    unwanted edits, locking options, 45
Select All button (worksheets), 27
selecting
    cell groups
        contiguous cells, 28-29
        noncontiguous cells, 28
    columns, 27-28
    individual cells, 5-6, 27
Series in area (Chart Wizard), 84-85
shading, adding to cells, 38
Sheet tabs (Page Setup dialog box)
    navigating between worksheets using, 3
shortcut menus
    accessing, 30
    charts
        Format Axis dialog box, 93-94
        Format Axis Title dialog box, 93
        Format Chart Title dialog box, 92
    Properties option, Auto hide feature, 4
Show Legend box (Chart Wizard), 85
slash (/) symbol
    comparison with backslash (\), 53
    in formulas, 53
Solver tool, 78
Spreadsheet Solutions tab (General Templates task pane)
    Expense Statement template, 22
spreadsheets
    uses for, 1
standard deviation, calculating, function for, 75
Standard toolbar
    Chart Wizard button, 84
    Copy button
        moving merged data, 111
    customizing location, 3
    display options, CE13, CE15
    Insert Hyperlink button/dialog box, 126
    Open dialog box, CE6-7, CE9
    Paste button
        moving merged data, 111
    Print button, CE16
    Print Preview button
        adding headers, 97
        previewing charts, 96
        setting font options, 97
    Redo button, 11
    Save button, 13
    Undo button, 11
Start button (Office taskbar), 3
starting Office applications, CE3-5, CE9-10
statistics, statistical functions
    AVERAGE function, 75
    frequency distributions, 77
    Histogram tool for, 77
    linear regression, 104
    MIN/MAX functions, 75
    STDEVP function, 75
    floppy disks, 8
subtraction
    basic formulas, 51-52
    referencing multiple cells, 54
summarizing expenses, example of, 21
summary sheets, 110-111
    creating, 111-112
    linking data sheets to, 112-114
sums, calculating, 12-13, 21-22

T

tab keys, navigating worksheets using, 6-7, 9
tables
    finding data in
        HLOOKUP function, 76
        VLOOKUP function, 76-77

Word tables, pasting into worksheets, 127
Task Pane
    closing, 4
    enabling/disabling, CE4
    functions, 3
    locating, 3
    New from Template section, 22
taskbar
    enabling/disabling, CE4
    with multiple open applications, CE10-11
    starting applications using, CE3
templates
    modifying, 22
    viewing list of, 3
text
    accommodating large/long text entries, 32-33
    entering into cells, 7-9
    formatting
        alignment options, 34-35, 44
        font options, 36
    text emphasis options, 36
    text wrapping, 34
Thick Border option (Borders button), 37
three-dimensional (3-D) effects, adding to pie charts, 105
Title bar, Close button, 16
titles, 85
    adding to column charts, 90
    adding to pie charts, 88, 92
        formatting axis labels, 93
        formatting axis title, 93
        modifying scale, 94
Titles tab (Chart Wizard), 85
toolbars, 4, 11
    adding or removing, CE16
    AutoShapes, Callouts button, 94
    customizing, CE3, CE14-15
    Formatting toolbar
        alignment buttons, 35
        Borders button, 37
        Comma Style button, 29
        Currency Style button, 29
        Decrease Decimal button, 29
        Fill Color button, 38
        Font Color button, 38-39
        Increase Decimal button, 30
        Merge and enter button, 33, 111
    selecting/deselecting, CE13
    Standard toolbar
        Copy button, 111
        Insert Hyperlink button, 126
        Open dialog box, 9
        Paste button, 111
        Print button, 16
        Print Preview, 96
        Redo button, 11
        Save button, 13
        Undo button, 11
Tools menu, CE11-12
    Data Analysis option, 77
    Goal Seek dialog box, 74
    Options, Edit tab, 8
    Solver option, 78
Top and Double Bottom Border option (Borders button), 38
totals, calculating, formulas for, 12-13, 21-22
transparencies, creating from charts, 98
trendlines, in X-Y charts, 104
trends, data, charts for, 83-86
two-digit dates, 45
typing errors, correcting, 9-12

U

underlining cell contents, 36
Undo button (Standard toolbar), adding to toolbar, 11

V

value axis (charts), formatting, 93
vertical scrollbar, navigating worksheets, 4-5
View menu
    enabling/disabling task panes, CE4
View menu (Windows Explorer), Options submenu, enabling/disabling filename extensions, CE13
VLOOKUP function, 76-77

W

Web browsers, previewing worksheets in, 119-120
Web pages
    saving workbooks as, 125-126
    saving worksheets as, 117-120
windows, maximizing, CE5
Windows Explorer
    enabling, disabling filename extensions, 13
    opening documents from, CE8
wizards
    Chart Wizard, 81
        column charts, 89-91, 101
        handling missing data, 104-105
        line charts, 84-86
        pie charts, 86-88, 92, 105
    for function arguments, 66-69
    types of, in Excel, 66
workbooks, 3
    opening existing workbooks, 3
    pasting into Word documents, 125
    prewritten templates for, modifying, 22

saving as Web pages, 125-126
saving to disk, 13-15
worksheets, 3
   adding borders in, 37-38
   adding fill colors/shading, 38
   calculations, 12-13, 21-22
   calculations in, 51
   cell formatting
      Comma Style, 29
      Currency Style, 29
      dates, 30-31
      Decrease Decimal, 29
      Increase Decimal, 30
   cell groups
      selecting contiguous cells, 28-29
      selecting noncontiguous cells, 28
   cells
      entering text and numbers, 7-9
      moving, 46
      selecting individual cells, 5-6
      splitting merged cells, 46
   closing, 16
   columns
      enlarging, 32-33
      formatting headers, 33
      selecting, 27-28
   filtering contents, 46
   formatting cell contents
      alignment options, 34-35, 44
      dates, 45
      font options, 36, 38-39
      organizing data visually, 44
   formulas
      basic operations with single cells, 51-53
      built-in, 65-69
      combining operations, 55-62
      loan repayment example, 63-64
      printing with worksheet, 59
      referencing multiple cells, 53-54
      viewing, 59
   functions in, 198-199
   in prewritten workbook templates, modifying, 22
   inserting document hyperlinks, 126
   locking cells, 45
   multiple data sheets, creating, 109-110
   named cells in, 126-127
   navigating between, 3
   navigating within
      horizontal scrollbar, 4-5
      keyboard arrows, 6
      tab keys, 7, 9
      vertical scrollbar, 4
   pasting into Word documents, 115-116
   pasting Word tables into, 127
   placing charts on, 103
   printing, 16
   saving to disk, 13-15
   saving as Web pages, 117-120
   selecting entire sheet, 27
   summary sheets
      creating, 110-112
      linking data sheets to, 112-114
Wrap text option (Format Cells, Alignment tab), 34

X-Y charts
   adding data labels, 104
   adding trend lines, 104
   creating, 103-104
XML (Extensible Markup Language) documents, 117-119
   previewing, 119-120
.xls filename extension, 13